EXTRAORDINARY EXPERIENCES

PERSONAL ACCOUNTS OF THE PARANORMAL IN CANADA

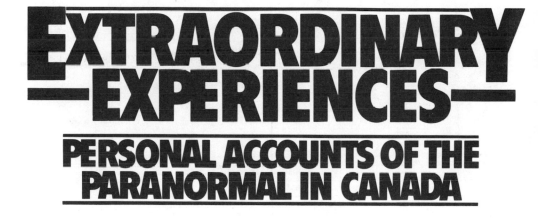

JOHN ROBERT COLOMBO

HOUNSLOW

Extraordinary Experiences
Personal Accounts of the Paranormal
in Canada

Copyright © 1989 by J.R. Colombo

ISBN 0-88882-108-5

Publisher: Anthony Hawke
Design: Gerard Williams
Editor: Shirley Knight Morris
Composition: Accurate Typesetting Limited
Printer: Gagné Printing Ltd.
Front Cover Photograph: Bill Brooks

Hounslow Press
A Division of Anthony R. Hawke Limited
124 Parkview Avenue
Willowdale, Ontario, Canada
M2N 3Y5

Publication was assisted by
The Canada Council and
The Ontario Arts Council.

Printed and bound in Canada.

To
Dwight Whalen
Tireless Researcher, Untiring Friend

Contents

Preface

In the pages of this book you will read accounts of experiences so extraordinary that you will find yourself wondering whether they could possibly be true. The incredible events narrated in the reports printed here seem to defy rational explanation. Yet the accounts themselves are described as true. They are not works of fiction. They were not imagined by professional writers of fantasy, but were written, in the main, by ordinary men and women who, through chance or circumstance, were eye-witnesses to astonishing and sometimes soul-searching events. These are first-hand accounts, as told by the witnesses themselves, unlike the second-hand tales written by journalists and investigators. Because of their immediacy, the evidence that they present, while partial, points to the reality of the experiences themselves.

The experiences are truly extraordinary. It should be noted that extraordinary experiences may be said to differ fundamentally from experiences that are out-of-the-ordinary. The former may appear to be impossible, yet they actually seem to have happened; the latter, though possible, are unlikely to occur. An out-of-the-ordinary experience is shooting Niagara Falls in a barrel or outfitting an expedition to scale Mount Everest. Such undertakings are real-life adventures for the fit and the foolhardy. Yet a question that will later be posed is the following puzzler: Are extraordinary experiences all that out-of-the-ordinary?

1

Still, no matter how fit and foolhardy one may be, no one could volunteer for the incredible adventures described in this book. You may visit a gypsy fortune teller and listen to her as she predicts your future, but how often does it happen that your future unfolds precisely as she predicted? Impossible? The account which appears herein suggests otherwise. Here is another instance of just such an incident. The media routinely report sightings of unidentified flying objects, yet how many people have ever claimed they have approached a landed UFO, have touched it, and have burn marks to prove it? Very few. Such adventures appear beyond the pale of human experience, outside the normal field of human understanding. So far off the beaten track are such accounts that in the normal course of human events they would be considered abnormal.

Or paranormal.

Perhaps these occurrences should be considered out-of-the-ordinary rather than extraordinary. Given the fact that such reports go back to time immemorial, and indeed that they are being reported widely even today, it would seem to be high time that investigators and researchers of such happenings shifted them from the wings of the stage to the centre of the human story.

This book has a number of purposes. One of them is to suggest that reports and accounts of such experiences are far from being rare or remarkable; indeed, they are fairly common. Historical records are replete with them; the contemporary media is full of them. Almost everyone knows someone who claims to have sighted a UFO or spotted a lake monster or sensed the presence of a spirit. Add all those mute witnesses — people who have experienced such things yet have remained silent because they felt uneasy about them, or feared that in relating them they would be ridiculed by listeners — and the ranks of witnesses swell.

Thus one of the purposes of this book is to suggest that extraordinary experiences occur often enough to be considered — well — out-of-the-ordinary. Another purpose is to document inexplicable occurrences and anomalous phenomena in Canada. Collections of this sort of material have been published in the United States, the United Kingdom, France, and other countries. Are there no Canadians who have experienced — who have reported experiencing — instances of the paranormal?

To prove otherwise, this book offers the reader over seventy reports, selected from the writings of the past and from the statements of present-day witnesses. Indicative representation has been given to the native peoples through the journals of explorers and early travellers. The thoughts of 19th-century spiritualists and 20th-century psychics find some elbow room here. Determined browsing along the paths and bypaths of Canadiana account for the discovery or recovery of out-of-the-way texts. For this reason the choice of selections in this collection is best described as eclectic.

The third purpose of this anthology is the practical one of finding a good way to use a number of the highly readable narratives that the present editor disinterred while in the throes of researching and writing *Mysterious Canada*. Published in the fall of 1988, this book was the first work to document and examine all aspects of the paranormal in the world's second-largest country. It surveyed immense areas, but only a few choice properties could be prospected. The format permitted the editor to handle with ease brief accounts of hauntings and sightings, etc., but the nagging problem remained of how to do justice to narrative accounts of some length. I had in mind Albert Ostman's detailed description of his abduction by a family of Sasquatches. That tale may be read with pleasure and profit, but only as a whole; in part, it loses all its appeal. The narrative's charm does not survive in excerpt or in paraphrase. A solution to this problem occurred to me. The place for such accounts is in an anthology of extraordinary experiences.

How did I go about finding new and unpublished reports? About one hundred daily newspapers are published in Canada. Why not appeal to the editors of these papers and ask them to publish requests for such material? The Editorial Department at Doubleday Canada Limited, the house responsible for publishing *Mysterious Canada,* agreed to participate. They mailed out one hundred copies of my request and agreed to forward the replies. A lot of thought went into the proper wording of the request, for the idea was to give the newspaper editor the opportunity to run it as a letter to the editor, a brief news item, or an unpaid notice in the Personal Column. Here is how the request was worded:

Dear Editor: I would appreciate it if you would consider publishing the following letter. I am preparing for publication a book about the supernatural in Canada, and I would be pleased to correspond with men and women who wish to share their psychic experiences, including sightings of ghosts, strange creatures, UFOs, etc.

John Robert Colombo c/o Editorial Department Doubleday Canada Limited 105 Bond Street Toronto M5B 1Y3.

More than twenty of the one hundred daily newspapers ran the request. The editor of one Calgary paper sent me a letter in which she explained that it was "against company policy" to run such letters. They were afraid that if they ran one they would set a precedent and have to run no end of similar requests!

As it happened, the notices appeared in newspapers published in all regions of the country (with the exception of the Far North). The result was that I received approximately 150 letters from correspondents across the country. In their initial letters the correspondents either stated that they had remarkable experiences they were willing to share if I requested them to do so, or they launched into their accounts right then and there. About the same time I made a number of media appearances during which I talked about my long-standing twin interests: Canadiana and the paranormal. I mentioned that I was working on "a Canadian ghost book" and was on the lookout for instances of "anomalistic phenomena." I spoke about these matters with Peter Feniak, host of the CTV Network show *Lifetime,* and with David Schatzky, host of CBC Radio's *Radio Noon.* Another fifty letters or phone calls followed these appearances. Word circulated that I was collecting "scary stuff." Friends and fellow writers with a residual interest in such matters mentioned their experiences or the experiences of others.

It goes without saying that I continue to collect "scary stuff." The invitation remains open to all readers to share their experiences with me for possible use in future collections. Feel free to write to me care of the address above.

The letters I received from readers, viewers, and listeners made a number of related points. These derived from the initial letters, but also from subsequent correspondence conducted with about half of the informants. Most of the correspondents thanked me for the opportunity — more than one referred to it as a privilege — to share the highly personal experiences with someone who was sympathetic, or at least not a scoffer. Many informants were still smarting from the way relatives and friends reacted to the telling of their tales. Many seemed relieved to have their incidents placed in a context of similar experiences. The majority of letter-writers felt that they wanted to tell their stories to someone who would appreciate what they had to say. The correspondents understood the fact that their experiences, while uniquely their own, shared characteristics with the experiences of others. A few went out of their way to make contact with such groups as the Aerial Phenomena Research Organization, and took pains to file detailed reports.

All the correspondents, judging by their letters to me, are still turning their experiences over in their minds, despite the fact that the episodes, or the majority of them, took place quite a while ago. In my follow-up letters, I made it a point to ask each informant, "Did the experience change your life in any way?" Most replied that no alteration had taken place in their lives, aside from the fact that a puzzling or enigmatic element or dimension had been added and that they now had to live with it. Yet a number found the occurrence so unsettling and intriguing that they found themselves contacting non-traditional religious organizations, and even subscribing to courses sponsored by New Age groups. A few informants felt that their lives had been enhanced by these experiences. One person, recording an out-of-body experience, claimed that death no longer held any terrors for him.

These contemporary accounts derive from correspondence and read like consistent narratives. They were reworked by the present editor from one or more letters. There was a deliberate attempt to make each account readable and self-explanatory. Each correspondent was sent a print-out of his or her experience along with a request to check it over for accuracy and emphasis. It should be noted that a fair amount of information extraneous to the experience in question was eliminated from each letter for reasons of space and dramatic effect. Nothing essential to any narrative was dropped. Many of the correspondents had not one but a number of experiences to relate.

At first this discovery dismayed me, for I felt that we were dealing with unique and hence non-recurring experiences. How often does one have the opportunity to view a UFO or to sense the presence of a spirit? Then I wondered why such experiences should be unique and non-recurring. Many of the correspondents felt themselves to be mediumistic, psychic, possessed of "second sight," or in possession of extrasensory powers. Psychologists might typify such people as "intuitive personalities" or as "fantasy-prone." Yet every psychologist recognizes that some people possess talents, abilities, or "gifts" that others lack, that some people are "lucky" whereas others are not. Is it not analogous that some people have a talent or a predisposition for extraordinary experiences? Perhaps they attract or collect them. Anyway, probably half the informants described themselves as somewhat psychic or sensitive. Then they went on to offer to relate a somewhat similar experience of a paranormal nature.

Although a good number of correspondents admitted that they felt themselves to be psychic — many of them are from the British Isles — a fair number described themselves as sceptics or non-believers. They said they belonged to no organized religious groups and subscribed to no particular beliefs about the existence of a deity, the possibilities of an afterlife, or the powers latent in man. Their paranormal experiences had nothing to do with their attitudes to life. I also heard from a handful of Christian fundamentalists who sent me religious tracts. In yellow ink they carefully highlighted passages predicting that hellfire and damnation would rain down upon the heads of those who had anything to do with the works of the devil. My favourite letter, however, was not of this sort. It was short and cryptic and it was sent from a correspondent in London, Ont. He said, simply, that he had lived a long life during which he had witnessed any number of strange and unusual things. "Come to London," he concluded, "and I will tell you about them."

It should be added that the correspondents are in no way publicity-seekers. They responded to my invitation to share their experiences, but not to capitalize on them. Nor are any of them proselytizers, though a number have spent considerable time pondering the particulars and implications of their experiences. It seems that what accompanies the anomalous event is the need to work it into one's life. This may require nothing more than the simple and repeated practice of relating what they believe happened. The telling of the tale may have therapeutic value. Certainly it is the easiest way of normalizing the incident, weaving it into the texture of modern life — life in the 1980s being surprisingly rationalistic (rather than strictly rational) and materialistic.

The reader need not believe in the truth of these accounts, but I hope readers will accept the fact that the informants themselves believe that these reports are full and true records of their experiences. Some of the occurrences described are more probable than others. The greater number fit into categories recognized by parapsychologists if not by psychologists. There is no gainsaying that the informants experienced something, but what and why are questions that will probably go unanswered, at least during the witnesses' lifetimes. An experience is not an occurrence. It is a subjective event, not an objective happening. There is no way to prove anything about the experiences themselves, merely about the nature of the reports, the accounts.

The experiences are accepted in good faith, although foolishness or fraud are not to be automatically dismissed. It was common practice in the 19th century for investigators with the British and American Societies for Psychical Research to speak of the "unimpeachable" character and "unassailable" conduct of a mediums or a subject during a séance held in a twilight of the parlour. It is a contemporary cliché for parapsychologists, who go about their work in the high noon of the research laboratories on university campuses, to speak about "well-designed" experiments and "unbreakable" protocols. Yet one must not forget that when tests for the paranormal are being conducted, what is being studied is not a mass of tissues or a tissue of theory, but human nature. As Iris and George Owen, the founders of the New Horizons Research Foundation, remind us: "Parapsychology is people."

It is possible to explain each and every one of the experiences in this book in a rational way. Yet the rational is not always the real, as philosophers are wont to note. It seems likely to me there is a surd factor in nature and in human nature. Something — or some things — may well at core remain puzzling, mysterious, paradoxical, or unintelligible, perhaps ultimately irrational. It is possible in the end the surd factor will be amenable to sweet reason; currently, it defies our limited logic. My feeling is that the accounts herein shed a little light on perverse and peculiar aspects of the nature of man — perhaps even on a wider and wilder sense of the state of the world and the status quo of the cosmos.

Whatever their interpretation, however well they fit into someone's world view, they are inexplicable in the present context. They offer anecdotal evidence of irrational experience in everyday life. The psychologist talks of confabulation — the tendency of informants to combine factual and non-factual elements into a consistent whole. Folklorists talk of memorates — narratives of personal happenings that are not quite legends and not quite accounts of experiences. These accounts may be fantastic, but they are not simply works of the conscious or unconscious imagination. They are more than that. But to what it is that they attest I do not know. They remain extraordinary experiences. I hope that they make for extraordinarily good reading, too.

*

A few acknowledgements are in order.

I am grateful to the contributors to this collection, both the living and the dead; their generosity allowed me to share their experiences with the readers of this book. The editors of the daily newspapers who published my request for contributions deserve to be thanked by name; if I had all their names on hand I would do so. In this regard the contribution of John Pearce of Doubleday Canada Limited requires acknowledgement.

As usual I am in the debt of Philip Singer and Michael Richardson of the North York Public Library. I conducted research at various branches of this library system as well as at the Metropolitan Reference Library, part of the Toronto Public Library system. Let me acknowledge assistance received from the librarians of two special collections, Lorna Toolis of the Spaced Out Library, and Robin Armstrong of the IAO Research Centre Library of Divine Sciences and Healing Arts, both in Toronto.

Assistance of other kinds was received from the following men and women: Joel Bonn, Montreal; Patrick Crean, Toronto; Edith Fowke, Toronto; William Gough, Toronto; Cyril Greenland,

Toronto; Jessica Hunt, Toronto; W. Edward Mann, Willowdale; Chris Rutkowski, Winnipeg; Donna Sinclair, North Bay; Allen Spraggett, Richmond Hill.

I am grateful to Tony Hawke, publisher of Hounslow Press, an inveterate reader of books on the paranormal, for his commitment to this book.

Extraordinary Experiences is dedicated to Dwight Whalen for the reasons given on the dedication page.

Native
Spirituality

Conjuring and Curing among the Indians

Samuel Hearne

The explorer and fur trader Samuel Hearne was a sharp-eyed observer of native customs in the Northwest in the late 18th century. He described the sights and sounds of the Barren Lands, as well as the feelings evoked by the wilderness, in his posthumously published memoirs, A Journey from Prince of Wales's Fort in Hudson's Bay to the Northern Ocean 1769, 1770, 1771, 1772 (1795). The volume is an invaluable record of native beliefs and customs. It is also a record of Hearne's long-lasting friendship with his guide and interpreter Matonabbee, who was the son of a Northern Indian and a slave woman of the Northern (or Chipewyan) Indians and a resident at Churchill River.

Three excerpts follow from Hearne's memoirs. The first excerpt, "Native Medicine," offers particulars about medical procedures which bear comparison with the present-day practices of so-called psychic surgeons. The second excerpt, "Conjuring-House," describes the erection of a Shaking Tent for the performance of magical effects. (The Shaking Tent is described more fully by Paul Kane later in this book.) The third excerpt, "Hexing," gives an instance of the interplay between native expectations and the white man's "magic."

The first two excerpts are taken from a passage written on the shore of Athapapuskow Lake in Northern Manitoba on 9 Aug. 1771. The second excerpt comes from an account written on 20 Nov. 1771 at Anaw'd Lake, also called Indian Lake, which empties into Athapapuskow Lake.

12

NATIVE MEDICINE Several of the Indians being very ill, the con-jurers, who are always the doctors, and pretend to perform great cures, began to try their skill to effect their recovery. Here it is necessary to remark, that they use no medicine either for internal or external complaints, but perform all their cures by charms. In ordinary cases, sucking the part affected, blowing, and singing to it; laughing, spitting, and at the same time uttering a heap of unintelligible jargon, compose the whole process of the cure. For some inward complaints; such as, griping in the intestines, diffi-culty of making water, &c., it is very common to see those jugglers blowing into the *anus*, or into the parts adjacent, till their eyes are almost starting out of their heads: and this operation is performed indifferently on all, without regard either to age or sex. The accumulation of so large a quantity of wind is at times apt to occasion some extraordinary emotions, which are not easily sup-pressed by a sick person; and as there is no vent for it but by the channel through which it was conveyed thither, it sometimes occa-sions an odd scene between the doctor and his patient; which I once wantonly called an engagement, but for which I was after-ward exceedingly sorry, as it highly offended several of the Indians; particularly the juggler and the sick person, both of whom were men I much esteemed, and, except in the moment of levity, it had ever been no less my inclination than my interest to shew them every respect that my situation would admit.

I have often admired the great pains these jugglers take to deceive their credulous countrymen, while at the same time they are indefatigably industrious and persevering in their efforts to relieve them. Being naturally not very delicate, they frequently continue their windy process so long, that I have more than once seen the doctor quit his patient with his face and breast in a very disagreeable condition. However laughable this may appear to an European, custom makes it very indecent, in their opinion, to turn any thing of the kind to ridicule.

When a friend for whom they have a particular regard is, as they suppose, dangerously ill, beside the above methods, they have recourse to another very extraordinary piece of super-stition; which is no less than that of pretending to swallow hatchets, ice-chissels, broad bayonets, knives, and the like; out of a superstitious notion that undertaking such desperate feats will have some influence in appeasing death, and procure a respite for their patience.

On such extraordinary occasions a conjuring-house is erected, by driving the ends of four long small sticks, or poles, into the ground at right angles, so as to form a square of four, five, six, or seven feet, as may be required. The tops of the poles are tied together, and all is close covered with a tent-cloth or other skin, exactly in the shape of a small square tent, except that there is no vacancy left at the top to admit the light. In the middle of this house, or tent, the patient is laid, and is soon followed by the conjurer, or conjurers. Sometimes five or six of them give their joint-assistance; but before they enter, they strip themselves quite naked, and as soon as they get into the house, the door being well closed, they kneel round the sick person or persons, and begin to suck and blow at the parts affected, and then in a very short space of time sing and talk as if conversing with familiar spirits, which they say appear to them in the shape of different beasts and birds of prey. When they have had sufficient conference with those necessary agents, or shadows, as they term them, they ask for the hatchet, bayonet, or the like, which is always prepared by another person, with a long string fastened to it by the haft, for the convenience of hauling it up again after they have swallowed it; for they very wisely admit this to be a very necessary precaution, as hard and compact bodies, such as iron and steel, would be very difficult to digest, even by the men who are enabled to swallow them. Besides, as those tools are in themselves very useful, and not always to be procured, it would be very ungenerous in the conjurers to digest them, when it is known that barely swallowing them and hauling them up again is fully sufficient to answer every purpose that is expected from them.

At the time when the forty and odd tents of Indians joined us, one man was so dangerously ill, that it was thought necessary the conjurers should use some of those wonderful experiments for his recovery; one of them therefore immediately consented to swallow a broad bayonet. Accordingly, a conjuring-house was erected in the manner above described, into which the patient was conveyed, and he was soon followed by the conjurer, who, after a long preparatory discourse, and the necessary conference with his familiar spirits, or shadows, as they call them, advanced to the door and asked for the bayonet, which was then ready prepared, by having a string fastened to it, and a short piece of wood tied to the other end of the string, to prevent him from swallowing it. I could not help observing that the length of the bit of wood was not more than the breadth of the bayonet; however, as it answered the intended purpose, it did equally well as if it had been as long as a handspike.

Though I am not so credulous as to believe that the conjurer absolutely swallowed the bayonet, yet I must acknowledge that in the twinkling of an eye he conveyed it to — God knows where; and the small piece of wood, or one exactly like it, was confined close to his teeth. He then paraded backward and forward before the conjuring-house for a short time, when he feigned to be greatly disordered in his stomach and bowels; and, after making many wry faces, and groaning most hideously, he put his body into several distorted attitudes, very suitable to the occasion. He then returned to the door of the conjuring-house, and after making many strong efforts to vomit, by the help of the string he at length, and after tugging at it some time, produced the bayonet, which apparently he hauled out of his mouth, to the no small surprise of all present. He then looked round with an air of exultation, and strutted into the conjuring-house, where he renewed his incantations, and continued them without intermission twenty-four hours. Though I was not close to his elbow when he performed the above feat, yet I thought myself near enough (and I can assure my readers I was all attention) to have detected him. Indeed I must confess that it appeared to me to be a very nice piece of deception, especially as it was performed by a man quite naked.

Not long after this sleight-of-hand work was over, some of the Indians asked me what I thought of it; to which I answered, that I was too far off to see it so plain as I could wish; which indeed was no more than the strictest truth, because I was not near enough to detect the deception. The sick man, however, soon recovered; and in a few days afterwards we left that place and proceeded to the South West.

*

CONJURING-HOUSE   As during our stay at Anaw'd Lake several of
the Indians were sickly, the doctors undertook to administer relief;
particularly to one man, who had been hauled on a sledge by his
brother for two months. His disorder was the dread palsey, which
affected one side, from the crown of his head to the sole of his foot.
Besides this dreadful disorder, he had some inward complaints,
with a total loss of appetite; so that he was reduced to a mere
skeleton, and so weak as to be scarcely capable of speaking. In this
deplorable condition, he was laid in the centre of a large conjuring-
house, made much after the manner as that which has been already
described. And that nothing might be wanting toward his recovery,
the same man who deceived me in swallowing a bayonet in the
Summer, now offered to swallow a large piece of board, about the
size of a barrel-stave, in order to effect his recovery. The piece of
board was prepared by another man, and painted according to the
direction of the juggler, with a rude representation of some beast of
prey on one side, and on the reverse was painted, according to their
rude method, a resemblance of the sky.

Without entering into a long detail of the preparations for this
feat, I shall at once proceed to observe, that after the conjurer had
held the necessary conference with his invisible spirits, or shadows,
he asked if I was present; for he had heard of my saying that I did
not see him swallow the bayonet fair; and on being answered in the
affirmative, he desired me to come nearer; on which the mob made
a lane for me to pass, and I advanced close to him, and found him
standing at the conjuring-house as naked as he was born.

When the piece of board was delivered to him, he proposed at
first only to shove one-third of it down his throat, and then walk
round the company afterward to shove down another third; and so
proceed till he had swallowed the whole, except a small piece of the
end, which was left behind to haul it up again. When he put it to his
mouth it apparently slipped down his throat like lightning, and
only left about three inches sticking without his lips; after walking
backwards and forwards three times, he hauled it up again, and ran
into the conjuring-house with great precipitation. This he did to all
appearance with great ease and composure; and notwithstanding I
was all attention on the occasion, I could not detect the deceit; and
as to the reality of its being a piece of wood that he pretended to

swallow, there is not the least reason to doubt of it, for I had it in my hand, both before and immediately after the ceremony.

To prevent a variety of opinions on this occasion, and to lessen the apparent magnitude of the miracle, as well as to give some colour to my skepticism, which might otherwise appear ridiculous, it is necessary to observe, that this feat was performed in a dark and excessively cold night; and although there was a large fire at some distance, which reflected a good light, yet there was a great room for collusion: for though the conjurer him self was quite naked, there were several of his fraternity well clothed, who attended him very close during the time of his attempting to swallow the board, as well as at the time of his hauling it up again.

For these reasons it is necessary also to observe, that on the day preceding the performance of this piece of deception, in one of my hunting excursions, I accidentally came across the conjurer as he was sitting under a bush, several miles from the tents, where he was busily employed shaping a piece of wood exactly like that part which stuck out of his mouth after he had pretended to swallow the remainder of the piece. The shape of the piece which I saw him making was this, ; which exactly resembled the forked end of the main piece, the shape of which was this, . So that when his attendants had concealed the main piece, it was easy for him to stick the small point into his mouth, as it was reduced at the small end to a proper size for the purpose.

Similar proofs may easily be urged against his swallowing the bayonet in the Summer, as no person less ignorance than themselves can possibly place any belief in the reality of those feats; yet on the whole, they must be allowed a considerable share of dexterity in the performance of those tricks, and a wonderful deal of perseverance in what they do for the relief of those whom they undertake to cure.

Not long after the above performance had taken place, some of the Indians began to ask me what I thought of it. As I could not have any plea for saying that I was far off, and at the same time not caring to affront them by hinting my suspicions of the deceit, I was some time at a loss for an answer: I urged, however, the impossibility of a man's swallowing a piece of wood, that was not only much longer than his whole back, but nearly twice as broad as he could extend his mouth. On which some of them laughed at my ignorance, as they were pleased to call it; and said, that the spirits in waiting swallowed, or otherwise concealed, the stick, and only left the forked end apparently sticking out of the conjurer's mouth. My guide, Matonabbee, with all his other good sense, was so bigotted to the reality of those performances, that he assured me in the strongest terms, he had seen a man, who was then in company, swallow a child's cradle, with as much ease as he could fold up a piece of paper, and put it into his mouth; and that when he hauled it up again, not the mark of a tooth, or of any violence, was to be discovered about it.

This story so far exceeded the feats which I had seen with the bayonet and board, that, for the sake of keeping up the farce, I began to be very inquisitive about the spirits which appear to them on those occasions, and their form; when I was told that they appeared in various shapes, for almost every conjurer had his peculiar attendant; but that the spirit which attended the man who pretended to swallow the piece of wood, they said, generally appeared to him in the shape of a cloud. This I thought very a-propos to the present occasion; and I must confess that I never had so thick a cloud thrown before my eyes before or since; and had it not been by accident, that I saw him make a counterpart to the piece of wood said to be swallowed, I should have been still at a loss how to account for so extraordinary a piece of deception, performed by a man who was entirely naked.

As soon as our conjurer had executed the above feat, and entered the conjuring-house, as already mentioned, five other men and an old woman, all of whom were great professors of that art, stripped themselves quite naked and followed him, when they soon began to suck, blow, sing, and dance, round the poor paralytic; and continued so to do for three days and four nights, without taking the least rest or refreshment, not even so much as a drop of water. When these poor deluding and deluded people came out of the conjuring-house, their mouths were so parched with thirst as to be quite black, and their throats so sore, that they were scarcely able to articulate a single word, except those that stand for *yes* and *no* in their language.

After so long an abstinence they were very careful not to eat or drink too much at one time, particularly for the first day; and indeed some of them, to appearance, were almost as bad as the poor man they had been endeavouring to relieve. But a great part of this was feigned; for they lay on their backs with their eyes fixed, as if in the agonies of death, and were treated like young children; one person sat constantly by them, moistening their mouths with fat, and now and then giving them a drop of water. At other times a small bit of meat was put into their mouths, or a pipe held for them to smoke. This farce only lasted for the first day; after which they seemed to be perfectly well, except the hoarseness, which continued for a considerable time afterwards. And it is truly wonderful, though the strictest truth, that when the poor sick man was taken from the conjuring-house, he had not only recovered his appetite to an amazing degree, but was able to move all the fingers and toes of the side that had been so long dead. In three weeks he recovered so far as to be capable of walking, and at the end of six weeks went a hunting for his family. He was one of the persons particularly engaged to provide for me during my journey; and after his recovery from this dreadful disorder, accompanied me back to Prince of Wales's Fort in June one thousand seven hundred and seventy-two; and since that time he has frequently visited the Factory, though he never had a healthy look afterwards, and at times seemed troubled with a nervous complaint. It may be added, that he had been formerly of a remarkable lively disposition; but after his last illness he always appeared thoughtful, sometimes gloomy, and, in fact, the disorder seemed to have changed his whole nature; for before that dreadful paralytic stroke, he was distinguished for his good-nature and benevolent disposition; was entirely free from every appearance of avarice; and the whole of his wishes seemed confined within the narrow limits of possessing as many goods as were absolutely necessary, with his own industry, to enable him to support his family from season to season; but after this event, he was the most fractious, quarrelsome, discontented, and covetous wretch alive.

Though the ordinary trick of these conjurers may be easily detected, and justly exploded, being no more than the tricks of common jugglers, yet the apparent good effect of their labours on the sick and diseased is not so easily accounted for. Perhaps the implicit confidence placed in them by the sick may, at times, leave the mind so perfectly at rest, as to cause the disorder to take a favourable turn; and a few successful cases are quite sufficient to establish the doctor's character and reputation: But how this consideration could operate in the case I have just mentioned I am at a loss to say; such, however, was the fact, and I leave it to be accounted for by others.

When these jugglers take a dislike to, and threaten a secret revenge on any person, it often proves fatal to that person; as, from a firm belief that the conjurer has power over his life, he permits the very thoughts of it to prey on his spirits, till by degrees it brings on a disorder which puts an end to his existence: and sometimes a threat of this kind causes the death of a whole family; and that without any blood being shed, or the least apparent molestation being offered to any of the parties.

HEXING   As proof of this, Matonabbee, (who always thought me possessed of this art,) on his arrival at Prince of Wales's Fort in the Winter of 1778, informed me, that a man whom I had never seen but once, had treated him in such a manner that he was afraid of his life; in consequence of which he pressed me very much to kill him, though I was then several thousands of miles distant: On which, to please this great man to whom I owed so much, and not expecting that any harm could possibly arise from it, I drew a rough sketch of two human figures on a piece of paper, in the attitude of wrestling: in the hand of one of them, I drew the figure of a bayonet pointing to the breast of the other. This is me, said I to Matonabbee, pointing to the figure which was holding the bayonet; and the other, is your enemy. Opposite to those figures I drew a pine-tree, over which I placed a large human eye, and out of the tree projected a human hand. This paper I gave to Matonabbee, with instructions to make it as publicly known as possible. Sure enough, the following year, when he came in to trade, he informed me that the man was dead, though at that time he was not less than three hundred miles from Prince of Wales's Fort. He assured me that the man was in perfect health when he heard of my design against him; but almost immediately afterwards became quite gloomy, and refusing all kind of sustenance, in a very few days died. After this I was frequently applied to on the same account, both by Matonabbee and other leading Indians, but never thought proper to comply with their requests; by which means I not only preserved the credit I gained on the first attempt, but always kept them in awe, and in some degree of respect and obedience to me. In fact, strange as it may appear, it is almost absolutely necessary that the chiefs at this place should profess something a little supernatural, to be able to deal with those people. The circumstance here recorded is a fact well known to Mr. William Jefferson, who succeeded me at Churchill Factory, as well as to all the officers and many of the common men who were at Prince of Wales's Fort at the time.

The Shaking Tent Mystery

Paul Kane

The Shaking Tent Mystery has been called the Delphic Oracle of the Indian People. There are many descriptions of it. One of the most graphic accounts is that of Paul Kane, the artist and explorer.

Kane was travelling with a "fur brigade" in the company of a Major McKenzie when he had the opportunity to observe the Indian oracle in action. At the time he was making his way from Norway House back to Toronto on the last leg of his epic sketching trip across the North American continent. The weather was so inclement and Lake Winnipeg was so choppy that the Cree voyageurs had to take to the shore at Dog's Head. Here the Cree erected their "jonglerie" or "medicine lodge" or "shaking tent" principally to bring about fair weather. Kane questioned the oracle about the whereabouts of his "curiosities" — actually a bundle of his painting supplies. The oracle told him where they were and when they would be retrieved. It transpired that the oracle was right. It was also right about the passing storm for dawn brought them fair weather. The brigade was able to leave Dog's Head and two days later arrived at Fort Alexander, then at Fort Francis, and in no time at all Paul Kane was back in Toronto after an absence in the wilderness of two years.

Kane expressed surprise that the Shaking Tent had worked, but hazarded no guesses as the reasons for its effectiveness. His account comes from his diary entry for 28 July 1848 as published in

Wanderings of an Artist Among the Indians of North America
(1859; edition of 1925, reprinted in 1974).

ABOUT 2 O'CLOCK P.M., we endeavoured to proceed, but only got as far as the Dog's Head, the wind being so strong and unfavourable, that it was thought useless to run any risk for the short distance that we would be able to make against it. In the evening our Indians constructed a jonglerie, or medicine lodge, the main object of which was to procure a fair wind for next day. For this purpose they first drive ten or twelve poles, nine or ten feet long, into the ground, enclosing a circular area of about three feet in diameter, with a boat sail open at the top. The medicine-man, one of whom is generally found in every brigade, gets inside and commences shaking the poles violently, rattling his medicinal rattle, and singing hoarse incantations to the Great Spirit for a fair wind. Being unable to sleep on account of the discordant noises, I wrapped a blanket round me, and went out into the woods, where they were holding their midnight orgies, and lay down amongst those on the outside of the medicine lodge, to witness the proceedings. I had no sooner done so than the incantations at once ceased, and the performer exclaimed that a white man was present. How he ascertained this fact I am at a loss to surmise, as it was pitch dark at the time, and he was enclosed in the narrow tent, without any apparent opening through which he could espy me, even had it been light enough to distinguish one person from another.

The Major, who, with many other intelligent persons, is a firm believer in their medicine, told me that a Canadian once had the temerity to peep under the covering which enclosed the jonglerie, but that he got such a fright that he never fairly recovered from it, nor could he ever be prevailed upon to tell what it was that had so appalled him. After about two hours' shaking and singing, the medicine-man cried out that he saw five boats with the sails set running before the wind, which communication was greeted by the whole party with their usual grunt of satisfaction and assent.

After this, many questions were asked him by the Indians, some inquiring after the health of their families at home, whom they had not seen for many months. Upon putting the question, the inquirer threw a small piece of tobacco over the covering of the tent, upon which the medicine-man agitated the tent, and shook his rattle violently, and then replied that he saw one family enjoying themselves over a fat sturgeon, another engaged in some pleasing employment, &c., &c. I then put a question to him myself, accompanying it with a double portion of tobacco, for which I got a double portion of noise. I asked about my curiosities which I had left at Norway House (for want of room in our boats), to be brought on by the canoes which had taken up Sir John Richardson on their return, they not being engaged to carry him further than Prairie River. The medicine-man told me that he saw the party with my baggage encamped on a sandy point, which we had ourselves passed two days before.

However singular the coincidence may appear, it is a fact, that on the next day we had a fair wind, for which the medicine-man of course took all the credit; and it is no less true, that the canoes with my baggage were on the sandy point on the day stated, for I inquired particularly of them when they came up to us.

The Last Sun Dance

"Hilarion"

This remarkable description of "the last authentic Sun Dance" witnessed near Beaver Crossing, Alberta, in July 1938, was recorded by a person who is identified only as "Hilarion." That name was carefully chosen. Theosophists know Hilarion to be one of the Masters or Mahatmas; he is a member of the Great White Brotherhood. Contemporary Canadian trance-channellers may recall that Hilarion is the source of those revelations published in a series of books by the Toronto businessman M.B. Cooke. The "Hilarion" above, who contributed the account of the last Sun Dance, was a Canadian resident in North Surrey, B.C. He supplied this memoir to Winifred G. Barton who first published it in Psychic Phenomena in Canada *(1967).*

THE YEAR WAS 1938. Western Canadians were still deep in the throes of a frustration and despair born of the greatest depression in our history. The streets of Saskatoon and Regina even saw blood, when bitter, jobless and hungry men rode the boxcars to Ottawa to demand the right to eat, to live and to work.

The earth lay parched under a blistering sun. Great clouds of dust, that had once been fruitful soil, billowed and swirled across the horizon. The former luxuriant vastness lay charred and naked. Army worms moved across this wilderness in battle formation;

grasshoppers invaded the prairies like miniature monsters from out of space, bent on complete destruction of all vegetable life.

The homesteaders, farmers, labourers, and ranchers endured not only the depression; but it seemed that all the forces of nature were pitted against the ineffectiveness of man — to beat him to submission. This was a case of the survival of the fittest.

It seemed that man and nature were in a furious battle for supremacy and the result was chaotic confusion. Man, the highest manifestation of natural law, was out of harmony with the Universe and on the verge of mortifying defeat. No rain had come to cool the earth and replenish its growth; only the burning sun filled the cloudless skies. Clumps of yellow matted grass entangled with dried Russian Thistle lay in mounds of powdered dust. This was the bleak picture of the prairies in the "dirty thirties," the era of the "Bennett Buggy" and the "Anderson Cart."

Our native Indians had long known, loved, and respected nature; had often demonstrated the effectiveness of natural law when they turned to their spirits for what they knew to be their just heritage. These people who lived close to the earth seemed ever aware of that "something" which had often proved to be a source of strength and protection in time of need..."the power of the spirits." Now was the time for testing the valour of the gods.

I was to witness such a manifestation of this "hidden power" of the spirit world, in a simple harmonious interaction between natural and supernatural. An interplay far beyond the scope and understanding of many in our day and age.

It was July, and for me it was vacation time. My uncle and I were discussing plans for a trip to Cold Lake in Northern Alberta when I suggested a stop at Frog Lake, since it was here, during the massacre of 1885, that his father (who was my grandfather) rescued Mrs. Gowanlock and Mrs. Delaney from the fate of an Indian torture and killing, trading horses for their freedom.

At this point, an old chief of the Cree tribe, overhearing our conversation, interrupted to tell of a proposed "Sun Dance" that was to be held at a secret rendezvous near Beaver Crossing, northeast of Frog Lake. The chief said he would arrange for us to be present for the occasion, to witness the last truly authentic demonstration of the powers of the gods. My uncle and I were intrigued with the idea, since we knew that such rituals as "the making of Braves" as well as many religious ceremonies and ancient customs had been outlawed by the Great White Fathers. I also learned that the primitive code of spiritual reality was not to be so easily discarded by those who knew their gods and how to communicate with them for decisions on vital matters.

The old Cree chieftain explained that the Indian who would be officiating at the ceremony was much older than himself, and that he was actually the only remaining "true brave" — a distinction earned in battle, in tortuous ceremony, in wisdom, and in ancient tribal ritual. He was the last Medicine Man, the only remaining initiate of an age-old tradition, the only one who could talk with the Sun-god in a language he understood. The Sun-god, in turn, would command the "Gods of Rain." Before this departure for the Buffalo Range in the sky, this Medicine Man would bring about the return of the rains; and my uncle and I were to witness this for ourselves — imagine!

So it was that a few days later, far from the normally travelled roads, we found the designated location, a remote clearing among some poplars. We presented ourselves to the young chief of the Blackfoot tribe. He advised us that under no circumstances could pictures be taken, that we were free to move about the encampment, that the dance would last for three days and within that time there would be rain. There was not a wisp of cloud in the blue-white skies at the time.

As our intended destination was Cold Lake, we decided that we would stop only long enough to look over the ceremonial hut nearing completion a short distance away. Sinewy young bucks and attractive budding squaws worked at a feverish pitch fashioning the circular edifice where the festivities would be held. Load after load of young poplar trees were brought by wagon from the surrounding bush; the rails were tied together to form the sides and the roof. Finally these rails were covered over with interlaced leafy branches to a teepee-type pinnacle. Evidently this was the contribution of the youth of the tribe to the faith of their elders.

On our return from Frog Lake, the gathering place had been completed and the festivities were well under way...the critical point was fast approaching. It was just after one o'clock in the afternoon of this, the third and final day; the sun blasted out its piercing rays in apparent mockery with not a cloud in sight.

We walked around the back of the leaf-covered dance hall, noting that there was only one opening at the opposite (southeast) side. Where we stood, on the north side, a small shaded roof had been built, under which sat the grand-old-man-of-the-hour with his ritual assistants. They sat in a semi-circle, cross-legged on the ground. The ancient Medicine Man lit the pipe-of-peace, took a puff, then exhaled.

With the pipe stem he pointed to the North, South, East and West; then to the buffalo skull on the ground in front of him before passing the pipe on to the next man. Each of the ritual assistants repeated the procedure in turn. This was followed by a quiet discussion before the old brave stood up. Solemnly he picked up the dried and shrivelled buffalo skull with a horn held in each hand. Now, with the forepart of the dried skull, he again pointed in the direction of the four points on the compass. Followed by his assistants, the Medicine Man circled the main enclosure three times before depositing the buffalo skull at the doorway and making his entrance into the hall proper.

Seated around a fire in the centre of the enclosure, the highly electrified singers and dancers swayed with increasing tempo to the beat of the tom-toms. I was told that it was a pure white dog that was boiling in the kettle over the fire. Just to the rear of this frenzy of emotion sat the Ancient and True Brave, now the centre of all attention. He seemed lost in deep meditation, closeted in the profound silence of "inner communication," that, by contrast, seemed to lift his presence above all others. All the ritual partici- pants took turns in "washing" their hands in the flames of the fire and partook of the feast, while the frantic rhythm of the dancing and chanting rose higher and higher to its climax.

Then, amidst frightening silence and the peak of expectancy, the Medicine Man rose slowly, every eye following each deliberate step toward the entrance of the hut. At the entrance he stopped and gazed into the outside distances, he studied the outer silences with all the gracious poise of a prophet of the ages; personified nobility, with deeply etched lines of wisdom radiating over his weather- beaten face. He turned and surveyed all those about him with eyes that penetrated to the very heart and soul. he turned again to look long and defiantly across the vastness of the skies, reverently he gazed at the buffalo skull at his feet.

With arms outstretched towards the blazing sun, he chanted aloud in the mournfully fascinating language of the spirits. No one could doubt the power that flowed from deep within this greatest-of-sages as he reached beyond mortals and boldly challenged the spirits.

Suddenly as we watched, a blinding ray of light seemed to pour down from the heavens to fill a void in the awesome silence in that ceremonial hut. Widening from a narrow prism into a broad arc, it spotlighted the sages, dancers, singers and drummers. The silent figure with his back to the gathering stood out in bold relief, reflecting humility in the radiance of victory. Had the gods been gracious?

Our host, the young chief, came up beside me and whispered... "You are driving a car; you had better get moving. The roads here are very bad when it rains." I thanked him but could not resist a smile as I glanced at the still cloudless sky. "Rain," I thought, "what a joke." It was now three o'clock and at the young chief's insistence I left the enclosure and moments later was bumping across the bleak prairie.

Then without warning the skies blackened, tremendous claps of thunder resounded across the open plains, lightning danced wildly in the distance in a matter of seconds torrents of rain poured from the inky-black skies. Real, true, honest-to-goodness rivers of wet rain!

Less than three miles from the encampment our faithful Durant was hub-deep in a sea of mud and we were unable to budge. I was too dumfounded for words, and uncle couldn't even swear.

After sitting it out for almost an hour, an Indian rider stopped to offer help; it was still pouring with rain. He roped the car to his saddle-horn and pulled the car in this way until we were back on a passable road (a seemingly impossible feat). He would accept no payment for his kindness, saying only, "Maybe this fall I will be down your way and you can help me get a job." I have not seen that rider since, nor have I ever met anyone who knew him.

The return of the rains brought new life and hope to the parched earth and to men lost in the greatest depression in our history.

Historians will some day date the phenomenal restoration from the great drought as the summer of 1938 when the rains came. But it is almost a certainty that only I will relate this transformation to the intervention of the Great Brave of the Blackfoot tribe of Alberta — the last Medicine Man, who stood alone in the remote wilderness between Frog Lake and Beaver Crossing and called upon his gods to disperse the evil spirits and bring peace and plenty to the faithful.

The Rainmaker has long since joined the old Cree chief in the Happy Hunting Grounds — may their traplines never be empty.

As for myself, I tell only what I saw: This last authentic Sun Dance, the return of the rains, the miles of mud. And I think I saw a greater light.

HILARION,
NORTH SURREY, B.C.

I Actually Went into the Astral Heaven

Norval Morrisseau

Woodland Indian Art has many admirers who speak approvingly of its technical and stylistic characteristics. Few people want to seek out or speak about its roots in the world of the spirit. One person who does want to speak about its rootedness in the larger world of nature and the spirit is Norval Morrisseau, the brilliant painter, whose brightly coloured canvases inaugurated the movement in 1962. Morrisseau continues to stress the basis of art in native spirituality.

Copper Thunderbird is Morrisseau's native name, and the artist identifies fully with the awe-inspiring Algonkian spirit of the Thunderbird. Indeed, Morrisseau has painted a series of six panels which depict a shaman being transformed into a magical, bird-like being. The series is called "Man Changing into Thunderbird (Transmigration)."

In the excerpts that follow, taken from an interview conducted by Lister Sinclair and Jack Pollock for the illustrated publication The Art of Norval Morrisseau (1979), the artist speaks revealingly about his upbringing, his visions, his influences, and his mission in life. His vision is at once traditional and contemporary, merging as it does at least three spiritual strands — the Ojibwa tradition of the dream quest, the imagery of classical Christianity, and the practice of astral travel associated with Eckankar.

...BEING A SHAMAN as well as a spiritual person, I do think I have visions. Some of the visions I have had are in many colours. Some are not. In a way, that is hard to explain. But I have seen imagery about Christ and about the Virgin Mary. In fact, one time I think I actually went into the Astral Heaven, and worked there for twelve hours. I was lying down at the time. It was amazing. In that vision I saw Christ and a room full of people. On one side of the room, the people were all dressed in green, flowing robes; on the other side, they were dressed in maroon robes. All at once there were choirs upon choirs upon choirs of angels and saints. They were all singing. It's something you just cannot explain. The music they were playing...and then I saw a shower of roses raining down...robes flowing...this burning fire...the Holy Spirit. Then someone in a black robe walks in. And you say, "What the hell is happening? What's all this rejoicing? What's going on?"

*

I have always been attracted to religious paintings, but only the ones that had that mystical or supernatural quality in them, especially Saint Teresa by Bernini. Just looking at Saint Teresa I get some kind of vibrations from it. I can close my eyes and feel them. That's great art, and it brings on that tingling sexual feeling. Other saints, like Saint Sebastian, do that as well. But the Christ figure was always the one that was dominant for me. That's why I say that Christ to me is still the greatest shaman, and that is why some religious visions are so complex, and so very hard to explain to people. So whenever you are looking at my pictures, you are looking at my visions, whatever they may be.

*

My grandfather showed me how to do interpretations of the shaman beliefs on birchbark. When I was playing with the other children, I was already playing the role of a shaman. I was away from the mainstream of these young people. Already I was acting a role.

*

Anyway, I am being taught what to put down on the bark, for only the shamans made the scrolls. You could say that through history, the shamans were the artists; they were the only members in the tribe allowed to do this. So all my painting and drawing is really a continuation of the shaman's scrolls.

*

I wanted to be a shaman and an artist. I wanted to give the world these images, because I felt this could bring back the pride of the Ojibway which was once great.

*

No matter how much I have abused my physical body, I was always spiritually strong. And I still am. It's as if someone somewhere is looking at me, saying, "Norval, you're going to make it! Get up there! But in the meantime, here is something to look at!" Then this being would take me up to the Astral Plane.... But there are always more questions and I'm still looking for the answers.

*

Now I know I can be a spiritual channel, and I can make my paintings beautiful. But sometimes, I feel physically lazy. Then I just say, "Spirit, you take over!" And, all of a sudden, I get up and start paintings. As for all those colours! The Spirit has chosen the colours. This way it comes so easy. It seems as if I had a whole art gallery, a whole museum of beautiful pictures to bring back from another plane. And when I show them to people on this plane, they can see that they have great power because they have come from a powerful place.

*

Now I say, I *am* a channel, because I realize magnificent things more often. But, of course, there are other little things around here that take up my attention.

*

We as natives believe in the following saying:
> Our God is Native.
> The Great Deity of the Five Planes is so.
> We are neither for nor against.
> We speak not of Christ nor of God.
> We say, "Let them be."
> We follow the Spirit on its Inward Journey of Soul through attitudes and attentions.
> Remember we are all in a big School and the Inner Master teaches us Experience over many Lifetimes.

Beasts and
Beings

The God of the Waters and of the Lakes

Venant St. Germain

Venant St. Germain was a trader with the North West
Company as well as the Seigneur of Repentigy in Lower Canada.
Researchers of remarkable occurrences recall him as "the man who
saw a mermaid" in Lake Superior. That description is inexact
because it was not a "mermaid" that St. Germain saw in Lake
Superior on 3 May 1782; nor was it a "merman." There is no word
in French or English to apply to the being or creature that he saw
and later described. He prepared an account of his experience in
Montreal on 13 Nov. 1812. It took the form of an English-language
affidavit which he swore before two judges of the Court of King's
Bench. Nowhere does the affidavit refer to a "mermaid." That word
was introduced in the preface to the account which appeared as "A
Mermaid in Lake Superior" in the May 1824 issue of The Canadian
Magazine. Here is how it was introduced:

The following relation of some particulars of an animal resembling the human form, which was seen in Lake Superior many years
ago, is given, if not as a proof of the existence of the mermaid, as an
undeniable testimony that even in these lakes, as well as in the
ocean, there are inhabitants with which our philosophers are not
yet acquainted. This account is given in the form of a deposition
before two of the Judges of the Court of King's Bench, and, as
appears from his character, the relator was entitled to belief;
although the opinion he had formed of the narrative being liable to
be doubted, induced him to give it under the solemnity of an oath.

APPEARED BEFORE US, Judges of the Court of King's Bench for the District of Montreal, Venant St. Germain, Esquire, of Repentigny, Merchant and Voyageur, who being sworn on the Holy Evangelists, sayeth: —

That in the year 1782, on the 3d of May, when on his return to Michilimackinac from the Grand Portage, he arrived at the south end of the Isle Paté, where he formed his encampment to stop for the night. That a little before sunset, the evening being clear and serene, deponent was returning from setting his nets, and reached his encampment a short time after the sun went down. That on disembarking, the deponent happened to turn towards the lake, when he observed, about an acre or three quarters of an acre distant from the bank where he stood, an animal in the water, which appeared to him to have the upper part of its body, above the waist, formed exactly like that of a human being. It had the half of its body out of the water, and the novelty of so extraordinary a spectacle, excited his attention, and led him to examine it carefully. That the body of the animal seemed to him about the size of that of a child of seven or eight years of age, with one of its arms extended and elevated in the air. The hand appeared to be composed of fingers exactly similar to those of a man; and the right arm was kept in an elevated position, while the left seemed to rest upon the hip, but the deponent did not see the latter, it being kept under the water. The deponent distinctly saw the features of the countenance, which bore an exact resemblance to those of the human face. The eyes were extremely brilliant; the nose small but handsomely shaped; the mouth proportionate to the rest of the face; the complexion of a brownish hue, somewhat similar to that of a young negro; the ears well formed, and corresponding to the other parts of the figure. He did not discover that the animal had any hair, but in the place of it he observed that woolly substance about an inch long, on the top of the head, somewhat similar to that which grows on the heads of negroes. The animal looked the deponent in the face, with an aspect indicating uneasiness, but at the same time with a mixture of curiosity; and the deponent, along with other three men who were with him at the time, and an old Indian woman to whom he had given a passage in his canoe, attentively examined the animal for the space of three or four minutes.

The deponent formed the design of getting possession of the animal if possible, and for this purpose endeavoured to get hold of his gun, which was loaded at the time, with the intention of shooting it; but the Indian woman, who was near at the time, ran up to the deponent, and, seizing him by the clothes, by her violent struggles, prevented his taking aim. During the time which he was occupied in this, the animal sunk under water without changing its attitude, and, disappearing, was seen no more.

The woman appeared highly indignant at the audacity of the deponent in offering to fire upon what she termed the God of the Waters and Lakes; and vented her anger in bitter reproaches, saying they would all infallibly perish, for the God of the Waters would raise such a tempest as would dash them to pieces upon the rocks; saying, that "for her own part, she would fly the danger," and proceeded to ascend the bank, which happened to be steep in that part. The deponent, despising her threats, remained quietly where he had fixed his encampment. That at about 10 or 11 o'clock at night, they heard the dashing of the waves, accompanied with such a violent gale of wind, so as to render it necessary for them to drag their canoe higher upon the beach; and the deponent, accompanied by his men, was obliged to seek shelter form the violence of the storm, which continued for three days, unabated.

That it is in the knowledge of the deponent, that there exists a general belief diffused among the Indians who inhabit the country around this island, that it is the residence of the God of the Waters and of the Lakes, whom in their language they call *Manitou Nibe Nabais,* and that he had often heard that this belief was peculiar to the Sauteux Indians. He farther learned from another voyageur, that an animal exactly similar to that which deponent described, had been seen by him on another occasion when passing from Paté to Tonnerre, and deponent thinks the frequent appearance of this extraordinary animal in this spot has given rise to the superstitious belief among the Indians, that the God of the Waters had fixed upon this for his residence.

That the deponent, in speaking of the storm which followed the threats of the Indian woman, merely remarked it as a strange circumstance which coincided with the time, without attributing it to any other cause than what naturally produces such an effect, and which is a well known occurrence to voyageurs: that fish in general appear most numerous near the surface, and are most apt to show themselves above water on the approach of a storm.

And further the deponent saith not.

Signed, VENANT ST. GERMAIN.

Sworn before us, 13th November, 1812.
Signed, P.L. Panet, J.K.B.
J. Ogden, J.K.B.

Abducted by the Sasquatches

Albert Ostman

This astonishing account is a "classic case" of a sasquatch abduction. It is also an amazingly readable narrative. Its
length and its feel of verisimilitude set it apart from all other
accounts of chance encounters between human beings and those
hairy, ape-like beings believed by some to inhabit the wild interior
of British Columbia.

Albert Ostman, a Canadian prospector of Scandinavian background, was sixty-four years old in 1957 and living near Fort
Langley, B.C. In longhand in a scribbler, he wrote out the account
of his 1924 abduction. Before a Justice of the Peace on 20 Aug. 1957,
he swore as follows: "And I make this solemn Declaration conscientiously believing it to be true, and knowing that it is of the same
force and effect as if made under oath and by virtue of the Canada
Evidence Act."

"Albert Ostman had written his story before I met him," noted
the journalist John Green in his publication On the Track of the
Sasquatch (1968). "When he was asked to recall all he could of his
encounter with the Sasquatch back in 1924, he went about it by
gathering whatever he could on hand from that period, including,
among other things, a shopping list used in getting ready for one of
his prospecting trips. Then he set about rebuilding the experience
in detail, including his own actions prior to and following the
actual encounter, in an attempt to re-enter, as much as possible, the
scene of events that took place more than 30 years ago.

"When he was later asked if he would swear to the accuracy of the account, he made it clear that he could do so only as to the main elements of the story, not the surrounding detail. Here is the story that he wrote...."

I HAVE ALWAYS FOLLOWED logging and construction work. This time I had worked over one year on a construction job, and thought a good vacation was in order. B.C. is famous for lost gold mines. One is supposed to be at the head of Toba Inlet — why not look for this mine and have a vacation at the same time? I took the Union Steamship boat to Lund, B.C. From there I hired an old Indian to take me to the head of Toba Inlet.

This old Indian was a very talkative old gentleman. He told me stories about gold brought out by a white man from this lost mine. This white man was a very heavy drinker — spent his money freely in saloons. But he had no trouble in getting more money. He would be away a few days, then come back with a bag of gold. But one time he went to his mine and never came back. Some people said a Sasquatch killed him.

At that time I had never heard of Sasquatch. So I asked what kind of an animal he called a Sasquatch. The Indian said: "They have hair all over their bodies, but they are not animals. They are people. Big people living in the mountains. My uncle saw the tracks of one that were two feet long. One old Indian saw one over eight feet tall."

I told the Indian I didn't believe in their old fables about mountain giants. It might have been some thousands of years ago, but not nowadays.

The Indian said: "There may not be many, but they still exist."

We arrived at the head of the inlet about 4:00 p.m. I made camp at the mouth of a creek. The Indian was in no hurry — he had to wait for high tide to go back. That would be about 7:00 p.m. I tried to catch some trout in the creek — but no luck. The Indian had supper with me, and I told him to look out for me in about three weeks. I would be camping at the same spot when I came back. He promised to tell his friend to look out for me too.

Next morning I took my rifle with me, but left my equipment at the camp. I decided to look around for some deer trail to lead me up into the mountains. On the way up the inlet I had seen a pass in the mountain that I wanted to go through, to see what was on the other side.

I spent most of the forenoon looking for a trail but found none, except for a hogback running down to within about a hundred feet of the beach. So I swamped out a trail from there, got back to my camp about 3:00 p.m. that afternoon, and made up my pack to be ready in the morning. My equipment consisted of one 30-30 Winchester rifle, I had a special home-made prospecting pick, axe on one end, and pick on the other. I had a leather case for this pick which fastened to my belt, also my sheath knife.

The storekeeper at Lund was co-operative. He gave me some cans for my sugar, salt and matches to keep them dry. My grub consisted mostly of canned stuff, except for a side of bacon, a bag of beans, four pounds of prunes and six packets of macaroni, cheese, three pounds of pancake flour and six packets Rye King hard tack, three rolls of snuff, one quarter sealer of butter and two one-pound cans of milk. I had two boxes of shells for my rifle.

The storekeepers gave me a biscuit tin. I put a few things in that and cached it under a windfall, so I would have it when I came back here waiting for a boat to bring me out. My sleeping bag I rolled up and tied on top of my pack sack — together with my ground sheet, small frying pan, and one aluminum pot that held about a gallon. As my canned food was used, I would get plenty of empty cans to cook with.

The following morning I had an early breakfast, made up my pack, and started out up this hogback. My pack must have been at least eighty pounds, besides my rifle. After one hour, I had to rest. I kept resting and climbing all that morning. About 2:00 p.m. I came to a flat place below a rock bluff. There was a bunch of willow in one place. I made a wooden spade and started digging for water. About a foot down I got seepings of water, so I decided to camp here for the night, and scout around for the best way to get on from here.

I must have been up to near a thousand feet. There was a most beautiful view over the islands and the Strait — tug boats with log booms, and fishing boats going in all directions. A lovely spot. I spent the following day prospecting round. But no signs of minerals. I found a deer trail leading towards this pass that I had seen on my way up the inlet.

The following morning I started out early, while it was cool. It was steep climbing with my heavy pack. After a three hours climb, I was tired and stopped to rest. On the other side of a ravine from where I was resting was a yellow spot below some small trees. I moved over there and started digging for water.

I found a small spring and made a small trough from cedar bark and got a small amount of water, had my lunch and rested here till evening. This was not a good camping site, and I wanted to get over the pass. I saved all the water I got from this spring, as I might not find water on the other side of this pass. However, I made it over the pass late that night.

Now I had downhill and good going, but I was hungry and tired, so I camped at the first bunch of trees I came to. I had about a gallon of water so I was good for one day. Of course, I could see rough country ahead of me, and I was trying to size up the terrain — what direction I would take from here. Towards west would lead to low land and some other inlet, so I decided to go in a northeast direction, but I had to find a good way to get down.

I left my pack and went east along a ledge, but came to an abrupt end — was two or three hundred feet straight down. I came back, found a place only about 50 feet down to a ledge that looked like good going for as far as I could see. I got down on this ledge all right and had good going and slight down hill all day — I must have made 10 miles when I came to a small spring and a big black hemlock tree.

This was a lovely campsite. I spent two days here just resting and prospecting. There were some minerals but nothing interesting. The first night here I shot a small deer (buck) so I had plenty of good meat, and good water. The weather was very hot in the daytime, so I was in no hurry, as I had plenty of meat. When I finally left this camp, I got into plenty of trouble. First I got into a box canyon, and had to come back to almost where I started this morning, when I found a deer trail down to another ledge, and had about two miles of good going. Then I came to another canyon, on the other side was a yellow patch of grass that meant water. I made it down into this canyon, and up on the other side, but it was tough climbing. I was tired and when I finally got there I dug a pit for water and got plenty for my needs. I only stayed here one night, it was not a good camping site. Next day I had hard going. I made it over a well-timbered ridge into another canyon. This canyon was not so steep on the west side, but the east side was almost plumb. I would have to go down hill to find a way out. I was now well below timber line.

I found a fair campsite that night, but moved on next morning. It was a very hot day, not a breath of wind.

Late that day I found an exceptionally good campsite. It was two good-sized cypress trees growing close together and near a rock wall with a nice spring just below these trees. I intended to make this my permanent camp. I cut lots of brush for my bed between these trees. I rigged up a pole from this rock wall to hang my packsack on, and I arranged some flat rocks for my fireplace for cooking. I had a really classy setup. I shot a grouse just before I came to this place.

Too late to roast that tonight — I would do that tomorrow.

And that is when things began to happen.

I am a heavy sleeper, not much disturbs me after I go to sleep, especially on a good bed like I had now.

Next morning I noticed things had been disturbed during the night. But nothing missing that I could see. I roasted my grouse on a stick for my breakfast — about 9:00 a.m. I started out prospecting. I always carried my rifle with me. Your rifle is your most important equipment.

I started out in a southwest direction below the way I had come in the night before. There were some signs (minerals) but nothing important. I shot a squirrel in the afternoon, and got back to camp at 7:00 p.m. I fried the squirrel on a stick, opened a can of peas and carrots for my supper, and gathered up dry branches from trees. There are always dead branches of fir and hemlock under trees, near the ground. They make good fuel and good heat.

That night I filled up the magazine of my rifle. I still had one full box of 20 shells in my coat pocket. That night I laid my rifle under the edge of my sleeping bag. I thought a porcupine had visited me the night before and porkies like leather, so I put my shoes in the bottom of my sleeping bag.

Next morning my pack sack had been emptied out. Some one had turned the sack upside down. It was still hanging on the pole from the shoulder straps as I had hung it up. Then I noticed one half-pound package of prunes was missing. Also most of my pancake flour was missing, but my salt bag was not touched. Porkies always look for salt, so I decided it must be something else than porkies. I looked for tracks but found none. I did not think it was a bear, they always tear up and make a mess of things. I kept close to camp these days in case this visitor would come back.

I climbed up on a big rock where I had a good view of the camp, but nothing showed up. I was hoping it would be a porky, so I would get a good porky stew. These visits had now been going on for three nights.

I intended to make a new campsite the following day, but I hated to leave this place. I had fixed it up so nicely, and these two cypress trees were bushy. It would have to be a heavy rain before I would get wet, and I had good spring water and that is hard to find.

This night it was cloudy and looked like it might rain. I took special notice of how everything was arranged. I closed my pack sack, I did not undress, I only took off my shoes, put them in the bottom of my sleeping bag. I drove my prospecting pick into one of the cypress trees so I could reach it from my bed. I also put the rifle alongside me, inside my sleeping bag. I fully intended to stay awake all night to find out who my visitor was, but I must have fallen asleep.

I was awakened by something picking me up. I was half asleep and at first I did not remember where I was. As I began to get my wits together, I remembered I was on this prospecting trip, and in my sleeping bag.

My first thought was — it must be a snow slide, but there was no snow around my camp. Then it felt like I was tossed on horseback, but I could feel whoever it was, was walking.

I tried to reason out what kind of animal this could be, I tried to get at my sheath knife, and cut my way out, but I was in an almost sitting position, and the knife was under me. I could not get hold of it, but the rifle was in front of me, I had a good hold of that, and had no intention to let go of it. At times I could feel my packsack touching me, and I could feel the cans in the sack touching my back.

After what seemed like an hour, I could feel we were going up a steep hill. I could feel myself rise for every step. What was carrying me was breathing hard and sometimes gave a slight cough. Now, I knew this must be one of the mountain Sasquatch giants the Indian told me about.

I was in a very uncomfortable position — unable to move. I was sitting on my feet, and one of the boots in the bottom of the bag was crossways with the hobnail sole up across my foot. It hurt me terribly, but I could not move.

It was very hot inside. It was lucky for me this fellow's hand was not big enough to close up the whole bag when he picked me up — there was a small opening at the top, otherwise I would have choked to death.

Now he was going downhill. I could feel myself touching the ground at times and at one time he dragged me behind him and I could feel was below me. Then he seemed to get on level ground and was going at a trot for a long time. By this time, I had cramps in my legs, the pain was terrible. I was wishing he would get to his destination soon. I could not stand this type of transportation much longer.

Now he was going uphill again. It did not hurt me so bad. I tried to estimate distance and directions. As near as I could guess we were about three hours travelling. I had no idea when he started as I was asleep when he picked me up.

Finally he stopped and let me down. Then he dropped my packsack, I could hear the cans rattle. Then I heard chatter — some kind of talk I did not understand. The ground was sloping so when he let go of my sleeping bag, I rolled head first downhill. I got my head out, and got some air. I tried to straighten my legs and crawl out, but my legs were numb.

It was still dark, I could not see what my captors looked like. I tried to massage my legs to get some life in them, and get my shoes on. I could hear now it was at least four of them. They were standing around me, and continuously chattering. I had never heard of Sasquatch before the Indian told me about them. But I knew I was right among them.

But how to get away from them, that was another question. I got to see the outline of them now, as it began to get lighter, though the sky was cloudy, and it looked like rain, in fact there was a slight sprinkle.

I now had circulation in my legs, but my left foot was very sore on top where it had been resting on my hobnail boots. I got my boots out from the sleeping bag and tried to stand up. I was wobbly on my feet but had a good hold of my rifle.

I asked, "What you fellows want with me?"

Only some more chatter.

It was getting lighter now, and I could see them quite clearly. I could make out forms of four people. Two big and two little ones. They were all covered with hair and no clothes on at all.

I could now make out mountains all around me. I looked at my watch. It was 4:25 a.m. It was getting lighter now and I could see the people clearly.

They look like a family, old man, old lady and two young ones, a boy and a girl. The boy and the girl seem to be scared of me. The old lady did not seem too pleased about what the old man dragged home. But the old man was waving his arms and telling them all what he had in mind. They all left me then.

I had my compass and my prospecting glass on strings around my neck. The compass in my left-hand shirt pocket and my glass in my right-hand pocket. I tried to reason our location, and where I was. I could see now that I was in a small valley or basin about eight or ten acres, surrounded by high mountains, on the southeast side there was a V-shaped opening about eight feet wide at the bottom and about twenty feet high at the highest point — that must be the way I came in. But how will I get out? The old man was now sitting near this opening.

I moved my belongings up close to the west wall. There were two small cypress trees there, and this will do for a shelter for the time being. Until I find out what these people want with me, and how to get away from here. I emptied out my packsack to see what I had left in the line of food. All my canned meat and vegetables were intact and I had one can of coffee. Also three small cans of milk — two packages of Rye King hard tack and my butter sealer half full of butter. But my prunes and macaroni were missing. Also my full box of shells for my rifle. I only had six shells beside what I had in the magazine of my rifle. I had my sheath knife but my prospecting pick was missing and my can of matches. I only had my safety box full and that held only about a dozen matches. That did not worry me — I can always start a fire with my prospecting glass when the sun is shining, if I got dry wood. I wanted hot coffee, but I had no wood, also nothing around here that looked like wood. I had a good look over the valley from where I was — but the boy and the girl were always watching me from behind some juniper bush. I decided there must be some water around here. The ground was leaning towards the opening in the wall. There must be water at the upper end of this valley, there is green grass and moss along the bottom.

All my utensils were left behind. I opened my coffee tin and emptied the coffee in a dishtowel and tied it with the metal strip from the can. I took my rifle and the can and went looking for water. Right at the head under a cliff there was a lovely spring that disappeared underground. I got a drink, and a full can of water. When I got back the young boy was looking over my belongings, but did not touch anything. On my way back I noticed where these people were sleeping. On the east side wall of this valley was a shelf in the mountain side, with overhanging rock, looking something like a big undercut in a big tree about 10 feet deep and 30 feet wide. The floor was covered with lots of dry moss, and they had some kind of blankets woven of narrow strips of cedar bark, packed with dry moss. They looked very practical and warm — with no need of washing.

The first day not much happened. I had to eat my food cold. The young fellow was coming nearer me, and seemed curious about me. My one snuff box was empty, so I rolled it towards him. When he saw it coming, he sprang up quick as a cat, and grabbed it. He went over to his sister and showed her. They found out how to open and close it — they spent a long time playing with it — then he trotted over to the old man and showed him. They had a long chatter.

Next morning, I made up my mind to leave this place — if I had to shoot my way out. I could not stay much longer, I had only enough grub to last me till I got back to Toba Inlet. I did not know the direction but I would go down hill and I would come out near civilization some place. I rolled up my sleeping bag, put that inside my packsack — packed the few cans I had — swung the sack on my back, injected a shell in the barrel of my rifle and started for the opening in the wall. The old man got up, held up his hands as though he would push me back.

I pointed to the opening, I wanted to go out. But he stood there pushing towards me — and said something that sounded like "Soka, soka." Again I pointed outside. He only kept pushing with his hands saying "Soka, soka." I backed up to about sixty feet. I did not want to be too close, I thought, if I had to shoot my way out. A 30 30 might not have much effect on this fellow, it might make him mad. I only had six shells so I decided to wait. There must be a better way than killing him, in order to get out of here. I went back to my campsite to figure out some other way to get out.

If I could make friends with the young fellow or the girl, they might help me. If I only could talk to them. Then I thought of a fellow who saved himself from a mad bull by blinding him with snuff in his eyes. But how will I get near enough to this fellow to put the snuff in his eyes? So I decided next time to give the young fellow my snuff box to leave a few grains of snuff in it. He might give the old man a taste of it.

But the question is, in what direction will I go, if I should get out? I must have been near 25 miles northeast of Toba Inlet when I was kidnapped. This fellow must have travelled at least 25 miles in the three hours he carried me. If he went west we would be near salt water — same thing if he went south — therefore he must have gone northeast. If I then keep going south and over two mountains, I must hit salt water someplace between Lund and Vancouver.

The following day I did not see the old lady till about 4:00 p.m. She came home with her arms full of grass and twigs of all kinds from spruce and hemlock as well as some kind of nuts that grow in the ground. I have seen lots of them on Vancouver Island. The young fellow went up the mountain to the east every day, he could climb better than a mountain goat. He picked some kind of grass with long sweet roots. He gave me some one day — they tasted very sweet. I gave him another snuff box with about a teaspoon of snuff in it. He tasted it, then went to the old man — he licked it with his tongue. They had a long chat. I made a dipper from a milk can. I made many dippers — you can use them for pots too — you cut two slits near the top of any can — then cut a limb from any small tree — cut down on the limb — down the stem of the tree — then taper the part you cut from the stem. Then cut a hole in the tapered part, slide the tapered part in the slit you made in the can, and you have a good handle on your can. I threw one over to the young fellow that was playing near my camp, he picked it up and looked at it then he went to the old man and showed it to him. They had a long chatter. Then he came to me, pointed at the dipper then at his sister. I could see that he wanted one for her too. I had other peas and carrots, so I made one for his sister. He was standing only eight feet away from me. When I had made the dipper, I dipped it in water and drank from it, he was very pleased, almost smiled at me. Then I took a chew of snuff, smacked my lips, said that's good.

The young fellow pointed to the old man, said something that sounded like "Ook." I got the idea that the old man liked snuff, and the young fellow wanted a box for the old man. I shook my head. I motioned with my hands for the old man to come to me. I do not think the young fellow understood what I meant. He went to his sister and gave her the dipper I made for her. They did not come near me again that day. I had now been here six days, but I was sure I was making progress. If only I could get the old man to come over to me, get him to eat a full box of snuff that would kill him for sure, and that way kill himself, I wouldn't be guilty of murder.

The old lady was a meek old thing. The young fellow was by this time quite friendly. The girl would not hurt anybody. Her chest was flat like a boy — no development like young ladies. I am sure if I could get the old man out of the way, I could easily have brought this girl out with me to civilization. But what good would that have been? I would have to keep her in a cage for public display. I don't think we have any right to force our way of life on other people, and I don't think they would like it. (The noise and racket in a modern city they would not like any more than I do.)

The young fellow might have been between 11-18 years old, about seven feet tall and might weigh about 300 lbs. His chest would be 50-55 inches, his waist about 36-38 inches. He had wide jaws, narrow forehead, that slanted upward round at the back about four or five inches higher than the forehead. The hair on their heads was about six inches long. The hair on the rest of their body was short and thick in places. The women's hair was a bit longer on their heads and the hair on the forehead had an upward turn like some women have — they call it bangs, among women's hair-do's. Nowadays the old lady could have been anything between 40-70 years old. She was over seven feet tall. She would be about 500-600 pounds.

She had very wide hips, and a goose-like walk. She was not built for beauty or speed. Some of those lovable brassieres and uplifts would have been a great improvement on her looks and her figure. The man's eye teeth were longer than the rest of the teeth, but not long enough to be called tusks. The old man must have been near eight feet tall. Big barrel chest and big hump on his back — powerful shoulders, his biceps on upper arm were enormous and tapered down to his elbows. His forearms were longer than common people have, but well proportioned. His hands were wide, the palm was long and broad, and hollow like a scoop. His fingers were short in proportion to the rest of his hand. His fingernails were like chisels. The only place they had no hair was inside their hands and the soles of their feet and upper part of the nose and eyelids. I never did see their ears, they were covered with hair hanging over them.

If the old man were to wear a collar it would have to be at least 30 inches. I have no idea what size shoes they would need. I was watching the young fellow's foot one day when he was sitting down. The soles of his feet seemed to be padded like a dog's foot, and the big toe was longer than the rest and very strong. In mountain climbing all he needed was footing for his big toe. They were very agile. To sit down they turned their knees out and came straight down. To rise they came straight up without help of their hands and arms. I don't think this valley was their permanent home. I think they move from place to place, as food is available in different localities. They might eat meat, but I never saw them eat meat, or do any cooking.

I think this was probably a stopover place and the plants with sweet roots on the mountain side might have been in season this time of the year. They seemed to be most interested in them. The roots have a very sweet and satisfying taste. They always seem to do everything for a reason, wasted no time on anything they did not need. When they were not looking for food, the old man and the old lady were resting, but the boy and the girl were always climbing something or some other exercise. His favourite position was to take hold of his feet with his hands and balance his rump, then bounce forward. The idea seems to be to see how far he could go without his feet or hands touching the ground. Sometimes he made 20 feet.

But what do they want with me? They must understand I cannot stay here indefinitely. I will soon be out of grub, and so far I have seen no deer or other game. I will soon have to make a break for freedom. Not that I was mistreated in any way. One consolation was that the old man was coming closer each day, and was very interested in my snuff. Watching me when I take of a pinch of snuff. He seems to think it useless to only put it inside my lips. One morning after I had my breakfast both the old man and the boy came and sat down only ten feet away from me. This morning I made coffee. I had saved up all dry branches I found and I had some dry moss and I used all the labels from cans to get a fire.

I got my coffee pot boiling and it was strong coffee too, and the aroma from boiling coffee was what brought them over. I was sitting eating hard-tack with plenty of butter on, and sipping coffee. And it sure tasted good. I was smacking my lips pretending it was better than it really was. I set the can down that was about half full. I intended to warm it up later. I pulled out a full box of snuff, took a big chew. Before I had time to close the box the old man reached for it. I was afraid he would waste it, and only had two more boxes. So I held on to the box intending him to take a pinch like I had just done. Instead he grabbed the box and emptied it in his mouth. Swallowed it in one gulp. Then he licked the box inside with his tongue.

After a few minutes his eyes began to roll over in his head, he was looking straight up. I could see he was sick. Then he grabbed my coffee can that was quite cold by this time, he emptied that in his mouth, grounds and all. That did no good. He stuck his head between his legs and rolled forwards a few times away from me. Then he began to squeal like a stuck pig. I grabbed my rifle. I said to myself, "This is it. If he comes for me I will shoot him plumb between his eyes." But he started for the spring, he wanted water. I packed my sleeping bag in my packsack with the few cans I had left.

The young fellow ran over to his mother. Then she began to squeal. I started for the opening in the wall — and I just made it. The old lady was right behind me. I fired one shot at the rock over her head.

I guess she had never seen a rifle fired before. She turned and ran inside the wall. I injected another shell in the barrel of my rifle and started downhill, looking back over my shoulder every so often to see if they were coming. I was in a canyon, and good travelling and I made fast time. Must have made three miles in some world record time. I came to a turn in the canyon and I had the sun on my left, that meant I was going south, and the canyon turned west. I decided to climb the ridge ahead of me. I knew I must have two mountain ridges between me and salt water and by climbing this ridge I would have a good view of this canyon, so I could see if the Sasquatch were coming after me. I had a light pack and was soon making good time up this hill. I stopped soon after to look back to where I came from, but nobody followed me. As I came over the ridge I could see Mt. Baker, then I knew I was going in the right direction.

I was hungry and tired. I opened my packsack to see what I had to eat. I decided to rest here for a while. I had a good view of the mountain side, and if the old man was coming I had the advantage because I was up and above him. To get me he would have to come up a steep hill. And that might not be so easy after stopping a few 30-30 bullets. I had made up my mind this was my last chance, and this would be a fight to the finish. I ate some hard tack and I opened my last can of corned beef. I had no butter, I forgot to pick up my butter sealer I had buried near my camp to keep it cold. I did not dare to make a fire. I rested here for two hours. It was 3:00 p.m. when I started down the mountain side. it was nice going, not too steep, and not too much underbrush.

When I got near the bottom, I shot a big blue grouse. She was sitting on a windfall, looking right at me, only a hundred feet away. I shot her neck right off.

I made it down to the creek at the bottom of this canyon. I felt I was safe now. I made a fire between two big boulders, roasted the grouse, made some coffee and opened my can of milk. My first good meal for days. I spread out my sleeping bag under a big spruce tree and went to sleep. Next morning when I woke up, I was feeling terrible. My feet were sore from dirty socks. My legs were sore, my stomach was upset from that grouse that I ate the night before. I was not too sure I was going to make it up that mountain. It was a cloudy day, no sun, but after some coffee and hard tack I felt a bit better. I started up the mountain side but had no energy. I only wanted to rest. My legs were shaking. I had to rest every hundred feet. I finally made the top, but it took me six hours to get there. It was cloudy, visibility about a mile.

I knew I had to go down hill. After about two hours I got down to the heavy timber and sat down to rest. I could hear a motor running hard at times, then stop. I listened to this for a while and decided the sound was from a gas donkey. Someone was logging in the neighbourhood. I made for this sound, for if only I can get to that donkey, I will be safe. After a while I heard someone holler "Timber" and a tree go down. Now I knew I was safe. When I came up to the fellows, I guess I was a sorry sight. I hadn't had a shave since I left Toba Inlet, and no good wash for days. When I came up out of the bushes, they kept staring at me. I asked where the place was and how far to the nearest town. The men said, "You look like a wild man, where did you come from?"

I told them I was a prospector and was lost. I had not had much to eat the last few weeks. I got sick from eating a grouse last night, and I am all in. The bucker called to his partner, "Pete, come over here a minute." Pete came over and looked at me and said this man is sick. We had better help him down to the landing, put him on a logging truck and send him down to the beach. I did not like to tell them I had been kidnapped by a sasquatch, as if I had told them, they would probably have said, he is crazy too. They were very helpful and they talked to the truck driver to give him a ride down to the beach. Pete helped me up into the truck cab, and said the first aid man will fix you up at the camp. The first aid man brought me to the cook and asked, "Have you a bowl of soup for this man?" The cook came and looked me over. He asked, "When did you eat last, and where did you come from?" I told him I had been lost in the wood. I ate a grouse last night and it made me sick.

After the cook had given me a first class meal, the first aid man took me to the first aid house. I asked, "Can you get me a clean suit of underwear and a pair of socks? I would like a bath, too." He said, "Sure thing, you take a rest and I will fix all that. I'll arrange for you to go down to Schelt when the timekeeper goes down for mail." After a session in the bathroom the first aid man gave me a shave and a hair trim, and I was back to my normal self. The Bull of the Woods told me I was welcome to stay for a day and rest up if I liked. I told him I accepted his hospitality as I was not feeling any too good yet. I told him about my prospecting but nothing about being kidnapped by a Sasquatch.

The following day I went down from this camp on Salmon Arm Branch of Sechelt Inlet. From there I got the Union Boat back to Vancouver. That was my last prospecting trip, and my only experience with what is known as Sasquatches. I know that in 1924 there were four Sasquatches living, it might be only two now. The old man and the old lady might be dead by this time.

The Profile of a Head

Hubert Evans

A sea serpent was first reported sighted off Victoria's Cadboro Bay on 8 Oct. 1933. That was the first modern sighting of the creature called Caborosaurus. Or was it?

It seems that a sighting took place a year earlier. The man who said he watched it as it cavorted in these waters in 1932 was the esteemed novelist Hubert Evans (1892-1986). Evans's recollections of that remarkable afternoon were taped almost fifty years later by Howard White, the editor and writer, who published his account of the conversation under the title "The Cadborosaurus Meets Hubert Evans" in Raincoast Chronicles, No. 16, 1983.

The conversation between the elderly novelist and the youthful editor took place in the front room of Evans's home at Roberts Creek, B.C. The two men were looking out across "the glassy calm" of the bay towards Nanaimo. On the radio they heard a news report about the Loch Ness monster. That triggered Evans's recollection. "When Hubert finished telling me this I was just as speechless as he must have been at the original event," White concluded.

White's estimation of Evans's veracity is apparent in his estimation of the man: "He is the sort of person who, if he tells you the Cadborosaurus exists, you suddenly discover you believe in Cadborosauruses. I would be hard put to say which is more remarkable."

"WE HAD ONE HERE, YOU KNOW."

"One what?"

"A sea serpent. Or some sort of sea creature quite similar to the way they describe that one over there."

"No!"

"Well, I've never told many people, but it's a fact," he said. "It was in 1932, right out there where you're looking. I was up on the back lot with Dick Reeve, our neighbour, working on the road — that same one you drove in on to get here. Bob Stephens, the old Scot from down the beach — he's dead these many years — came puffing up the hill and said, 'By God now, you've got to come down and see what you make of this. We've had the glass on it for half an hour. It's the damnedest thing.'

"It was late afternoon with the water dead calm just as it is now, and the sun was low so the water was just a sheet of gold. And here, out just beyond that deadhead, was a series of bumps breaking the water, all in dark silhouette and circled with ripples.

"'Sea lions,' I said. 'They run in a line like that sometimes.'

"'You just keep watching,' old Scotty said. And just a minute or so later, along at the end of this series of bumps, up out of the water comes a shaft — this was all in silhouette, so we couldn't see detail, although the outlines were very clear — up, up, up until it must have been six or eight feet out of the water. There was a spar buoy out on the reef then, which was about twelve inches through, and I could see this thing was about the same thickness — certainly no smaller.

"'You know, it could be a log,' I said. I'd seen a crooked log sometimes catch in the current and roll, so a limb comes up like that — when you see something you don't know what to make of, you keep trying to explain it by the things you know.

"But right there as we stood watching, none of us breathing a word, the top end of this shaft began to elongate horizontally, until we were presented with the profile of a head, very much like a horse's in general shape, with eye bumps, nostrils, and something in the way of ears or horns. The neighbour down the way said it had stuff hanging down like hair but I didn't see that. I tell you, it was a feeling, watching that head come round as if to look at us. It just put the hair up on the back of your neck."

Maybe This Was a Sasquatch

William Roe

Not much is known of William Roe except that he was a hunter and trapper who was also a roadworker on the highway near Tête Jaune Cache, B.C. One day in Oct. 1955, he climbed Mica Mountain in the Monashee range, close to the Alberta border, to explore the site of an old deserted mine. Instead of exploring the mine he made a much, much more interesting discovery....

Two years later Roe felt it was necessary to prepare a sworn statement that he was telling the truth. So on 26 Aug. 1957, before a Commissioner for Oaths in Edmonton, he attested to the truth of this account of his strange encounter.

Roe's report of this encounter is reproduced here in its entirety as it appeared in the publication On the Track of the Sasquatch (1968) by John Green. Green corresponded with Roe and from him gained the following additional information about the creature:

"The nails were not like a bear's, but short and heavy like a man's finger nails are. Its eyes were not light and large but small and black like a bear's. You couldn't see any knotted corded muscles. This animal seemed almost round. It was as deep through as it was wide, and I believe if this animal should have been seven feet tall, it would have weighed close to 500 pounds.

"We have to get away from the idea of comparing it to a human being as we know them."

EVER SINCE I WAS A SMALL BOY back in the forest of Michigan, I have studied the lives and habits of wild animals. Later, when I supported my family in Northern Alberta by hunting and trapping, I spent many hours just observing the wild things. They fascinated me. But the most incredible experience I ever had with a wild creature occurred near a little town called Tête Jaune Cache, British Columbia, about eighty miles west of Jasper, Alberta.

I had been working on the highway near Tête Jaune Cache for about two years. In October 1955, I decided to climb five miles up Mica Mountain to an old deserted mine, just for something to do. I came in sight of the mine about three o'clock in the afternoon after an easy climb. I had just come out of a patch of low brush into a clearing, when I saw what I thought was a grizzly bear, in the brush on the other side. I had shot a grizzly near that spot the year before. This one was only about seventy-five yards away, but I didn't want to shoot it, for I had no way of getting it out. So I sat down on a small rock and watched, my rifle in my hands.

I could just see part of the animal's head and the top of one shoulder. A moment later it raised up and stepped out into the opening. Then I saw it was not a bear.

This, to the best of my recollection, is what the creature looked like and how it acted as it came across the clearing directly toward me. My first impression was of a huge man, about six feet tall, almost three feet wide, and probably weighing somewhere near three hundred pounds. It was covered from head to foot with dark brown silver-tipped hair. But as it came closer I saw by its breasts that it was female.

And yet, its torso was not curved like a female's. Its broad frame was straight from shoulder to hip. Its arms were much thicker than a man's arms, and longer, reaching almost to its knees. Its feet were broader proportionately than a man's, about five inches wide at the front and tapering to much thinner heels. When it walked it placed the heel of its foot down first, and I could see the grey-brown skin or hide on the soles of its feet.

It came to the edge of the bush I was hiding in, within twenty feet of me, and squatted down on its haunches. Reaching out its hands it pulled the branches of bushes toward it and stipped the leaves with its teeth. Its lips curled flexibly around the leaves as it ate. I was close enough to see that its teeth were white and even.

The shape of this creature's head somewhat resembled a Negro's. The head was higher at the back than at the front. The nose was broad and flat. The lips and chin protruded farther than its nose. But the hair that covered it, leaving bare only the parts of its face around the mouth, nose and ears, made it resemble an animal as much as a human. None of this hair, even on the back of its head, was longer than an inch, and that on its face much shorter. Its ears were shaped like a human's ears. But its eyes were small and black like a bear's. And its neck also was unhuman. Thicker and shorter than any man's I had ever seen.

As I watched this creature, I wondered if some movie company was making a film at this place and that what I saw was an actor, made up to look partly human and partly animal. But as I observed it more, I decided it would be impossible to fake such a specimen. Anyway, I learned later there was no such company near that area. Nor, in fact, did anyone live up Mica Mountain, according to the people who lived in Tête Jaune Cache.

Finally, the wild thing must have got my scent, for it looked directly at me through an opening in the brush. A look of amazement crossed its face. It looked so comical at the moment I had to grin. Still in a crouched position, it backed up three or four short steps, then straightened up to its full height and started to walk rapidly back the way it had come. For a moment it watched me over its shoulder as it went, not exactly afraid, but as though it wanted no contact with anything strange.

The thought came to me that if I shot it, I would possibly have a specimen of great interest to scientists the world over. I had heard stories about the Sasquatch, the giant hairy Indians that live in the legends of British Columbia Indians and also, many claim, are still in fact alive today. Maybe this was a Sasquatch, I told myself.

I levelled my rifle. The creature was still walking rapidly away, again turning its head to look in my direction. Although I have called the creature "it," I felt now that it was a human being and I knew I would never forgive myself if I killed it.

Just as it came to the other patch of brush it threw its head back and made a peculiar noise that seemed to be half laugh and half language, and which I can only describe as a kind of a whinny. Then it walked from the small brush into a stand of lodge-pole pine.

I stepped out into the opening and looked across a small ridge just beyond the pine to see if I could see it again. It came out on the ridge a couple of hundred yards away from me, tipped its head back again, and again emitted the only sound I had heard it make, but what this half-laugh, half-language was meant to convey, I do not know. It disappeared then, and I never saw it again.

I wanted to find out if it lived on vegetation entirely or ate meat as well, so I went down and looked for signs. I found it in five different places, and although I examined it thoroughly, could find no hair or shells of bugs or insects. So I believe it was strictly a vegetarian.

I found one place where it had slept for a couple of nights under a tree. Now, the nights were cool up the mountain, at that time of year especially, and yet it had not used a fire. I found no sign that it possessed even the simplest of tools. Nor a single companion while in this place.

Whether this creature was a Sasquatch I do not know. It will always remain a mystery to me, unless another one is found.

I hereby declare the above statement to be in every part true, to the best of my powers of observation and recollection.

The Monster of
Lake Massawippi

Ronald Sutherland

Cryptozoology is a department of zoology that deals with hitherto unknown forms of animal life. Cryptozoologists routinely study reports of sightings of Sasquatches and Ogopogos, subjecting them to the principles of rational and scientific inquiry.

Ronald Sutherland is no cryptologist but a novelist, an essayist, a literary critic, and a Professor of Comparative Literature at the Université de Sherbrooke in Quebec's Eastern Townships. He contributed the impressionistic essay "The Monster of Massawippi" to "The Mermaid Inn" column of The Globe and Mail *on 5 Dec. 1981.*

Sutherland's essay intriguingly complements the multitudinous descriptions of encounters with the strange marine life said to inhabit the loch-like lakes of the Eastern Townships, notably Lake Memphremagog which adjoins the author's own Lake Massawippi.

IT WAS A LITTLE PAST MIDNIGHT as I paddled my canoe across Lake Massawippi in the hills of southern Quebec near the Vermont border. The water was still quite calm, but the increasingly loud rumblings and flashes of lightning in the distance indicated that a storm was closing in fast. Every few minutes the moon emerged from behind the clouds to pour shimmering white light over the waves. The effect was eerie, almost otherworldly.

Taking my eyes off the yellow porch lamp on the far shore which was serving as my guide beacon, I stopped paddling for a moment to survey the night and the lake, gloriously silent now that the motor boats were all tied to their docks. Then I heard a splash...and a hissing sound, like some creature drawing breath. I turned, and what I saw literally took away my breath.

The moonlight glared from two greenish eyes and from huge, hideous, protruding fangs. Curving upward snakelike to twin points, the head was a foot or so out of the water, and it was definitely coming toward me, bobbing slightly up and down. I admit I froze in panic, gripping my paddle with both hands, and in the next few seconds all the stories I had dismissed with a wink and a chuckle came thundering back into my mind.

An old man in a bar, shortly after I settled by Lake Massawippi, told me how he had once hooked a large sturgeon, at least six feet long, originally. After playing the fish for two hours, suddenly he was able to haul it in without a struggle. Then he discovered that the sturgeon had been bitten in half. "Sliced clean right across in one bite. Now what yuh figure could do that?" he asked, staring into his beer and breaking a pickled egg in two to emphasize his point.

A woman I know who types university theses rented a house up the lake one summer. Conscientious and hard-headed, Paulette used to get up at 5:00 a.m. and work on the front veranda of her cottage. One morning, just as she was lining up a page in the machine, a movement on the lake caught her eye. She looked out to see, in her own words, "a fin about a foot and a half out of the water, tearing across the lake at a terrific speed, leaving a wake like an ocean liner."

The moon slipped behind the clouds again, plunging me into pitch darkness. The frightful hissing grew louder and quicker, and I could actually feel hot breath on my arms, but I still could not force myself to paddle and at least try to escape.

Oddly enough, a few days earlier, my wife and I had gone out for a midnight canoe ride and had tipped the canoe. She can't swim but was wearing a life belt, so we simply held on for an hour or so, cheering each other as we kicked our feet and stroked with one arm, and eventually we managed to propel the boat to shore.

My God, I thought, the breath growing hotter on my frozen arms, what if we had known that there was really a monster in the lake? How could we have kept our presence of mind? They're in Loch Ness for sure. Why not Massawippi? Plumb lines, I had once heard, have never reached the murky bottom of some parts of the lake. Great caves are down there, and quite probably an underground channel connecting with vast Lake Memphramagog, which is shared by Canada and the United States.

The creature might even be American. The adjoining State of Vermont is apparently full of leaky nuclear plants, which can cause horrible mutations, I'm told — in other words, monsters.

Just this summer a panel of two hundred scientists met in Shelburne, Vt., to study the photographs, sonar readings and 144 sightings over four hundred years (explorer Samuel de Champlain saw a "large, snake-like beast" in 1609) of "Champ," the monster of Lake Champlain. Dr. George Zug, chairman of the Smithsonian Institute's Department of Vertebrate Zoology, summed up the panel's findings by saying, "There's at least a population of large animals of some kind." Serious scientists, they were; two hundred of them.

That guy who disappeared two years ago. They said that he was having an affair with a young thing and wanted to get away from his unsympathetic wife. They'll no doubt say the same thing about me when no trace of my body can be found. The gossips will have a field day for sure. I knew my wife couldn't swim. Tried to get rid of her a few nights earlier by tipping the canoe, but it didn't work. So I faked a disappearance. Always was a dubious character. Oddball friends. Weird habits. Too many kids. Obscure books. Kept bees up on the hill.

A matter of seconds now. The moonlight is spreading across the lake again. The storm is veering to the south. And as I stare transfixed toward the head in the water, resigned now to go to my fate like a blubbering zombie, suddenly the head barks at me.

A familiar bark. A familiar old yellow mutt.

I'll never know why my dog took a notion to swim out to the canoe. He loves the water, and all summer he has been trying to catch water skiers. But in the middle of the night with a storm brewing? And in a lake full of monsters?

The Art of
Healing

The Laying on of Hands

Professor Seymour

The following account of the form of healing known as "the laying on of hands" is reprinted from Glimpses of the Unseen *(1898), compiled by Benjamin Fish Austin, where the source of the passage is given as being from "Professor Seymour's little work on Psychology." There is no further information on the identity of "Professor Seymour" or the details of publication concerning his "little work," which seems to be a pamphlet or a booklet concerned with the curative properties of "animal magnetism," Mesmerism, auto-suggestion, or hypnotism. Perhaps the procedure or the principle described in the passage refers to a form of naturopathy, chiropractic, or acupuncture.*

IN THE CITY OF TORONTO, on the 14th day of December, 1888, Dr. J. Hunter Emory, 33 Richmond Street East, invited me to his office to try an experiment of this kind upon a gentleman by the name of Charles Armstrong, who lives at 247 Spadina Avenue. The operation to be performed was the amputation of a finger. I went to the doctor's office at the time appointed, and was introduced to the patient, and the object of my presence was made known. Mr. Armstrong stated that he objected to taking ether, and was willing that I should try my power of magnetizing the arm; but at the same time he said he had but little confidence in my success, as he had been tried by several professional mesmerists, and had never been controlled. I told him I did not intend to mesmerize him, but simply intended to control the circulation of the blood and nerve fluid, so as to prevent his suffering. When he had seated himself in the chair, and the doctor was ready, commencing with the tips of the fingers of my right hand at the end of his fingers, and with the assurance of mind that the blood in his hand would recede back into his arm, as I drew my hand back over his arm. I moved slowly backward, and when I had drawn my hand clear back over his arm to the shoulder, I told the doctor I was ready. I then placed my right hand upon the patient's forehead, and the left hand just back of the hand that was being cut. The finger was taken off, and the patient was conscious of all that was going on during the operation; and, according to his own testimony (not only given to those who were present on the occasion, but also before the Canadian Institute, on the 22nd of the same month), he did not feel the slightest sensation of pain during the entire amputation, nor in sewing up the flesh, until the last stitch was being put in, which took place after I had withdrawn my influence from him. Nor was there a loss of more than from about six to eight drops of blood, during the ten or fifteen minutes that must have expired in sewing up the wound.

The Endless Power of the Human Spirit

Lindsay G. King

The Rev. Lindsay G. King has been Minister of the Willowdale United Church in Metropolitan Toronto since 1966. He was born at Bell Island, Nfld., in 1930, educated at Mount Allison University, Sackville, N.B., theologically trained at Pine Hill Divinity Hall, Halifax, and ordained to the United Church Ministry in 1953. He holds a Master's degree from Boston University and a Master of Divinity from Pine Hill.

Pneumatology is his special interest, and he has described it in the following words: "The word pneumatology literally means 'the study of the human spirit.' Pneumatology recognizes the fact that we as human beings express ourselves in three ways — physically, mentally, and spiritually. Think of an equilateral triangle. Think of the right side of the triangle as representing the physical body. Think of the left side of the triangle as representing the mental body. And think of the base of the triangle as representing the spiritual body. If all sides are equal, then you can draw a perfect circle in the centre of the triangle. That perfect circle represents a whole person. It doesn't take too much imagination to realize that if anything happens to any one of the sides of the triangle, it affects the shape of the circle."

MY WIFE AND I were at our wit's end. Our eight-year-old daughter, Catherine, was ill again, seriously ill. For the fifth time in the winter of 1963-64, the congestion in her lungs had turned into pneumonia.

Problems with her lungs began in 1959 when she was about two-and-one-half years old. Cathy was born in 1956 in a rural area of northern New Brunswick where I served as a United Church minister. In 1958 we moved to Pointe Claire, P.Q. When her problem started we presumed she had just a minor infection. The first time it happened, she responded fairly well to the usual medication for pneumonia.

However, it happened again and again. Because of my interest in psychology, I suspected the medical problem had a psychological component. Here was a young, sensitive child who was uprooted from her birthplace and friends. I assumed that as she made new friends things would improve.

They didn't. As a matter of fact, they got worse. In addition to her lungs, her throat and tonsils became inflamed. The antibiotics were of little value. Our family doctor, who was very helpful and concerned, suggested that we take her to a specialist at the Hospital for Sick Children in Toronto. The result? "Your daughter should have her tonsils removed. She is also allergic to many things, but especially to animals and birds. We'll prepare a desensitizing serum. When she recovers from the surgery and returns home, have your family doctor see her each week for her shots. She may have to take them for the rest of her life." We followed the specialist's orders to the letter, but the periodic bouts with pneumonia persisted.

My intuition that something was seriously wrong was confirmed when one of the doctors at Sick Kids warned us not to expect too much. "Your daughter may not live to maturity," he said. "All we can do is keep giving her the medicine and hope for the best." Years later, in the 1970s, I discovered from several medical friends of mine that the medicine — chloromycetin, a broad-spectrum antibiotic — had been removed from general use because of its negative effect upon the kidneys and the immune system. At the time the admission by one of the doctors that modern medicine is not infallible shocked me. It motivated me to look for help in another direction.

Since the days when I was a student for the Ministry, I have been interested in the relationship between religion and the healing of the whole person. I have all the respect in the world for medicine and physical science. But I soon became aware that only a few medical scientists are aware of the dynamic and practical role that faith can play in healing. So I went back and re-read two books that had influenced me: *Prayer Can Change Your Life* and *Psychology, Religion and Healing.*

The first book was written by two psychologists, Dr. William Parker and Elaine St. John, and it dealt with the power of rational faith. The Rev. Dr. Leslie D. Weatherhead was the author of the second book, and in it he recommended the setting up of a total health clinic within the church setting, a clinic wherein doctors, psychologists, and clergy can work together.

I preached a series of sermons on faith-healing. I also presented a five-part series on the subject over the CBC. The editor of the religion page of the *Toronto Star* heard my comments on the CBC and got in touch with me. He told me he was very interested in how religion and psychology can work together to promote the healing of the whole person, adding that he was particularly interested in remarks I had made about the role of hypnosis. Then he said, "I know of two or three people I would like to bring to Toronto to tell us of their experience in this field. If you would be interested in having them speak at your church, I am sure the *Star* would cover any expenses involved. In return for this, we would get a good story." I agreed, after securing the approval of the church board.

Dr. Franklin Loehr, the first of the two guest speakers, talked dramatically about the technique of hypnosis, the trance state, and the power of suggestion. Not long after this, a group of us witnessed a close-up demonstration of hypnosis in action. The demonstrator told the subject that the tap-water tasted like Coca-Cola. It did. I thought to myself: If by hypnosis and suggestion, one can change ordinary water into Coca-Cola, then why should one not be able to change negative thinking into positive thinking, disease into health?

The second speaker was the Rev. Joseph Wittkofski, then Minister at St. Mary's Episcopal Church, Charleroi, Pennsylvania, U.S.A. He had been using a form of spiritual hypnosis since 1939. He gave his lecture and demonstration on 26 Jan. 1964, a few weeks after the talk by Dr. Loehr.

I remember sitting there and listening to his speech and demonstration and thinking: I wonder if this would help Catherine. Following his presentation, I explained the problem and asked him, "Do you think that hypnosis would be of any help?"

"Yes," he said. "It could do nothing but help and I would suggest that you do it. She is very young and you, as a parent, are very close to her."

"What if I say the wrong thing?" I asked.

He replied, "If you love your daughter, you will not make a mistake."

With this assurance, the next evening I went into Cathy's room. As she lay there coughing and heaving, I explained: "Cathy, I've discovered a way to help you get a good night's sleep. Would you like to try it?"

"Yes!" she said. "What do you want me to do?"

"All you have to do," I said, "is to look up at the ceiling and breathe as deeply as you can." I instructed her to do this three times. By the time she had taken her third breath, she closed her eyes. At this point I said, "I get the feeling you would like to ride your bicycle."

Immediately she responded, "Yes, but I'm too tired, aren't I?"

I replied, "In your mind's eye — your imagination — you can do anything. Now, take yourself, in spiritual form, outside your body and get your bicycle." I could almost see her do it. I waited a moment, then I said, "Okay, get on your bike. I'll clear the streets for you. In about an hour I'll come back and see how you're doing."

I came back to her room about an hour later and there she was, holding her hands and moving her feet as if she were riding her bicycle. I suggested to her, "You can come back now. Get off your bike. Put it away and listen to me."

For the next few minutes I offered her a series of positive suggestions: "You are in control of your circumstances. You have the ability to breathe deeply, to help your body deal with and drive out whatever it is that is causing your congestion. [I noticed that she was sweating. The exercise and deep breathing were working.] Tonight, you will have a deep sleep. In your dreams you can be anyone you want to be and have all kinds of adventures. When you awaken in the morning, you will be able to cough freely and thus remove all the nasty old phlegm from your lungs."

She slept soundly. When she got up around 8:00 a.m., she coughed for about twenty minutes. She must have removed a cup of mucus from her lungs. She was never bedridden again.

It needs to be pointed out that all this was done with the approval of our family doctor. He even agreed to co-operate when I suggested that we would continue to bring Cathy to him for her needle, but that he would space them out and weaken the contents until all he was injecting was sterile water. Several weeks later she was still well and he agreed that no more needles were needed.

Amazingly, she was soon able to play with animals belonging to our neighbour. Later we got her a pet budgie; later still, a cat. She returned to her dance lessons, in which she excelled. She advanced rapidly in school, taking two grades in one year. In high school she participated in gym, arts, and drama. Outside the school she took advanced lessons in dance and was co-host for a CBC-TV youth program. She graduated from York University's School of Fine Arts in the physically demanding dance program when she was twenty-two.

Beyond university she has taken a massage therapy program and is a registered massage therapist. She has also taken studies in diet, herbs, and meditation, all of which, she says, have helped her to remain healthy. Currently she is teaching others what she has learned from her own experience. Because of her own personal experience, she can speak with sincerity and authority.

Why have I put this story on the record? I do so in the hope that it may help others deal with similar problems, and that it may encourage people not to be shy about using the tremendous resources of the mind and spirit when dealing with problems of the body. Your wit's end is not the end. Beyond it is the power of the spirit which is endless.

Calling upon a Witch

Robin Skelton

Witches are present-day practitioners of the Old Religion, the pagan rites which preceded latter-day religions like Christianity. Robin Skelton, the distinguished man-of-letters, who lives in Victoria, B.C., calls himself a witch. He practises the rites of wicca. He writes in a modest and even matter-of-fact fashion about his calling — or cast of mind — in the last chapter of The Memoirs of a Literary Blockhead *(1988). In this excerpt from that volume he tells of a cure or the lifting of a curse of some kind.*

SOMETIMES ONE COMES ACROSS people who have been cursed. One middle-aged woman was sent to me for help by her hairdresser. She had been married several times, and her last husband had died from the consequences of alcoholism. She sat on the edge of the sofa and accepted a small glass of wine as if she thought it would bite her. She told me she hated living alone and, therefore, took rooms in people's houses where she would share the kitchen and feel, at least a little, part of the household. Everything always went well for the first ten days and then the family "turned against" her, and she became unhappy and had to move on. This kept happening. She was now so nervous she could not even contemplate getting a job and working with people. She knew they would "turn against" her too. It sounded like paranoia, but I probed a little further and discovered that her husband, shortly before his death, had given her a ring with the jovial words "I'm putting my brand on you, my girl." She always wore the ring.

I said, "Let me have it," and as I held it I could feel the energy field of the thing. It was like holding a hot coal. I said, "May I keep this for a week?" and she said I could. I cleansed the ring of its energy field and she came back a week later to get it back. This time she sat on the sofa in a relaxed manner, accepted two full glasses of wine, chatted easily, and spoke of getting an apartment for herself and maybe taking a few courses and visiting her family in Alberta. I told her that I would vet any apartment she found, as she was clearly sensitive to psychic influences, but she never came back to me, though I did make inquiries and her hairdresser told me she was doing fine. I am sure that her husband had not really intended to curse her; he had done so unwittingly. Ever since then, whenever I get a new ring myself — and I collect rings and wear one on every finger (another result of collector's disease) — I feel them out most carefully in case I am picking up something with an energy field I do not want or need.

Most people who call on the which do so because they are at the end of their tether and know nowhere else to go. Many of them do not believe in witchcraft or magic of any kind, but can see no harm in trying this last resource.

Crisis
Apparitions

The Awful Sight Aroused Her

H.T. Crossley

The following experience is related by the Rev. H.T. Crossley, who is identified as an "evangelist" by Benjamin Fish Austin in his tome Glimpses of the Unseen *(1898). Crossley is the narrator of this account and the compiler of the one that follows. The latter one is told in the words of his sister, Mrs. W.J. Parkhill. Prophetic dreams like the two retold here are familiarly encountered in psychical literature. They are known as crisis apparitions.*

MY SISTER, Mrs. W.J. Parkhill, has had several exceptional and wonderful manifestations....

My eldest brother, Levi, was drowned about midnight on Saturday, Sept. 10th, 1881, when the steamer *Columbia* foundered on Lake Michigan. That night my sister, while sleeping, saw him drowning. The awful sight aroused her from slumber, and she sprang out of bed screaming with fright; and as Mr. Parkhill, awakened by her cries, anxiously asked, "What is the matter?" she told him that she had seen Levi drowning and felt sure that she would never behold him alive again.

He tried to dissuade her from the impression; but she never wavered in her belief that Levi was drowned at the time of her dream.

On Monday the following telegram was received: "The Columbia foundered Saturday night and your brother Levi is drowned."

My sister was living at Randwick, Ont., and my brother was drowned near Frankfort, Mich., some hundreds of miles away.

The Sinking of the Asia

Mrs. W.J. Parkhill

"My sister, Mrs. W.J. Parkhill, has had several exceptional and wonderful manifestations," wrote the evangelist H.T.
Crossley to Benjamin Fish Austin, referring to Mrs. Parkhill's
clairvoyance and clairaudience. Crossley's two accounts of his
sister's wild talents were reproduced by Austin in his compilation
Glimpses of the Unseen (1898).

One of the accounts of Mrs. Parkhill's abilities appears under
Crossley's name because it was presented in his own words; the
other account appears here, under Mrs. Parkhill's name because
she was its narrator. Crossley commented on the unusual and tragic
incident: "It occurred in connection with the drowning of Mr.
William Henry, with whom my brother-in-law had been in business
for over twenty years, and who had been almost as a brother to my
sister. I shall give the account in the words of my sister as they
appear in a letter she sent me."

The sinking in Georgian Bay in 1882 of the Asia marked the
greatest loss of life in a marine disaster to that time.

ON SEPTEMBER 14TH, 1882, between eleven and twelve o'clock in the
day, as I was in the kitchen helping with the dinner, a peculiar
sensation passed over me, and clasping my hands tightly together
and walking through the dining room to the front door, I exclaimed: "Oh, I feel so strange."

The upper part of this door, as you will remember, consists of one large pane of glass.

As I stood there I seemed to lose sight of the mill, lawn, and everything before me, and I distinctly saw William tossing on great waves. I do not know whether I stood there one minute or ten, but this I know, that I saw William as plainly as I ever saw him. I saw his bald head and his long locks as they were lifted by the water. As I beheld him struggling in the waves, I seemed to be quite near and gazed horror-stricken at the awful sight. At length I saw him throw up his hands and sink beneath the waters.

I then rushed into the parlour where there was a lady friend. I could not speak. The lady looked wonderingly at me and said, "Why, what is the matter? You look as if you had seen a ghost."

I cried out, "Oh, William Henry is drowned; I saw him drowning, I saw him tossed on the waves. I saw him going down and coming up again. I saw him sink to rise no more."

The lady looked incredulously at me and smiled as she said: "Mrs. Parkhill, you have only imagined all this. If he were drowning you could not see him. You are crossing the bridge before you come to it. Why, it is impossible, for he told you where he would be today, and he is not even on the water, much less drowned."

I implored her not to ridicule my fears, for I saw the waves go over him.

I was so prostrated that I lay down on the sofa and for a time gave way to convulsive sobs, after which I tried to calm myself and shut out the awful sight that I had witnessed.

William was a good Christian man, and was one of our particular friends for whom I prayed every night. That night, however, I could not pray for him as usual, for I felt sure that he was beyond the reach of our prayers.

"This 14th day of September was a Thursday. On Friday afternoon my husband returned home, and when he saw me he exclaimed: "I see that you have been having another one of your awful headaches."

I relied, "No, I have not had a headache, but yesterday I saw William drowning."

He urged me not to distress myself, and said, "William is all right; I saw him in Toronto on Tuesday before he started for the Manitoulin Islands."

I cried out, "Oh Park, I know he is dead, for I saw him drowning."

My husband was much disturbed by my seeming hallucination, and requested me not to speak of the matter again, but to take a good rest and all would be right.

I went about the house quietly, with that strange feeling which I cannot describe, but never doubting the truth of what I had seen.

The next day, Saturday afternoon, I went out to the Post Office, where Mr. Parkhill sat at the desk writing. Looking up, he said, "I'm writing a letter to William." I answered, "Oh please don't write to him, he will never get it; he is dead."

After much persuasion I got him to put the letter away until the paper would come in the afternoon, when he would see an account of the disaster.

Something happened to the newspaper part of the mail, so that the Toronto Saturday papers did not come; but my mind remained unchanged.

On Sunday morning, while we were sitting on the verandah, I feeling very poorly and still weighed down with grief, Mr. Parkhill looked up and said, "Why, there is Mr. Wade driving in; I wonder what is bringing him on Sunday?" He was the Postmaster at Lisle.

I replied, "He has yesterday's papers, and is coming in to tell you that William is drowned."

He got up quickly, saying, "You must not talk that way, I cannot bear it; it would be too dreadful," and went into the house.

A few moments later Mr. Wade assured him that William was drowned, and handed him the paper in which the news of the wreck of the *Asia* was printed; and the truth was forced upon him that what I saw had really happened.

When the body of William was found, his watch was stopped at the hour I saw him drowning; and Mr. Tinkiss and Miss Morrison, the only two surviving passengers of the ill-fated steamer, stated that it was on Thursday at the hour I have named when the steamer was wrecked on the Georgian Bay.

I never could understand or explain the phenomenon; but this I know, that I never saw anything more distinctly in my life than the scene I have faintly described to you.

Apparition of a Person about to Die

G.J. Romanes

George John Romanes (1848-1894) was born in King-ston, Ont., and educated at Cambridge University. He was elected a Fellow of the Royal Society in 1879. A distinguished psychologist and zoologist, he lectured at Cambridge and Edinburgh, contrib-uted to scientific journals, and published books on science and notably on the theory of evolution.

The apparition of a person about to die appeared to Romanes, who recorded the experience. On 20 Nov. 1899 he sent his account F. W.H. Myers, a friend and fellow scientist, who was collecting such accounts with the object of classifying and publishing them. Following Romanes' own early death, Myers incorporated the account in the paper he wrote on crisis apparitions. It appeared as "Subliminal Self" in Volume XI of the Proceedings of the Society for Psychical Research.

Myers added the following postscript: "The impression made by this incident upon the late Dr. Romanes, F.R.S., was, as he has more than once told me, very deep; nor was there, he thought, any such anxiety in his mind at the time with regard to his sister as could have predisposed him to this unique hallucination. There were, I may add, other unpublished circumstances which confirmed him in this view of the matter." It is unfortunate that Myers did not elaborate on that latter point.

TOWARDS THE END OF MARCH, 1878, in the dead of the night, while believing myself to be awake, I thought the door at the head of my bed was opened and a white figure passed alongside the side of the bed to the foot, where it faced about and showed me it was covered head and all in a shroud. Then with its hands it suddenly parted the shroud over the face, revealing between its two hands the face of my sister, who was ill in another room. I exclaimed her name, whereupon the figure vanished instantly. Next day (and certainly on account of the shock given me by the above experience) I called in Sir W. Jenner, who said my sister had not many days to live. [She died, in fact, very soon afterwards.]

I was in good health, without any grief or anxiety. My sister was being attended by our family doctor, who did not suspect anything serious, therefore I had no anxiety at all on her account, nor had she herself.

I have never, either before or after this, had such an experience.

G.J. Romanes.

A Death in Ireland

James L. Hughes

The folklorist might call the following story a memorate. A memorate is a family tradition or tale that is passed from member to member, from generation to generation. Its maximum impact is felt by members of the immediate family, not members of the general public. James L. Hughes, Inspector of Public Schools, Toronto, disclosed this memorate to B.F. Austin who reproduced it in Glimpses of the Unseen *(1898).*

MY FATHER WAS BORN in the northern part of Ireland. His grandmother was especially fond of him, and her affection was returned warmly. Soon after his marriage he came to Canada. His grandmother was still alive; her health was good, and her love for him had lost none of its vitality. She remained in Ireland.

I am his oldest child, and I well remember one Sunday morning hearing him relate the following experience to my mother:

"I was awakened about three o'clock by a loud rapping at the door of my bedroom. I sat up in bed, and asked, 'Who's there?' I heard the answer distinctly and very definitely: 'Your grandmother is dead.' I got up and opened the door, but could find no one; and I heard no more."

He aroused my mother and told her at once the strange story I heard him repeating in the morning. He told the story to his brother and other neighbours after church the same day. Some of these neighbours had known his grandmother in Ireland. In due time a letter came announcing the old lady's death. Making the necessary allowance for the difference in time in Ireland and in Canada, she died at the exact time the announcement was made to him.

How was the message conveyed? To say, "He dreamt it," leaves the mystery unsolved. The fact still remains that he announced the death of his grandmother, thousands of miles away, weeks before the fact was communicated by letter, and a few seconds after she passed away. It makes the case still more remarkable to know that he had no knowledge of her illness.

My father is a man weighing more than two hundred pounds, and possessed of extraordinary physical strength. He has always had receptive telepathic power which frequently enabled him to announce events of importance occurring to members of his family at a distance without any information by the ordinary channels of communication.

A Crisis Apparition

Duncan Cameron

A crisis apparition is a vision of a dying person which is experienced by a relative or a loved one immediately prior to the moment of death. The crisis apparition described below occurred to Malcolm Macdonald, a Montreal tea merchant, sometime in the 1880s. Macdonald related the experience to his friend and fellow Methodist congregant Duncan Cameron in 1889. At the time Cameron was a bank employee in Montreal. Thereafter he was appointed manager of the Merchants' Bank of Halifax, Maitland, N.S. He set down the details of the experience eight years after hearing about it for the use of Benjamin Fish Austin who included the report in his copious volume Glimpses of the Unseen *(1898) under the title "An Account of a Remarkable Vision." Little is known of Macdonald but more is known of Cameron who was trained in accountancy in Scotland where he was converted to evangelical Christianity. He was much interested in visions and testimonials to Gospel truth.*

IN 1889 I was living in Montreal and was well acquainted with Mr. Malcolm Macdonald, who then carried on a tea business on Seigneurs Street, and who was well known as a leading member of the West End Methodist Church. He told me the following experience of a vision which he had. It was shortly before dawn on a certain morning. He wakened to find himself in an interview with an unmarried brother, who for some time had been pursuing his fortune in the

State of Ohio, and another brother who resided in Toronto. He was at the self-same time perfectly conscious of being in bed in his own home, and in his ordinary environment, and also perfectly conscious of a real, personal interview with his two brothers, both of whom he knew also were hundreds of miles distant from him and from each other. In his vision he saw the interview begin by their lovingly greeting one another, whereupon the brother from Ohio solemnly informed the other two that he was dying then, and that before departing he wished to give them certain instructions and counsel. These instructions and counsel he gave, but they need not here be related; only let me state that they were truly wise and truly appropriate, and, as the surviving brothers found out afterwards, they were to them of great value. The interview finished with a tender farewell, and the vision ended.

Malcolm at once informed his wife of what he had just experienced, and he prepared himself for news from Ohio. Sure enough, early in that forenoon, a telegram arrived containing the announcement of the death of the brother in Ohio. Malcolm at once arranged by wire with the brother in Toronto to meet him and proceed together to look after the remains. As soon as they met, the Toronto brother said: "Malcolm, I had a wonderful vision this morning." Malcolm, feeling surprised, asked him what it was, but he was more than surprised when his brother went on to give what was a perfect description of the vision he himself also had at Montreal, and at the very same time.

They reached the home of strangers in Ohio, where lay the remains of the dead brother. Kind friends had watched by him during his last hours, and they informed the men from Canada how, for a time ere he breathed his last, he seemed to be in a trance, at the commencement of which he spoke out distinctly, as if giving a loving greeting to two brothers. Then he said to them many things as to family matters, and matters of eternity, which the watchers related so faithfully as to be recognized by the two brothers as a perfect account of their respective visions in Montreal and Toronto.

Duncan Cameron,
Manager, Merchants' Bank of Halifax,
Maitland, N.S.

16 March, 1897.

Thousands of Miles
Away in Spain

Irene M. Ashby

*Irene M. Ashby volunteered the following informa-
tion about her personal life:*

*"I was born on Feb. 11th, 1915, in Toronto, of a father who was
Viennese and a mother who was American of German parentage.
I'm a homemaker who loves music, art, literature, and travel,
besides my family. I have been married fifty years this year and am
the mother of a son who works for the National Research Council
in Ottawa and a daughter who is a librarian, teacher, and editor
who holds five degrees, including a doctorate."*

*In the narrative that follows she has described a curious, clair-
voyant dream that she had while she was travelling with her husband in Spain. It corresponded to reality in Toronto, though she was
not to know that until some days later. The narrative is based on
her correspondence with the editor, dated 12 June and 21 July 1987.*

IN 1986 we were touring the cities of Spain, and on the morning
of Feb. 28th I had a dream in which I saw an older lady being
struck from behind, blood gushing out of her head, her purse
taken, and left unconscious and bleeding in the snow. It was made
very plain to me that this was taking place in Toronto on Victoria
Park Avenue. Later that day, in Seville, I was hit from behind and
my purse was snatched by a kid who got away on a motorbike. I
realized that I'd been warned, because all my life dreams have been

prophetic for me; I just couldn't figure out the Victoria Park Avenue aspect of this one. Why there?

We returned home on Saturday, March 8th, and on Monday, March 10th, I picked up the *Toronto Star* for that day, and inadvertently opened it at the page whereon "Crimestoppers" was featured. Although I don't usually read the feature, the headline that day compelled me to do so. It was about an elderly lady who'd been attacked from behind, coming out of Parkway Plaza on *Victoria Park Avenue*, on Feb. 28th, her purse snatched, and left bleeding and unconscious in the snow. The police were asking for help in solving the crime.

In figuring out the time difference between Spain and here I'm almost certain that what I saw in the dream took place as it was happening here in Toronto.

I did not know or recognize the elderly lady in my dream and police don't publish names in "Crimestoppers." I've no way of finding out who she was except by going to the police, but what good would it do? There was nothing in the dream that would provide a clue as to who did the dastardly deed.

What detail of Parkway Plaza did I recognize? None, except that it seemed to have happened near a fence and, according to the report, she was taking a short cut from the Plaza at the back where there is a fence. How did I know it was Victoria Park Avenue? It is hard to believe but in the dream someone was shouting at me, "This is Victoria Park Avenue!"

Now how was it that I, thousands of miles away in Spain, saw the whole thing in a dream? As I said, all my life my dreams have been prophetic, and the more vivid the dream, the more it is an omen of what is about to happen. I believe there are more things on earth than we poor humans will ever be able to solve. Two books by John G. Fuller — *Arigo, Surgeon of the Rusty Knife* and *The Airmen Who Would Not Die* — pose more questions than we can answer. I hope to read more of Fuller's books....

The Death of Roger

Kathleen Belanger

Did Kathleen Belanger see an apparition of her son Roger at the time of his death? In this memoir, written on 6 June 1987, the grief-stricken mother, a native of Port Mellon, B.C., gives an account of what she felt and what she saw that awful day. It is her feeling and belief that Roger, who suffered a fatal logging accident, appeared to her to offer some sort of consolation.

AS I AWOKE on the morning of May 16th, 1985, a feeling of dread spread over me... but *why?* It should be a good day; after all, my husband has finally gone back to work after months of illness. Finally he will be receiving a regular pay cheque. Maybe we will have steak tonight!

About mid-morning, my girl friend and I decide to go into the town of Gibsons. Naturally our talk on the way in is of my son Roger, his wife Myra, and their two boys — Dale is three and his little brother Ryan is only three months old. They had spent Mother's Day with us. Myra and the two boys had gone home to Mission and Roger was off to work near Mile 47, up the Elaho Valley. How they will be missed!

My feeling of dread persists. As a matter of fact, it is getting stronger and stronger... *what is going to happen?* We go for coffee with friends. It doesn't help. I am unable to concentrate on shopping. I don't even feel like looking at things.

It is two o'clock now and we may as well go home. As we turn into the driveway, I notice that the garage door is wide open. I enter the basement and every door there is wide open. As I turn, there stands Roger, with a big grin on his face. I'm about to ask him what happened, when all of a sudden he is no longer there!

Is my imagination working overtime?

My husband returns home from work. No supper is ready so we go back into town and have a pleasant meal while we watch all the boats coming into the bay. This is usually good therapy, but not tonight. My feeling of dread is still with me.

It is now eight in the evening and we are back home. The fire alarm is heard. My husband is the local fire chief so he has to leave. Then neighbours who rarely come to visit us drop in for a few minutes. The police come. As soon as I see them I knew that Roger is gone.

Roger was hit by a tree 165 feet high and died instantly. I do feel that he came to tell me that he is happy and has not suffered. I am sure that one day we will meet again and that he will most likely still be opening doors for me — maybe this time to let me in.

A Thanatological
Experience

Patient X

W*hat does the conscious person experience at the
moment of death? In the absence of a scientific answer to that
question, folk beliefs abound. Traditionally, the dying person
watches as scenes from his or her life unfold (the life review); then
the spirit separates from the body and surveys it dispassionately
(autoscopy); finally, there is the voyage into realms of radiance (the
soul's flight).*

*Something approaching the traditional pattern of the near-death
experience was recorded by a patient in the coronary unit of the
Toronto General Hospital. The details were set down by the patient
himself at the request of his two physicians who then added their
own observations. They published the account under the heading
"Cardiac Arrest Remembered" in the correspondence column of
the* Canadian Medical Association Journal, *22 May 1971.*

*The two physicians contributed the two paragraphs which ap-
pear here; in the journal, these preceded and succeeded the patient's own narrative. For present purposes the 68-year-old man has
been identified as Patient X.*

A 68-year-old man who previously had suffered no symptoms
of coronary artery disease awoke with aching pain in the left
arm. Squeezing retrosternal pain developed several hours later
and persisted until his admission to hospital in the late afternoon. He was transferred without delay to the coronary unit,
where his general condition was found to be satisfactory. Blood

pressure was 126/78, heart sounds were normal, and there were no signs of cardiac failure. A 12-lead electrocardiogram was normal. The heart rhythm was monitored continuously and only an occasional ventricular premature beat was seen that followed the T wave by a comfortable distance. Ten hours after admission, the chest pain became worse, and the patient was given 50 mg. of meperidine. Suddenly a ventricular premature beat fell on a T wave, causing ventricular fibrillation. One of the coronary unit nurses recognized the cardiac arrest and immediately defibrillated the patient. After this there were no further serious arrhythmias, and convalescence was uneventful apart from an episode of pulmonary infarction. The ECG was normal the morning after defibrillation, and it was not until the 10th day that changes of anterior subendocardial infarction became evident. Changes in SGOT and CPK levels, however, were diagnostic of recent myocardial infarction from the first day in hospital. The patient remembered in detail the events surrounding his cardiac arrest, and the following account is his own vivid description of the experience. (The right leg mentioned was badly scarred from osteomyelitis suffered in childhood.)

*

It is unusual for patients to remember the events surrounding cardiac arrest. More often there is a period of amnesia of several hours duration before and after the event. This description is extremely interesting. The patient saw himself leaving his body and was able to observe it "face to face." This could be the concept of the soul leaving the body which is found in many religions. The delightful feeling of floating in space and the tranquillity, the yellow light, the rectangular shape with holes in it, associated with the wish of not wanting to be brought back again, may provide comfort and reassurance to patients suffering from coronary artery disease as well as to their relatives.

R.L. MacMillan, M.D., F.R.C.P.[C] and
K. W.G. Brown, M.D., F.R.C.P.[C]

Coronary Unit,
Toronto General Hospital,
Toronto 2.

AS I PROMISED, I am setting down my experiences as I remember them when I had the cardiac arrest last May.

I find it hard to describe certain parts — I do not have words to express how vivid the experience was. The main thing that stands out is the clarity of my thoughts during the episode. They were almost exactly as I have written them and in retrospect it seems that they are fixed in my memory — more so than other things that have happened to me. It seemed at times that I was having a "dual" sensation — actually experiencing certain things yet at the same time "seeing" myself during these experiences.

I had been admitted into the intensive care ward in the early evening. I remember looking at my wrist watch and it appeared to be a few minutes before 4:00 a.m. I was lying flat on my back because of the intravenous tubes and the wires to the recording machine. Just then I heave a very, very deep sigh and my head flopped over to the right. I thought, "Why did my head flop over? — I didn't move it — I must be going to sleep." This was apparently my last conscious thought.

Then I am looking at my own body from the waist up, face to face (as though through a mirror in which I appear to be in the lower left corner). Almost immediately I saw myself leave my body, coming out through my head and shoulders. (I did not see my lower limbs.) The "body" leaving me was not exactly a vapour form, yet it seemed to expand very slightly once it was clear of me. It was somewhat transparent, for I could see my other "body" through it. Watching this I thought, "So this is what happens when you die" (although no thought of being dead presented itself to me).

Suddenly I am sitting on a very small object travelling at great speed, out and up into a dull blue-grey sky, at a 45-degree angle. I thought, "It's lonely out here. — Where am I going to end up? — This is one journey I must take alone."

Down below to my left I saw a pure white cloud-like substance also moving up on a line that would intersect my course. Somehow I was able to go down and take a look at it. It was perfectly rectangular in shape (about the same proportions as a regular building brick), but full of holes (like a sponge). Two thoughts came to me: "What will happen to me when it engulfs me?" and "You don't have to worry; it has all happened before and everything will be taken care of." I have no recollection of the shape catching up with me.

My next sensation was of floating in a bright, pale yellow light — a very delightful feeling. Although I was not conscious of having any lower limbs, I felt something being torn off the scars on my right leg, as if a large piece of adhesive tape had been taken off. I thought, "They have always said your body is made whole out here. I wonder if my scars are gone," but though I tried I could not seem to locate my legs. I continued to float, enjoying the most beautiful tranquil sensation. I had never experienced such a delightful sensation and have no words to describe it.

Then there were sledge-hammer blows to my left side. They created no actual pain, but jarred me so much that I had difficulty in retaining my balance (on whatever I was sitting). After a number of these blows, I began to count them and when I got to six I said (aloud I think), "What the....are you doing to me?" and opened my eyes.

Immediately I was in control of all my faculties and recognized the doctors and nurses around me. I asked the head nurse at the foot of my bed, "What's happening?" and she replied that I'd had a bad turn. I then asked who had been kicking me, and a doctor pointed to a nurse on my left, remarking that she really had to "thump" me hard and that I would be black and blue on my left side the next day. (I don't think I was.)

Just a few comments as I think over what happened to me. I wonder if the bright yellow surroundings could have been caused by someone looking into my eyes with a bright light?

I have read about heart transplants where it is claimed the brain dies before the heart stops. In my case, my brain must have been working after my heart stopped beating for me to experience these sensations.

If death comes to a heart patient in this manner, no one has cause to worry about it. I felt no pain (other than what I had when I entered hospital), and while it was a peculiar experience it was not unpleasant. The floating part of my sensation was so strangely beautiful that I said to a doctor later that night, "If I go out again, don't bring me back — it's so beautiful out there," and at that time I meant it.

Ghosts and Spirits

Completely Clad in White

"QUIS."

This account of the sighting of an apparition, ten or twelve feet in height and "completely clad in white," appeared under the heading "A Strange Apparition" in the correspondence column of the St. Catharines Evening Journal *on 17 Aug. 1866. It was signed "QUIS.," which is the Latin word for "who" or "what." The identity of "QUIS." has yet to be determined. No other letter about the appearance of the strange apparition or similar disturbance connected with the fire appeared in the* Evening Journal.

TO THE EDITOR OF THE JOURNAL: —

SIR, — I would beg leave to call your attention to a very strange incident in connection with the fire the other night, which at the time made a strong impression on my mind; but believing that it was perhaps a mere hallucination of my own brain, induced by the sudden awakening at or near the hour of midnight, when the mind is most susceptible of supernatural influences, I did not give expression to my thoughts or the matter until I learned to-day that others beside myself witnessed the same startling phenomenon.

When awakened that night by the most startling of all cries — the cry of fire at midnight — I jumped out of bed, and dressing myself as hastily as possible, I ran down Queen street on the south side, and when I had reached that part of it situated between

St. Paul and King streets, where the shade of the trees are deepest, I distinctly saw a figure moving on the other side to that on which I was going. Now, Sir, I think I am not superstitious, in fact I have always prided myself on my total want of faith in spiritual visitations, but there before my vision, and evidently with the consent of all my other senses, was a figure the first view of which brought me to a sudden halt and recalled lines long since impressed on my memory —

"For he reared at the sight of the lady in white,
    And he paused in his mad career.
She spoke and her words, when I heard them aright,
    They curdled my blood with fear."

The light from the burning building was just casting its lurid glare upon the dark and mazy atmosphere which prevailed at the time, and was bringing into view, in exaggerated proportions, every object within its influence. Whether it was this strange effect or my excited imagination I dare not say, but there, directly between me and the light of the conflagration, rose up a figure which I should judge was at least 10 or 12 feet in height and was from the knees upwards completely clad in white. Below the knees I thought I could discover a pair of legs and feet, which, considering the strides they were making, ought to have been enveloped in the seven league boots, which I remembered to have read of in my young days, but which were not, if my eyes were at all faithful to their trust, for they appeared to be as naked and bare, as if they were prepared for footing turf or searching for flax in a bog hole in the Emerald Isle. The head was surmounted with a cap, the climax of which, owing I suppose to the velocity with which the feet moved, stuck out behind to a great distance and left a trail which enabled me to follow its course for some time.

You may judge, Mr. Editor, what the effect of such an apparition was upon me at the moment, but as I watched it moving it suddenly disappeared before it reached the corner of King street and I saw no more of it. I am not, as I said before, superstitious, but I am certain there was something in it, and I would like to know what it was. I could not tell whether it was male or female, for I am not sure whether such distinctions exist in the spiritual world, but I am inclined to think it belonged to the latter gender. However this is not of material importance — but I would like to know from you whether you have had any intimation before this of such an apparition, or whether I am really the victim of my own imagination. I have thought that perhaps if followed up it might be made to account in some way for the origin of the fire; but this is a mere speculative hint, not worth much in itself. Do, Mr. Editor, try and unravel the mystery and you will confer a great favour on the community generally and myself particularly.

QUIS.

St. Catharines, August 16.

One May Imagine My Astonishment

Joshua Slocum

The master mariner Joshua Slocum (1844-1909) was the first man to sail solo around the world. It took him two years to accomplish this feat and he did it in his favourite vessel, a thirty-seven-foot yawl, Spray. *He described the voyage in a breezy and salty manner in a book of memoirs titled* Sailing Alone Around the World *(1900). The book was a bestseller — and a steady seller, for it remains in print more than eighty years later.*

Slocum, who was born on a farm at Wilmot, Annapolis County, N.S., personifies the "old-salt" tradition of the Maritimes during the days of sail. The master mariner was last seen taking his beloved Spray *from Boston harbour, heading into the region of open sea which later acquired notoriety as "the Bermuda Triangle."*

In the following passage, excerpted from his memoirs, Slocum tells the story of the strange appearance aboard his tiny vessel of a sailor who identifies himself as a member of the crew of Christopher Columbus's vessel the Pinta! *Twice the phantom deckhand appears to Slocum — once while delirious, once while sound asleep. The incident took place during a squall on the high seas between the Azores and Gibraltar, 26-7 July 1895.*

SINCE REACHING THE ISLANDS I had lived most luxuriously on fresh bread, butter, vegetables, and fruits of all kinds. Plums seemed the most plentiful on the *Spray*, and these Iate without stint. I had also a Pico white cheese that General Manning, the American consul-general, had given me, which I supposed was to be eaten, and of this I partook with the plums. Alas! by night-time I was doubled up with cramps. The wind, which was already a smart breeze, was increasing somewhat, with a heavy sky to the sou'-west. Reefs had been turned out, and I must turn them in again somehow. Between cramps I got the mainsail down, hauled out the earrings as best I could, and tied away point by point, in the double reef. There being sea-room, I should, in strict prudence, have made all snug and gone down at once to my cabin. I am a careful man at sea, but this night, in the coming storm, I swayed up my sails, which, reefed though they were, were still too much in such heavy weather; and I saw to it that the sheets were securely belayed. In a word, I should have laid to, but did not. I gave her the double-reefed mainsail and whole jib instead, and set her on her course. Then I went below, and threw myself upon the cabin floor in great pain. How long I lay there I could not tell, for I became delirious. When I came to, as I thought, from my swoon, I realized that the sloop was plunging into a heavy sea, and looking out of the companionway, to my amazement I saw a tall man at the helm. His rigid hand, grasping the spokes of the wheel, held them as in a vise. One may imagine my astonishment. His rig was that of a foreign sailor, and the large red cap he wore was cockbilled over his left ear, and all was set off with shaggy black whiskers. He would have been taken for a pirate in any part of the world. While I gazed upon his threatening aspect I forgot the storm, and wondered if he had come to cut my throat. This he seemed to divine. "Señor," said he, doffing his cap, "I have come to do you no harm." And a smile, the faintest in the world, but still a smile, played on his face, which seemed not unkind when he spoke. "I have come to do you no harm. I have sailed free," he said, "but was never worse than a *contrabandista*. I am one of Columbus's crew," he continued. "I am the pilot of the *Pinta* come to aid you. Lie quiet, señor captain," he added, "and I will guide your ship tonight. you have a *calentura*, but you will be all right tomorrow." I thought what a very devil he was to carry sail. Again, as if he read my mind, he exclaimed: "Yonder is the *Pinta* ahead; we must overtake her. Give her sail; give her sail! *Vale, vale, muy vale!*" Biting off a large quid of black twist, he said: "You did wrong, captain, to mix cheese with plums. White cheese is never safe unless you know whence it comes. *Quien sabe*, it may have been from *leche de Capra* and becoming capricious — "

"Avast, there!" I cried. "I have no mind for moralizing."

I made shift to spread a mattress and lie on that instead of the hard floor, my eyes all the while fastened on my strange guest, who, remarking again that I would have "only pains and calentura," chuckled as he chanted a wild song:

High are the waves, fierce, gleaming,
   High is the tempest roar!
High is the sea-bird screaming!
   High the Azore!

I suppose I was now on the mend, for I was peevish, and complained: "I detest your jingle. Your Azore should be a roost, and would have been were it a respectable bird!" I begged he would tie a rope-yarn on the rest of the song, if there was any more of it. I was still in agony. Great seas were boarding the *Spray*, but in my fevered brain I thought they were boats falling on deck, that careless draymen were throwing from wagons on the pier to which I imagined the *Spray* was now moored, and without fenders to breast her off. "You'll smash your boast!" I called out again and again, as the seas crashed on the cabin over my head. "You'll smash your boast, but you can't hurt the *Spray*. She is strong!" I cried.

I found, when my pains and calentura had gone, that the deck, now as white as a shark's tooth from seas washing over it, had been swept of everything movable. To my astonishment, I saw now at broad day that the *Spray* was still heading as I had left her, and was going like a race-horse. Columbus himself could not have held her more exactly on her course. The sloop had made ninety miles in the night through a rough sea. I felt grateful to the old pilot, but I marvelled some that he had not taken in the jib. The gale was moderating, and by noon the sun was shining. A meridian altitude and the distance on the patent log, which I always kept towing, told me that she had made a true course throughout the twenty-four hours. I was getting much better now, but was very weak, and did not turn out reefs that day or the night following, although the wind fell light; but I just put my wet clothes out in the sun when it was shining, and lying down there myself, fell asleep. Then who should visit me again but my old friend of the night before, this time, of course, in a dream. "You did well last night to take my advice," said he, "and if you would, I should like to be with you often on the voyage, for the love of adventure alone." Finishing what he had to say, he again doffed his cap and disappeared as mysteriously as he came, returning, I suppose, to the phantom *Pinta*. I awoke much refreshed, and with the feeling that I had been in the presence of a friend and a seaman of vast experience. I gathered up my clothes, which by this time were dry, then, by inspiration, I threw overboard all the plums in the vessel.

The Ghost of the Boy on the Bridge

J. W. Gattrell

An incident that occurred in 1936 at the bridge over the Souris River at Treesbank, Man., was recalled in a letter written by J. W. Gattrell to the present editor. The letter is dated 14 July 1987; Mr. Gattrell is now retired and living in Delta, B.C. But to this day he recalls with great clarity the sight of the ghost of the boy on the bridge.

I HAD LEFT HOME just after my 16th birthday on December 11th, 1936, from Shortdale, to live with my Aunt Mabel and Uncle Albert Dack in Wawanesa, Manitoba.

But as it was hard times in the middle of the so-called Dirty Thirties, my uncle in his harness and shoe shop couldn't keep himself employed, let alone hire and pay me. So I was to cut firewood for the heaters and cookstoves on a farm along the Souris River about two miles from the town of Treesbank. The farm was owned by an older couple, a Mr. and Mrs. Aylesbrey. The arrangement had been made by my uncle and the said farmer as they could both use the wood and I would get room and board and some money.

There was a good stand of poplar trees along the river valley on the Aylesbrey farm, so for many winter days I cut trees down to be sawed into firewood by a buzz saw. The nights were long and lonely for me, as there was no T.V. then and few books. The old couple went to bed early, as I did also.

But on one clear night with a bright moon, I went for a walk about two miles to the town of Treesbank. On my return from the town, downhill to the Souris River and the bridge I had to cross on my way, there was no traffic. As I remember it, I had a lonesome walk, or so I thought.

As I came close to the bridge I saw someone waiting for me, so I began to hurry, as I thought there was a message for me from my aunt or from home. Then, as I came onto the bridge, I was all alone.

The next morning I told Mr. Aylesbrey about it, as it made me feel quite funny and I couldn't forget it. He said, "Oh, you are not the first one to see the ghost of the boy that fell trying to cross the arch of the bridge on his bike."

Twenty-five or thirty years later, I drove back from B.C. to visit some folks I knew at Wawanesa. Morley Leachman, my good friend, and now a big farmer there, took me for drives around the countryside. We came to the bridge at Treesbank. It had been washed out at one end, as the water had been backed up by a dam in the U.S.A.

Morley pointed out to me an old house that had been empty for years. He said that the house was haunted. It was so close by the bridge I guess the ghost had moved from the bridge to the house.

That was my first visit back to the bridge. I could see the old wide arch that would tempt a boy to ride over it on his bike. But for the sake of situation and circumstance, that boy could have been myself.

Now They Had
My Attention

Lois Mulhall

Are spectral figures forerunners of tragedies to come? Are they premonitions or warnings? These are some of the questions raised by Lois Mulhall's account of the appearance of two ghostly figures in an old house near Bridgewater, N.S., in July of 1978. The account comes from a letter written to the present editor on 2 June 1987. Mrs. Mulhall was born in Montreal and joined the RCAF at age nineteen. She now works as a Medical/Legal Secretary with the Department of Veteran's Affairs in Ottawa.

NOW FOR THE UNUSUAL.

It was during Schooner Week in Nova Scotia. That's when all the schooners from Nova Scotia and the U.S. get together for races. My son, an airforce pilot, and his wife were at home visiting. In the house were those two, my husband, myself, a friend from Toronto, my daughter, a stepson, another son, and who knows who else? But here's what happened.

By mid-week, on Wednesday, we were all exhausted from racing and partying so we went to bed early. It was a very quiet night, foggy, no wind.

Our bedroom had a very thick shag area-carpet on the floor and we had to drag the door across it with force when we wanted to close it. The door was wide open, well past the area-carpet.

Near the door there was a mobile of abalone shells that tinkled when there was a breeze.

When everyone was asleep in this big old remodelled farmhouse, I was suddenly awakened by the sound of our bedroom door slamming shut. I heard the doorknob rattle and thought someone wanted to come talk to me. I was too exhausted — people always bring me their problems — so I woke my husband, saying, "Someone's trying to open the bedroom door!"

He asked how it got closed and locked and I replied that I had heard it slam shut and the knob must have turned and it locked itself. It sounded unlikely but he got up to investigate. I rolled over and tried to go back to sleep. He walked across the room, opened the door, and then came back to bed, saying, "You won't believe what just happened to me." But I hardly heard him and promptly dropped off to sleep.

Next morning I rose at five o'clock because I had to feed tne gang and we had to pack lunches for the day's sailing. While enjoying my first cup of coffee in the quiet, Ria, my friend from Toronto, came into the kitchen and said, "You won't believe what happened to me last night." Well, I'm not really a sociable person before coffee and really wasn't listening. Then my husband Les, a dentist, entered the kitchen. Ria said to him, "Les, you'll never believe what happened to me last night." He interrupted, "It can never top what happened to me!" Now they had my attention....

Les reminded me that I had awakened him and asked why. I explained what had happened. He said the abalone shells were still tinkling but there was no wind. Somehow the door had slammed shut. He said that when he walked across the floor to open the door, he saw a woman coming toward him. She was tall and slender, wearing a white nightgown with a tie around the waist. She had one arm raised, as though she was touching her hair. Her other arm was down at her side. He could not see her feet, but she seemed to be gliding across the floor. (Our bedroom was very long. We had taken down a wall to make two rooms into one.)

My husband said he thought the woman was Cheryl, my son's wife, and that she was sleepwalking. Not knowing what else to do (you know the old thing about not waking up sleepwalkers), he was going to turn her around and guide her back to the third floor where she and my son Peter were sleeping. But when he reached out to turn her around, he walked right through her. Thinking he was hallucinating from too much "ocean time," he went and opened the door and found nobody there. Then he came back to the bed and said to me, "You won't believe what just happened to me!"

Having heard that story, my friend Ria began hers. She was awakened by the loud slam on our door. She was in her room which is next to ours. Her door was closed. She said she saw someone standing just inside the door. It was a tall young man, and she thought it was my son Peter. Then she noticed that only half of him appeared to be standing in the doorway and the door was closed! She thought she must be hallucinating, so she sat up and moved sideways for another perspective. But he was still there, half of him. I can't remember now whether she said he disappeared or went back out the door. But I am sure she will remember it well if I ask her.

The odd part of it is that both Les and Ria identified the people they saw, tentatively, as Cheryl and Peter. Nine days later Peter and Cheryl were killed in a small aircraft accident on their way back to Chatham (New Brunswick) Airforce Base where Peter was stationed.

Almost everyone has weird stories to tell. But this one has more than one individual involved, and may well be worth noting in the light of the subsequent deaths.

The Graveyard

Nadine McMullin

Nadine McMullin *was born in Chipman Memorial Hospital (which no longer exists) in Charlotte County, N.B., in the year 1945. The oldest of twelve children, she is now the mother of three grown daughters and a grandmother three times over. She is also a member of the Writer's Federation of New Brunswick and has published poems, stories, and articles. She is currently writing a fictional family saga.*

"The Graveyard," as a factual and not a fictitious narrative, recalls an earlier, accidental trip through time. It specifically brings to mind the highly detailed account of the two English travellers, Miss J.A. Moberly and Miss Frances Jourdain, who, it seems, while vacationing in France during the summer of 1901, were granted admission, for a few hours, to everyday life at Versailles prior to the French Revolution.

IN THE PRETTY TOWN of St. Andrews by the Sea in the year of 1963, my husband was playing amateur hockey at the Sir James Dunn Arena. His family lived on Carleton Street near the arena and we were invited to stay overnight with them.

My husband, his brother, and his sister went to the rink. I decided instead to visit my mother-in-law. After an hour-long visit, I decided to walk up to the arena and then walk home with my husband and my in-laws.

It was a cool winter evening, but it was not cold. I knew my way. Straight up Carleton Street, at the end of the road, was the arena. Even if by some weird circumstance I took an unnecessary turn, I would be able to see the lights of the arena.

It was no more than a thirty-minute walk. I didn't meet anyone else walking. As I walked I looked down at the paved roadway. Houses became fewer. But when I raised my head I could see a dim light up ahead. It looked as if fog was moving in.

I looked down again because some parts of the roadway were snow-packed and a little slippery. There was now a heavy mist all around me. When I looked up again, directly in front of me there loomed several grey tombstones!

I took a deep breath and turned around. There were tombstones everywhere. Somehow I had walked into a graveyard. How? I don't know. I didn't make any turns on the way.

There was a light in the mist and I stared at it. Through the fog-like atmosphere, I could see an iron gate slowly swinging back and forth. It appeared to be beckoning. I walked toward the gate and discovered the light was an old-time lantern. I stood with my hand on the iron gate, holding it open.

I started to step through it when a group of people made me change my mind. The women were dressed in the clothing of bygone days. They were wearing shawls and bonnets. Long skirts swept dust from the ground. Dust on a paved roadway?

Each one walked with his or her head down. I didn't pay too much attention to them because each one of them wore a huge hat which hid most of the head. They looked like mourners. Mourners leaving the grave of a loved one. Slowly, with all the time in the world, they filed past me. When the last one was a safe distance away from me, I went through the iron gate and ran a few steps up the roadway.

It shook me. But I didn't tell anyone what I had seen. Who would believe me? A graveyard three feet from the site of the Sir James Dunn Arena? Not likely!

The Woman Appeared to Me with Perfect Clarity

Sylvia Taylor

The following account of a ghost appearing in a small house in a quiet suburb of Vancouver is derived from letters dated 4 June and 15 July 1987. They were sent to the present editor by Sylvia Taylor who, like her husband, was born and educated in England. Both Taylors hold degrees in the biological sciences. They came to Canada in 1968, settled in Vancouver, and are now Canadian citizens. What is remarkable about this report is that the single sighting, so brief and yet so intense, made such a strong impression on the sole witness.

MY HUSBAND AND I bought a small house in Vancouver in early 1972. The two-bedroom house is located in a middle-class neighbourhood in the southern part of the city about half a mile north of the Fraser River. The assessor could not find any information on the exact date that the house was built, but he estimated that 1943-45 was the probable period of its construction, as these were the years that services were laid onto the site. Therefore the house was about twenty-eight years old when we bought it. At the time we were in our early thirties and had no children.

Some weeks after moving into the house in March, my husband and I were sitting around the dining-room table enjoying dinner and chatting merrily. I was seated with my back to the window at the front of the house, facing a door which led into a small squarish hallway from which opened two more doors. The door directly opposite the dining-room door led to the bathroom, while the other door opened to the left into the kitchen. The kitchen and dining-room doors were open, and my husband was sitting with his left shoulder towards the hallway, facing the side of the house.

I suddenly stopped talking, as I saw a woman walk through the dining-room doorway and stop about two feet away from my husband. My face apparently changed in appearance, as my husband turned to his left to see what I was staring at. The woman had disappeared. He did not see her. He is skeptical when it comes to ghosts, but he is convinced that I did see something.

The whole incident lasted only a few seconds, but the woman appeared to me with perfect clarity. She was an elderly person, in her late fifties or early sixties, with a pleasant face and dark grey hair seemingly drawn back into a bun or similar hairstyle. She was wearing a high-necked, long-sleeved, light-coloured blouse and a skirt of dark, heavy material. I got the impression that the skirt was longish (falling well below her knees) and that she was wearing heavyish stockings and sensible shoes. In other words, she was somewhat old-fashioned in dress.

Over the blouse and skirt was a flowered apron with a bib top and straps over the shoulders. She had one corner of the apron skirt in her hands as if wiping them. Her attitude was one of coming to see that guests were comfortable and satisfied. I could almost hear her say, before she disappeared, "Is everything all right? Good!"

The incident was in no way scary. In fact, it was rather the opposite, as though we had been checked by a caring hostess and as if she herself was satisfied with what she saw.

The previous owners of the house were a childless couple, a few years older than ourselves, who had moved into a larger, more expensive place. The realtor had told us that they had owned the house for about six years. After the appearance of the lady, we asked some gentle questions of the neighbours (without telling them the reason for our curiosity) about previous occupants.

Their information was that the childless couple had lived in the house for no more than three years. The owners before them had been two middle-aged ladies. One or both of them were school-teachers, and one of them had committed suicide in her car, presumably by carbon-monoxide poisoning. There were a number of stories of where this had taken place. One story said that she had done it either in the carport or at the back of the house.

The sequel to the episode of the lady came about six months later. It was late fall or winter and my husband was involved in amateur sports in Vancouver. He invited two of his cohorts to dinner. One of them brought his wife and the other his girl friend. The girl friend walked into the house looking white and somewhat disturbed. She was very quiet through most of the evening. We put it down to the fact that possibly she had not wanted to come to an evening that would, in all likelihood, be devoted to sports talk.

However, sitting comfortably in the living room after dinner, over coffee and liqueurs, we talked about many things. The conversation turned to the subject of *déjà-vu* and ghosts. My husband suddenly said that I had seen a ghost in that very house. The girl almost sat up in her chair and became more animated, wanting to know all the details. It finally emerged that she had been very close to one of her lady teachers during the latter part of her high-school years, and had often visited the teacher at her house, which she shared with another lady. The teacher had committed suicide, and this had badly shaken the student. Her boy friend had told her only that they were invited out for dinner, not where they were going, and it was not until she was walking up the garden path to our front door that she realized she was revisiting the teacher's old house. She had not been there since the suicide. This was the reason for the white face. She had been very quiet because she did not know whether or not we knew about what had happened and she did not want to be the one to tell us. Her description of the school teacher fitted the appearance of the lady, both in body and in attitude.

We obtained no further information, as our guests departed soon after the revelation. We had been so excited by what the girl had said that we never even thought to ask for such details as the lady's name or the year that it had all happened.

We still live in the house, although we have made many changes over the years. These included closing doorways and extending the building. We have had no further manifestations since that one occurrence. My daughter affectionately describes the lady as Mum's ghost.

The striking thing about the episode is the clarity of the lady and the amount of detail I was able to amass during the few seconds — probably fewer than ten — that it lasted. The feeling it left with me was that we had been checked out and found to be satisfactory, both in character and in our attitude to the house. The school teacher had apparently been very house-proud. I had the feeling that she left happy.

The other thing that occurs to me is that this is the first time I have written a description of the occurrence since it happened. Yet everything is still very clear. We have told some friends about the incident, and their reactions vary from total disbelief to not wanting to return to the house until we can assure them that the lady has not returned.

I might add that both my husband and I are scientists. Our scientific training makes us wary of things that are not tangible; although we are reluctant to jump to conclusions without solid evidence, we must be flexible because we need to be able to countenance research experiments that produce results different from those anticipated. We have to be curious to know why something is happening.

We were somewhat skeptical of ghosts until the incident of the lady. My husband, I believe, is not quite sure what to think — he knows that I saw something, judging from my appearance at the dining-room table, but he saw nothing himself. I would say that my husband would probably consider himself a skeptic, but not a non-believer about ghosts, etc. He does not discount their occurrence, but has not had any experiences himself. I have to count myself as a believer in extraordinary experiences, if only because of "my lady."

I do not believe that the experience has changed our lives at all. The topic has come up only a handful of times during the last fifteen years, usually during one of those wide-ranging, after-dinner conversations that touch on all kinds of topics. I am not sure why, except one does get the feeling that some people will ridicule such an experience, while others seem to be terrified of the very thought of ghosts!

Incidentally, my daughter, when she learned about the incident, did not seem to be worried, upset, or frightened at the thought that her mother had once seen a lady in the house. In fact, she rather seems to wish that it would happen again!

Poltergeists and Hauntings

The Baldoon Mystery

William S. Fleury

William S. Fleury was a simple farmer and a member of the Highland Scots settlement known as Baldoon. The settlement was located on the north shore of Lake St. Clair not far from the present-day city of Wallaceburg, Ont. Just down the road from the Fleury farm was the large frame house of a fellow farmer, John McDonald, and his family.

Notorious is the word for the McDonald farmhouse which was the site of a three-year haunting, a haunting that was known far and wide in its day. Since then its notoriety has lingered, and the events are recalled (when they are recalled at all) as the "Baldoon Mystery." Fleury, along with other Scottish farmers and curiosity-seekers, witnessed a series of strange and inexplicable events unfold in and around the McDonald farmhouse. Between 1829 and 1831 the house was the focus of hails of bullets, stones, and lead pellets; water and fire descended upon the house as if from the heavens. No one was hurt by the flying and flaming objects, yet it is reported that the farmhouse heaved from its foundations and caught fire and burnt to the ground.

Was the devil making his haunt the McDonald farmhouse? Was the cause of the commotion a poltergeist, a "noisy spirit"? Students of such matters believe that the Baldoon Mystery follows the worldwide poltergeist pattern. Others maintain that the disturbances were, pure and simple, the product of hysteria, gossip, fear, and superstition.

Whatever the cause of what was reported to have happened,
forty years later Fleury and other farmers who had visited the
farmhouse were interviewed by Neil T. McDonald, the younger son
of the original owner. From twenty-six of the older residents of the
community, he collected statements. He published their accounts
serially in the Wallaceburg News. *These were collected and pub-*
lished in the form of a booklet called The Baldoon Mystery. The
booklet appeared in 1871 and has frequently been reprinted.

IT WAS RUMOURED that there was a great mystery going on at
McDonald's, and I, like a great many others, went to see for myself.
I saw stones and brick bats coming through the doors and windows, making the hole whatever size the article was that came in.
Parties would take these same things and throw them into the river,
and in a few minutes they would come back again. I saw a child
lying in a little cradle, when the cradle began to rock fearfully and
no one was near it. They thought it would throw the child out, so
two men undertook to stop it, but could not, still a third took hold,
but stop it they could not. Some of the party said, "Let's test this,"
so they put a Bible in the cradle and it stopped instantly. They said
that was a fair test.

The gun balls would come in through the windows and we
would take them and throw them into the river, which is about
thirty-six feet deep, and in a few minutes they would come back
through the windows, so we were satisfied that the evil one was at
the helm. I saw the house take fire upstairs in ten different places at
once. There were plenty to watch the fires, as people came from all
parts of the United States and Canada to see for themselves. Not
less than from twenty to fifty men were there all the time. The
bedsteads would move from one side of the room to the other, and
the chairs would move when someone was sitting on them and they
could not get off. They thought the devil was going to take them,
chair and all. I saw the pot, full of boiling water, come off the
fireplace and sail about the room over our heads and never spill a
drop, and then return to its starting place. I saw a large black dog
sitting on the milk house while it was burning, and thinking it
would burn we threw sticks at it, but it would not stir, but, all at

once, he disappeared. I saw the mush pot chase the dog that happened to come with one of the neighbours, through a crowd, and the people thought the devil was in the pot. It chased the dog all over the house and out of doors, and mush stick would strike it first on one side and then on the other. The dog showed fight, and turning round caught hold of the ring in the stick, which swinging, would strike him first on one side of the face and then on the other. It finally let go of the dog's teeth and went back to the pot. I was acquainted with Mr. McDonald and knew him to be an upright man and in good standing in the Baptist Church.

This is my true statement of what I saw.

William S. Fleury.

Story of the Haunted House

George H. Ham

George H. Ham (1847-1926) was born in Trenton and educated in Whitby, Ont. He moved to Winnipeg in 1875 and two years later settled into the house that caused him all the difficulties described in this excerpt, "Story of the Haunted House," from his lively book of memoirs called Reminiscences of a Raconteur (1921).

In 1891, Ham left the world of journalism in Winnipeg to become advertising manager of the Canadian Pacific Railway in Montreal. He had an eye for the odd and the unusual; although a strong Protestant, he wrote a book called The Miracle Man of Montreal (1922). It told the story of Brother André, the Roman Catholic miracle-worker whose faith inspired the construction of St. Joseph's Oratory.

WHILE I AM ON THIS SUBJECT, I might as well tell you that I once lived in a haunted house for a couple of years. Here's the story, which in every particular can be corroborated by Major George H. Young, formerly of the Customs office, Winnipeg, the owner and previously the occupant of the house, and by Charlie Bell, for many years secretary of the Winnipeg Board of Trade, who also lived in the place, and by others.

It was on St. Patrick's Day, 1877, that my wife and I took possession of the little house just south of old Grace Church on Main

Street, Winnipeg, our landlord being Mr. Geo. H. Young. Tradition said it was built on an old Indian burial ground. The house was not fully furnished the first day and we fixed up a bed in what was to be the parlour. During the night queer noises were heard. The stove in the adjoining room rattled like mad, and investigation proved nothing. There was no wind or anything else visible that should cause a commotion. A door would slam and on going to it, it was found wide open. One night there was a loud noise as if some tinware hanging up on the wall in the kitchen had fallen. Saying: "There goes the boiler lid," my mother, who had come from Whitby on a visit, ran downstairs and returned with the assertion that nothing had fallen on the floor to make such a noise. And so it went on.

I spoke to George Young about it, and he laughingly said: "You're hearing those noises too; well, I won't raise the rent anyway on that account." And he didn't — but that's not the custom nowadays.

One time the cellar was filled with water, coming from where, goodness only knows, though it was said that there was a slough through that property years ago. Anyway the cellar was full of water, and it had to be baled out. I said, "Leave it to me. Let George do it." My motto is "Do it now" — "now" being an indefinite time.

After a few days, despairing of any decisive action on my part, my wife engaged the Laurie boys (who came from Whitby) to empty the cellar. They came one fine morning with pails and ropes and everything was ready to put the cellar in its normal condition. But lo and behold, when the trap door was opened, there wasn't a blamed drop of water in the blooming cellar. It was dry as a tin horn. Of course I triumphantly boasted, "There, didn't I tell you? Always leave things to me." The Laurie boys were puzzled, for they had seen the cellar full the previous day. And I gloated. We never ascertained whence came the water or where it went, but by this time I had got accustomed to the prances and pranks of the house and didn't care a continental.

After a couple of years' occupancy of the house, which in the meantime had been purchased by the late George McVicar, we sought a new residence on Logan Street, next to Ald. More's' and the Main Street house was leased to a Mr. Conlisk, a cigar man-

ufacturer, who hitherto had boarded at John Pointz's hotel, diagonally opposite. We were to move out on a Saturday morning, but
the rain came down in torrents and the muddy streets were almost
impassable. Besides our new house wasn't ready.

I went to Mr. Conlisk and asked him if he would let us stay a
couple of days longer and I would pay his rent and his board at the
hotel. But he wouldn't. He had leased the house and he was going
into it Saturday afternoon. And he did. I don't like to think of
unpleasant things, so I'll skip telling about how we — and our
furniture — fared. In less than a week, Jimmy Bennett, a well-
known citizen who had a room with the Conlisks, left for other —
and doubtless quieter — quarters, and before the month was up
Conlisk paid another month's rent in advance, and gave the landlord notice that he was quitting. George McVicar came to me and
angrily wanted to know why I was spreading reports that his house
was haunted. I told him I had not done anything of the kind, but
that it was the spooks who had spoken. The building was removed
to the north end, and some years after, on recognizing it, I called to
see if the noises still continued. But they wouldn't let me in.

I don't pretend to be able to explain the queer noises, nor could
George Young, nor Charlie Bell, and Johnny Bennett would not
even speak of them. Whether they were the spirits of the past and
gone Indian braves showing their displeasure at our intrusion in
their domain, or were caused by some peculiarity in the construction of the house and its environments, I can not offer an
opinion. But, as we got accustomed to them, they didn't disturb us
at all, and we got rather proud of our ghostly ghosts whose board
and lodging cost us nothing.

A Singular Case of
Poltergeist Haunting

Sir Arthur Conan Doyle

Sir Arthur Conan Doyle and his wife travelled across North America in 1922 lecturing on the subject of spiritualism. In one hundred days he spoke no less than forty times about "spirit return" and "spirit communication." He delivered his fortieth and final lecture in Montreal and devoted an entire book to the North American tour and the public's reactions to his views. He called the book Our Second American Adventure *(1923).*

"I had not expected large audiences at Montreal, as the heat was great, and as the community is largely Roman Catholic, and of the opinion that the psychic phenomena which occur within its own ranks are saintly, while those experienced by others are diabolical," *he wrote. "However, the two lectures were splendidly attended, and the second was quite full. It was my last appearance in this series, and so it was rather a solemn moment for our little party. I took the occasion to thank with all my heart the Canadian and American Press and public for the splendid way in which they had treated me."*

It was in Montreal that Doyle's attention was caught by a newspaper report of a poltergeist.

A SINGULAR CASE of *poltergeist* haunting came under my notice whilst at Montreal. It had occurred to a couple, the man an experienced journalist, the wife a rather nervous lady of middle age. They lived alone, their only child having gone out into the world. These people were haunted by a very active and mischievous but at the same time harmless spirit or spirits. The box of bricks which had been their child's toy was dragged out and fantastic buildings erected, which were put up again as soon as dismantled. When one of these buildings was photographed, a queer little mannikin figure came out in the photograph behind the bricks, and beside it what looks like a female head. There seemed to be two haunters, for presently direct writing began to appear upon pieces of paper scattered over the house. I examined these and found distinctly two scripts, one of a grown-up person and the other of a child, which corresponded with the photograph. A picture of a house was also drawn, an extraordinary high, thin erection of twelve stories, with "the Middlesex House" written underneath. It was very well drawn. Occasionally the pranks were of a less harmless nature. The electric lights were switched off at untoward moments, and the pictures were stripped from the walls. Twice the husband was assaulted by pillows until his incredulity had been buffeted out of him. Prayer seemed of no avail. Unhappily it seldom is in such cases. I have notes of one where a large fur hearthrug was the centre of the disturbance. A priest was brought in to exorcise the force, and whilst he was in the midst of his exorcism the rug sprang at him and enveloped his head and shoulders, so that he ran terrified from the house. One is dealing with a mischievous and rather malicious child, and reason together with kindness is the only weapon. In this particular case at Montreal the couple were finally compelled to abandon the house. The haunting seemed to be local, for it did not follow them.

The Old House on
MacGregor Side Road

Ronald W. Cook

*R*onald *W. Cook is now in his mid-fifties. He and his
wife Carol live in an apartment building, where he handles the
maintenance, in Lethbridge, Alta., about as far removed from the
old house on MacGregor Side Road on the outskirts of Sarnia,
Ont., which he described in a letter to the present editor on 5 June
1987. The events that he described took place in the early 1950s.
Who knows whether or not the old house with the chequered
history is still standing; whether it is still occupied; and if it is still
occupied, whether its dwellers have experienced anything like the
events that occurred to Ron and Carol Cook?*

MY WIFE AND I were in the second year of our marriage when we
moved into an old house on MacGregor Side Road, outside Sarnia,
Ontario. It was a long, narrow house with a living room, a hall,
and a small room making up the main downstairs, with an add-on
at the back of the house making up the kitchen and a bathroom.

Upstairs was one large bedroom and a very narrow room with a
walk-in closet at the top of the stairs. The stairs had one turn near
the bottom and a false wall on the upstairs railing to privatize the
bedroom from the stairs. The small room at the foot of the stairs
gave us the chills, so we used it only for storage.

The first strange thing to happen was one night we had just gone
to bed when we heard an indescribable noise, low and violent.

124

Then the whole room took on a blue-green colour. It came through the windows. That too was just indescribable.

A couple of nights later, we had just gone to bed when we heard the door to the small room downstairs close ever so quietly. Then we heard distinct footfalls until they reached the closet at the top of the stairs. The door creaked open, then slammed shut. I finally got up enough courage to get out of bed, grab my .22 rifle, and headed for the closet, with my wife at my back like a second skin. When I got to the closet and opened the door, there was nothing to be seen.

Our two mixed collie and shepherd dogs were downstairs. We could hear them whimpering. So we snuck down the stairs and out to the kitchen across the back of the house. There we had an old, four-legged gas stove that was converted to propane. The outside door of the kitchen was one of those doors with six panels and a deadbolt. The storm door was a home-made door with a diamond-shaped window and a big hook and eye to lock it securely. Our closest neighbour was over a quarter-mile away, so we always kept both doors securely locked. In fact, the front door was nailed shut and had a chesterfield in front of it. Well, we got to the kitchen and those two dogs were whimpering and cowering under the stove. Both back doors were wide open.

A couple of days later my wife, who was pregnant at the time with our second child, was admitted to the hospital. It was false labour, so when she came out, I had her and our first child, a baby daughter, stay at her mother's. I stayed in the house.

The first day there by myself was a Wednesday. It started when I got home from work. I let myself in by the back door and found that there was water all over the place. It was coming from the bathroom. Well, I figured, the water tank was ruptured. So I shut the water line off and proceeded to mop up. Then I found on the kitchen floor a galvanized plug. It had been unscrewed from the bottom of the tank that was fastened to the other side of the wall in the bathroom.

On Friday I had Corey Oil from Petrolia come and fill my propane tank and heating oil tank. The heating oil tank took two hundred gallons. Our main source of heat was an oil space heater that sat in the living room and heated the upstairs by way of a hardwood grid in the ceiling.

On Saturday I spent the whole day in town with my wife and daughter and got home between 11:00 and 12:00 p.m. When I got into the house the place was cold. I figured the carburetor on the back of the oil stove had fouled up. But when I checked it out, it worked fine. Yet no oil was coming through the line, so I grabbed the flashlight — believe me, out there you need one when it is dark — and went outside to see if it had been shut off at the tank. But the tank wasn't there.

I found it fifty yards from the house, on its side, with the oil running out of it. But there was no trail of oil from the house to where it lay. Believe me, I couldn't get out of there fast enough!

The next day I drove my wife out there and showed her the oil tank. No one that we knew was strong enough to carry a two-hundred gallon tank a foot, let alone fifty yards, and leave no marks in the snow! The only marks on the ground were my own footprints coming and hastily leaving.

We learned later that the house we were living in had, at one time, been over twice its present size. It was built in Guelph or Kitchener. It had caught fire and suffered damage. The damaged part had been removed and the balance had been moved to Camlachi, Ontario. (There again it had suffered fire damage.) What was left had been moved to the MacGregor Side Road, where we had found it and moved into it.

We also found out both fires took human lives. The first one was lost in the part that had been removed — we suspect where the add-on kitchen and bath were located. The second one was lost in the small room at the foot of the stairs, the little room that always gave us the creeps — there an old lady had died.

It was not long before we found another house in which to live.

The Farmhouse on Bow Park Farm Road

Patricia Greathead

Are old houses haunted? Certainly some people are haunted... haunted by their experiences in old houses, especially old farmhouses, like the one that may be found on Bow Park Farm Road on the outskirts of Brantford, Ontario.

Patricia Greathead is a housewife in her mid-forties. She works in a retirement home and is married to an employee of Uniroyal. The Greatheads now reside in a non-haunted house with their family in Brantford. Mrs. Greathead wrote the letter which follows on 26 May 1987.

AFTER SEEING YOUR LETTER in the *Brantford Expositor*, I decided I would tell you of one of my strange experiences. The most vivid experience that happened to me occurred four or five years ago, when our family was looking for a house just outside the city of Brantford.

My husband, my younger son, and I were taken by a realtor to look at a farmhouse. The farm was located off a country road and had a lot of acreage. The farmhouse was two storeys in height and empty at the time of our inspection.

As soon as I entered the front door a feeling of *crawliness*, a *prickly sensation*, came over me. At the time I didn't give it a second thought. We looked around the downstairs and then proceeded to mount the stairs. I was very reluctant to follow the others up the stairs, but I didn't let on. For a few seconds it felt as if my feet were glued to the very stairs. The prickly sensation grew stronger and I felt a *chill* in the air. I really did feel strange, but I mounted the stairs and with the others went into a bedroom to look around, all the while trying to act calm and collected.

All of a sudden I thought, "Something terrible has happened here." I couldn't wait to get out of that house. I quickly left. As soon as I was outside, the sensations themselves vanished, though I still felt creepy or weird. But I didn't say a thing to anyone.

When we got back to our own house, my younger son turned to me and said, "That house was spooky!" He must have felt something too. I told him how I had felt. My husband laughed and said we were both nuts. I didn't realize how weird my son felt or how shaken up he was from the experience until a few minutes later. He went out to start his car. It backed up, smacking into our neighbour's car. No one was hurt and there was no damage, but I shook inside for a good hour after that.

My older son came home and wanted to know what house we had seen and what we had thought of it. When we told him where the farmhouse was located, I was really shaken by his reply. He said, "That house you went to see on Bow Park Farm Road is haunted! Didn't you know that? Everyone else does!"

Well, we didn't know that it was haunted. We had never heard about it before. Apparently there had been a triple murder committed in the house forty-five or so years ago. It was a lover's triangle or something like that. I learned from a friend that whoever had lived in that house since then had experienced bad luck, or had been driven out by some tragedy or other while living there. I wondered if the realtor who took us there knew of this story.

I also learned that a red, driverless truck had been periodically spotted in the vicinity of the house. I didn't get the particulars of the truck or the murders. Just out of curiosity I have meant to follow up the details, but I have not got around to it. One visit to the farmhouse was enough for me. I didn't want to go back. I have always wanted to forget the experience, but it's still on my mind.

The Spoon that Moved

Frank McInnis and Iris M. Owen

This account is a scientific report. It requires a host of explanations.

An event that occurs — or seems to occur — without apparent cause is called a psychokinetic event. The cause of the movement or kinesis is held to be psychic rather than material. The word poltergeist is German and means "noisy ghost," but in English the word describes the disturbances that accompany a haunting, not the haunting itself, since no ghost or spirit is present or witnessed, just the disturbances. The disturbances accompany a ghostless haunting, so to speak.

This account describes the unaccountable movements of an ordinary spoon. Its movements were witnessed by two level-headed Torontonians: Frank McInnis is a family physician; Iris M. Owen is an author and researcher; both are members of the Toronto Society for Psychical Research. Their report "A Psychokinetic Event of Poltergeist Type" appeared in the Summer 1972 issue of New Horizons: The Journal of the New Horizons Research Foundation.

ABSTRACT: an isolated event of poltergeist type is described by the two eye-witnesses.

The event took place on Saturday, November 21st, 1971. A buffet supper had been arranged in the dining room of Dr. and Mrs.

Owen's home, the guests at that time having a pre-dinner drink in the living room. Frank McInnis and Iris Owen were having a conversation in the kitchen, which adjoins the dining room. Frank was standing at the sink, (having collected some glasses up), and Iris was standing in the doorway, half turned towards him, and halfway towards the table. Frank was completely facing the dining table, as he had turned to answer a remark by Iris. His eyes went past and he said, "Look at that spoon." Iris turned, completely, and saw the spoon referred to just landing on the floor underneath the rung of one of the dining chairs, and some three feet away from the table. Frank saw the spoon rise from the bowl on which it was laid, float horizontally for a couple of feet, and then go down under the rung of the chair. It made just a tinkling sound as it landed.

The spoon had been placed some minutes before on the top of the bowl of rice, in the centre part of the table. The rice was only warm, not hot, as there had not been room for it to be heated in the oven. If the spoon had fallen in the normal way, it would have landed on the table; the bowl was fully 18 inches from any edge of the table. Nothing else moved at all.

(Signed) Frank McInnis, M.D.
Iris M. Owen.
23 November, 1971.

Toronto Society for Psychical Research

The Ghost of Rock Creek

Frank Western Smith

The events described in this memoir took place in 1975-76 in a cottage at Rock Creek, B.C. Humour is not at all characteristic of hauntings or scenes of poltergeist-like effects. But Frank Western Smith has the gift of humour and has recalled the disturbances at the cottage in an amusing fashion.

Smith's biography appears on his letterhead in capsule form: "Born July 20, 1917, New Westminster, B.C. Graduate, Art Centre College, Los Angeles, California. B.C. Lecturer for Forest Service. Banff National Park Warden and Vancouver Businessman. Now Retired and Resident Artist for the Town of Osoyoos, B.C."

WHEN IT CAME TO GHOSTS, I was a disbeliever. People talked about funny "goings on" in the cottage I had just rented, but I thought it was a lot of nonsense. If I had known how the "goings on" were going to affect me that winter, I would have stayed on in the summer cottage, and shivered with cold instead of fright.

No sooner had I moved into my new abode than things began to happen. I was still busy unpacking and putting things away when there was a loud knock on the front door. "Visitors," I thought, glad of a break from boring duties. Wearing my "welcome" smile, I flung open the door. There was nobody there. Puzzled, I looked around outside, but there was not a soul in sight.

Then came a knock on the back door. "Ah, they've gone around the back," I thought, and hastened to let them in. There was nobody there either. I would have attributed the knocking to pranksters, but there was no place they could have hidden.

That was the start of many weeks of door-knockings that began to be very disturbing. Real visitors who knocked must have wondered at my surprise at finding human beings on the doorstep!

One night, just as I was dropping off to sleep, I heard footsteps in the kitchen. All the doors were locked, but someone was inside, walking over the old floor boards. They squeaked at every footfall. Then the steps approached my bedroom door.

Quietly, I got up and reached for the 30-30 rifle on the wall near the bed. The footsteps had stopped, but an icy wind blew across my face. The windows were closed. Suddenly, the room was filled with the strong, pungent smell of pipe tobacco. I stood there with the rifle in my hands, wondering what the hell to do, while the wind grew colder and the pipe smoke seemed to be puffing right under my nose by some unseen presence. Then I heard footsteps retrace their route, away from my bedroom and across the kitchen floor. The wind stopped; the smoke disappeared.

I walked through the house, but nothing was altered. I returned to bed, but slept with one eye open.

Shortly after this experience with the invisible prowler, a friend asked me if I'd adopt his Belgian Shepherd. The dog was a good house-guarder. The request couldn't have been better timed. I met Major, we hit it off right away, and he moved in with me. At night, Major slept beside my bed; by day, between outings, he lay under my art table while I worked.

Shortly after Major's arrival, as we both had gone to bed, we had another "visitation." Again, the footsteps were coming across the kitchen. Major growled. I switched on the light. He was crouched, ready to spring, his lips drawn back. We waited. Nothing happened. Then we went out and looked around, and once again everything was normal.

This was just one of a series of "alerts," when we both heard footsteps of something that didn't exist. Then the footsteps were heard no more. Both Major and I relaxed, though we both kept one ear cocked.

Then one night, while I was busy at my art table, with Major lying beneath, without a moment's warning, the dog sprang up in a single bound. Whambo! The table flew up, throwing art supplies in all directions.

Snarling, Major leapt five feet in the air, opened his jaws, and closed his fangs on something I couldn't see. When he landed on the slippery tile floor, it took him a few seconds to get traction, then he shot through the kitchen to the back door, which he tried, frantically, to gnaw through.

Eventually Major calmed down, and so did I. Whatever his sixth sense had detected, whatever he had attacked and chased, it never came back again. There were no more mysterious "goings on" in the cottage.

I'll never know for sure what caused these disturbances, but if it was a ghost, Major saw to it that it is now haunting around with a big chunk removed from its transparent rear end!

I Tried to Imagine What It Could Be

Norma Metz

Readers with jaded tastes who prefer their accounts of haunted houses to be as scary and gory as the Amityville Horror are well advised to skip the next account. The residence in North Bay that is described in this letter is haunted (to the degree that the word applies in this instance) not by a ghoul but by a spirit of love and approval!

This account is based on a letter sent to the present editor and dated 15 May 1987. The author, Norma Metz, was born in Washington, D.C., in 1939. She spent ten years with a French-Canadian, Roman Catholic missionary community in Montreal and is also a graduate of the University of Ottawa, having majored in English literature. Metz, a freelance writer, settled in North Bay where she wrote about the uniqueness of her home in a column for the North Bay Nugget *on 7 Feb. 1987.*

Shortly after writing the letter upon which this account is based, Metz moved out of the house into a smaller one. That move was made with a degree of regret.

I WAS ALWAYS AFRAID to be alone. As a child I would sometimes be so petrified when hearing some unexplained noise that I'd freeze, unable to move for the longest time. My imagination ran wild. It still does. However, now I have developed more rationalizing power.

When my friend Ruby and I first visited this three-storey house at 918 Algonquin Avenue in North Bay — prior to buying it in the spring of 1985 — I was standing outside looking up towards the roof. The third-floor dormer has two windows. The house stands so tall that these windows appeared to be eyes peering down, almost daring me...to do what I don't know, just daring me. I thought they were attic windows, but when we toured the house I discovered they were the windows of the third floor. There was still an attic above that! My apprehension grew and secretly I prayed that I'd never be left alone in the house.

We moved in on May 17. During the first month, we renovated the third floor, which already consisted of two bedrooms and a very large room that the previous owners used for entertaining and dancing. We converted this entire third floor into a three-bedroom apartment, complete with bathroom, kitchen, and living room.

The incident occurred while in the midst of this construction. I was awakened in the middle of that night by the sound of strong winds outside. Suddenly I heard a strange sound coming from the third floor and focused my attention on it, trying, through my drowsiness to imagine what it could be. A ball? Maybe a golf-ball or a very large marble being rolled across the hardwood floor? The noise would stop, start again, rhythmical and continual.

Now at that time we had a cat named Smokie. I thought perhaps that we had left the door to the third floor open and that she was up there playing with something. But the noise was too steady, too regular. Besides, when I sat up, Smokie was still lying on my bed! With head and ears perked up, she was looking out towards the hallway. She must have heard the noise too. Naturally I froze right then and there!

Finally, with all the courage I could muster, I got out of bed and woke Ruby. She's always so brave. I knew she would investigate, hopefully without me. However, out of curiosity, I did venture up to the third floor with her and found the door to the attic was ajar. One of the windows was open and the wind was blowing through the apartment. We turned on all the lights. I told Ruby about the sound of a ball rolling on the floor but we didn't find anything resembling a ball. And Ruby, always so brave and perhaps sleepy, didn't seem too concerned. We went back to bed. I never heard the noise again.

The next day, in broad daylight, I looked over every inch of the third floor and found nothing that even came close to being a golf ball, a marble, or a rolling stone! Ruby concluded, "It was just the door blowing in the wind." But does a door blowing in the wind sound like something rolling across the floor? As I said I never heard that noise again and strangely enough, after that night, I was never afraid of being alone in the house.

I do believe there was a presence letting me know it was there. But why only me? (And my cat?) Why not Ruby?

Sometimes I like *not* knowing all the answers to such mysteries. When I do think about that incident and others similar to it, I can devise all sorts of stories. As I said, I do have quite an imagination! For sure though, I'll continue to believe in spirits. (I don't like the word "ghost.") I believe in a spirit of goodness, a spirit of evil, one of love, and one of hate, but whether such spirits can produce sound effects, I don't know.

I believe that a good, loving spirit permeates that house on Algonquin Avenue. When people ask me about my "ghost," I say it must be the spirit of the man who built the house. I think D.J. Morland, Sr., its original owner, built it in 1926 with a great deal of love for his family, that he still keeps watch over it, and that maybe, on that night two years ago, he was letting us know he approved of the manner in which we were maintaining his house and of the improvements we were making on the third floor.

Whatever the explanation may be, my "friendly ghost" was calm and non-violent. And that's the way I like my life.

But it'll remain a mystery to me why he chose to roll a ball of some sort across the floor just to announce his presence. Could it be he was practising his golf putts?

I discovered more information about D.J. Morland, Sr., after that incident. He, all his sons, and all their sons, were and still are avid, renowned, prize-winning golfers!

Not the Creakings or Groanings that Haunt Old Houses

Graeme Gibson

During the 1970s the novelists Graeme Gibson and Margaret Atwood lived with their young daughter in an old farmhouse outside Alliston, Ont. Their experiences were such that Gibson has reason to believe the farmhouse was and remains haunted. He described his experiences in a letter addressed to the present editor on 11 Jan. 1988.

Gibson has been an active force in the creation of the Writers' Union and the Writers' Development Trust. He is the author of three novels: Five Legs *(1969),* Communion *(1971),* Perpetual Motion *(1982). The latter work is set in rural Ontario in the last century and tells about a farmer who is obsessed with the notion of constructing a perpetual-motion machine.*

MY ENCOUNTER with the following inexplicable events occurred in the farmhouse we lived in during most of the 1970s.

Built in the 1860s, the frame house had a wooden staircase, with worn bare steps, that rose from a small front hall to the back of the second and upper floor. The narrow upstairs hallway, which ran to the front of the house, had a single small window (perhaps a foot square) at the top of the stairs, from which one could see the barnyard, one of the barns, and the wooded creek bed beyond. Three doorways opened off that hall; two on the north side and one, which was our bedroom, on the south. The bedroom door was at the front of the house, or the end of the upstairs hall.

We had not been in the house six months. Margaret was away somewhere, probably giving a poetry reading. It was winter. In memory, it was a still, cold night. After turning off all the lights, I retired (as they say) just before midnight and was on the verge of sleep when I heard something downstairs. It wasn't a noise I could immediately identify. Then I heard someone in the vestibule. Almost immediately there was the sound of footsteps on our stairs. These were not the creakings or groanings that haunt old houses, but the very specific and unmistakable noise of a woman's shoes as she ascended towards the back of the house....

Now it is important to emphasize several points. There had been no sound of a car on our curving drive, yet through my partially open window I could hear trucks half a mile away on Highway 89. Moreover, we'd recently acquired a stray Blue-tick hound who insisted upon sleeping in a pile of hay in the drive shed. Max, as we'd named him, had proved himself a reassuring addition to our menagerie by baying alarms at every provocation — both real and imagined. Yet he'd made not a whimper. To top it off we'd had the locks changed; only Margaret and I had keys and she was miles away.

And yet there was a woman in my house wearing solid shoes. I called "Hello!" in the darkness. "Who's that?" I heard her reach the small window at the top of the stairs; then she began walking along the hall towards my bedroom door. She walked methodically, or so it seemed to me, with a kind of comfortable assurance in the dark, as if she was familiar with the house. Again I called out but there was no answer. Only the clear sound of heels on the pine floorboards.

In retrospect, I believe I remained in my bed out of puzzlement. If it had been a man's shoes I'd heard, I'd have been more immediately apprehensive, and therefore self-protective. As it was, I left it too late. She was almost to the door when it came to me with a genuine shiver (as if someone were walking on my grave?) that it was a ghost. It had to be....

We had no bedside lamp so the only light switch was on the wall beside the door, which opened towards me and was ajar. In order to turn on that light I'd have to reach past eight or ten inches of dark space that contained whatever it was that waited out there. I'd like to say that I did so, that I went over to see who or what she was. But I didn't. In some fundamental way I didn't want to know.

So I lay there while assuring myself that she could have no quarrel with me. We had not been in the house long enough. Anyway, try as I might, I could remember no instance of a so-called spirit actually harming anyone. Eventually I went to sleep.

I told Margaret, of course, but as time passed we forgot about it, as one does. Perhaps I was melodramatic in my response to the sounds of an old house. Perhaps I'd drunk more than I'd thought; perhaps, as Scrooge protested, it was merely a scrap of undigested mutton. Certainly, without confirmation, that would have been the end of it.

Almost two years later we arranged with a new-found friend to mind the house while we went north for our annual escape into the bush. We had not told her about our "ghost," nor, to my knowledge, had we told anyone she might have known. Certainly she had no recollection of the story.

On our return we discovered that our friend had been visited, not once but three times, exactly as it had happened to me. The noise in the vestibule, the sound of footsteps on the stairs, and then in the hall. The alarming difference, for her, was that she took the footsteps to be those of a man. She didn't open the door either. Instead, she threw herself against it to keep him out. But there had been no attempt to enter . . . .

After moving back to Toronto, we had a series of tenants before finally selling the farm. Each lasted about a year before moving on. One day, when I was visiting the second family, who were from Northern Ireland, the woman said, "Tell us about the ghost." I asked her to tell me first, whereupon she reported that her husband had been wakened by a woman who seemed to walk past him into a small room behind the bedroom.

At first he'd thought it was his wife, but immediately discovered she was still asleep beside him. Their bed was placed as ours had been, so whatever it was had apparently entered the room through the doorway from the hall. A married daughter was coming to visit, and they had put a child's crib in the back room because logically it had seemed to be a nursery of some kind. We all wondered if it was the crib that had encouraged, permitted, or whatever, the "spirit" to actually enter the bedroom.

After that there were a number of incidents that are harder to verify. She appeared at least once again to the couple. They were all convinced, for example, that the covers and pillows in the crib were moved about and some stuffed toys were rearranged.

And then, about four years later, we met, once more, a young woman who had lived in our house as a mother's helper for almost a year. She told us that she had actually seen the woman from her bedroom which opened onto the hall at the top of the stairs. She said she called out, "Hey, can I help you?" Neither young nor old, wearing a plain, vaguely archaic blue dress, the apparition seemed to pause, and then continued along the hall. There had been a great sadness about her. Our young friend hadn't said anything at the time because she feared we'd think she was nuts, or a witch, and she needed the work.

While the unconfirmed episodes give convincing substance to this story, it has been the repetition of an almost identical experience that has forced me to believe that some ghostly phenomenon really was outside my door that night....

Exorcism by Two Witches

Robin Skelton

Robin Skelton is unique among Canada's poets and authors in that he is a practising witch. Welsh blood flows through his veins. He has published two books on and about spells and incantations, Spellcraft (1978) and Talismanic Magic (1985), and he writes with first-hand or hands-on experience about wicca.

Indeed, witchcraft is the subject of the final chapter of Skelton's book The Memoirs of a Literary Blockhead (1988). In the following excerpt from that book, he describes the exorcism of a house in Victoria, B.C., and its happy outcome. The deed was accomplished not by the author alone, but by Skelton in the company of a fellow witch, Jean Kozocari, and her daughter Tara.

SKEPTICISM IS FINE and healthy and sensible, and presents no real obstacle on most occasions. One couple who called us in were very doubtful. Nevertheless, they had a problem and the wife was particularly disturbed. She had seen a spectre which had upset her, and there was an area at the top of the stairs which felt so unpleasant that even the dog would not go there, while once a small black shape had been seen running across the landing just outside the door to the roof space. The basement felt so threatening that the wife would not go there. The husband had seen nothing and was not particulary disturbed, except by his wife's disquiet.

Jean and I went round one evening and answered their questions about ghosts and kindred phenomena; then we went upstairs and opened the door to the roof space. There was a definite "something" there and Jean said it seemed to her that it was an elemental, which is to say an entity made of pure energy and originating in the earth on which the house was built. The house was set upon what had been agricultural land and the earth had been very much disturbed. Moreover, there was running water under it and running water is a great conductor of psychic energies. The elemental was black and long, rather like a ferret; we "saw" it in our heads, or, one might say, with the "third eye." We talked to it and put an open paper bag into the roof space and told it to get into it. Then we wandered round the rest of the house. When we returned we could feel that the creature was in the bag, so we picked it up and took it away and wondered where to release it. We thought of one or two back gardens where a little disturbance might be amusing, but of course we did not do anything like that, one of the basic rules of the Old Religion being "Do what you will but harm no one," so we let it free in a wild wooded area where we thought it would be at home.

This sounds so absurd in the telling that I have difficulty in believing it myself. Nevertheless, it happened, and I am still astonished at the simplicity of the manoeuvre. The basement of the house was trickier. Jean, Tara, and I went down there the next day when the house was empty and felt it out again. There had been young people in there we knew, and we'd been told that when the present owners moved in there had been signs in red paint on the walls. We were not told what signs but we suspected hexagrams and pentagrams, as the wife seemed to avoid looking at the pentagrams we wore while she was telling us this. I sensed that there had been some amateur magic going on, and not pleasant magic, and also that some kind of ritual dancing had occurred. I tried to tune in to what had happened and found myself doing a little foot-shuffling dance as I did so, and then I knew suddenly I was in touch, and I commanded the presences to go, and in moments the air that had been chill began to regain its normal temperature and the job was done, apart from the necessary following blessing.

We told the house-owners to expect trouble within the next twenty-four hours, for when the energy field of a house has been altered there is always an after-shock. In this case it was most unpleasant. The wife heard her son's voice saying "Hello" in her ear about twenty minutes after she had watched him drive away to work, and she immediately feared for his safety. She became dreadfully depressed and tearful and had to go to bed. I told her that after all she had been warned, but she admitted that she had not taken the warning seriously. A few days later, on the phone, I heard from her husband that all was well; his wife was livelier and happier than she had ever been since they moved into the house. The wife, separately, told me her husband was much more vigorous and happy. They were both profoundly grateful. They asked me what they owed me, and I explained that no true witch accepts payment for any magical act, whether exorcism or healing.

Ecstatic States

One Drop of the Brahmic Bliss

Richard Maurice Bucke

Richard Maurice Bucke (1837-1902), a man of many
and varied accomplishments, was the greatest Canadian exponent of
the mystical experience. For the record: the country's most famous
mystic was the Métis leader Louis Riel; the Dominion's most active
spiritualist, the late Prime Minister W.L. Mackenzie King.

Dr. Bucke was one of the leading psychiatrists of his day. He
served with distinction as the Superintendent of the Asylum for
the Insane at London, Ont. He made numerous contributions to
the advancement of medicine and psychiatry in North America.
Although not a poet himself, he was passionately devoted to the
free verse of Walt Whitman. Bucke sponsored Whitman's visit to
Ontario and Quebec in 1880 and was the author of record of the
first formal biography of the American bard.

The decisive influence on Bucke's life was his own mystical
experience. This occurred while on a visit to England in 1872. At
the moment of the illumination, he was travelling across London in
a hansom cab. Bucke prepared a third-person account of his experience. It was first published by the historian James H. Coyne in
"Richard Maurice Bucke — A Sketch" included in the Transactions
of the Royal Society of Canada, Series II, Volume 12, 1906.

Bucke's major opus is the tome Cosmic Consciousness: A Study
in the Evolution of the Human Mind (1901). In its pages he surveys
the history of Western and even Eastern mysticism and examines
the lives of the principal religious and artistic leaders of the past

146

and the present for evidence of instances of "cosmic consciousness."
The psychologist William James has credited Bucke with the first
use of this term. Bucke employs it in the sense of "a higher form of
consciousness than that possessed by the ordinary man," an aware-
ness that is beginning to dawn on the human race as a whole, not
just on extraordinary members of that race. According to Bucke,
the experience possesses the power to transform. His own physical,
emotional, mental, moral, and spiritual life was certainly deepened
by it.

HE AND TWO FRIENDS had spent the evening reading Wordsworth,
Shelley, Keats, Browning, and especially Whitman. They parted at
midnight, and he had a long drive in a hansom (it was an English
city). His mind, deeply under the influence of the ideas, images and
emotions called up by the reading and talk of the evening, was calm
and peaceful. He was in a state of quiet, almost passive, enjoy-
ment. All at once, without warning of any kind, he found himself
wrapped around as it were by a flame-coloured cloud. For an instant
he thought of fire, some sudden conflagration in the great city, the
next he knew that the light was within himself. Directly afterwards
came upon him a sense of exultation, of immense joyousness, accompanied or immediately followed by an intellectual illumination quite
impossible to describe. Into his brain streamed one momentary light-
ning-flash of the Brahmic-Splendour which has ever since lightened his
life; upon his heart fell one drop of the Brahmic Bliss, leaving hence-
forward for always an after taste of Heaven.

Among other things he did not come to believe, he saw and
knew that the Cosmos is not dead matter, but a living Presence,
that the soul of man is immortal, that the universe is so built and
ordered that without any peradventure all things work together for
the good of each and all, that the foundation principle of the world
is what we call love, and that the happiness of every one is in the
long run absolutely certain. He claims that he learned more within
the few seconds during which the illumination lasted than in
previous months or even years of study, and that he learned much
that no study could ever have taught.

A Giggle in a Guru's Throat

Patricia Joudry

The playwright Patricia Joudry achieved early success with Teach Me How to Cry, *a play about young love in a prairie town. It was professionally produced in Toronto, London, and New York and even filmed by Hollywood in 1958 as* The Restless Years. *Flush and flushed with success, Joudry and her husband John Steele moved to London to be closer to the heart of the theatrical world. Then they acquired and renovated Shornhill, a 14th-century farmhouse in the Cotswolds, which they occupied from 1961 to 1971.*

An exuberant yet frank account of her life during the Shornhill years appears in her autobiography, Spirit River to Angels' Roost: Religions I Have Loved and Left *(1977). It tells how she rejected her parents' "compulsive Catholicism," yet there was no denying her innate spirituality. She describes her inner journey from one occult, religious, therapeutic, or human-potential system to another: psychoanalysis, Buddhism, yoga, George de la Warr's Radionics, Spiritualism, Maharishi Mahesh Yogi's Transcendental Meditation, Wilhelm Reich's Orgone Box, Paramahansa Yogananada's Self Realization Fellowship, "Complete Christianity," and what is now known as "trance-channelling."*

She was inspired when she wrote her plays; in fact, she took them down as if they were being dictated from beyond. At first she used one of George de la Warr's Black Boxes to spell out the words — it is mentioned in the passage that follows — but before long no inter-

mediary at all was required, for the words simply occurred to her. She co-credited these full-length plays (which attracted much interest but went unproduced) to the spirit of George Bernard Shaw. Following a trip to Ireland in 1962, she designated herself "Saint Patricia," announcing to the press the parthenogenesis of her fifth child.

In later years she completed and published a novel and found a degree of detachment. She wrote... And the Children Played (1975), an account of the home education of her children, as well as her autobiography, on the grounds of the Trappist monastery of Notre Dame du Lac in Quebec's Eastern Townships.

THE DATE WAS JULY 1ST, 1961. Way back in Canada it was Dominion Day. With me, as usual, it was Shopping Day. There were a lot of nick-nacks I had to buy in Cheltenham, the nearest town, nine miles away. So after breakfast John and I set out in the Rolls.

It was a beautiful route, once you got past our mile-long private lane, which was dying of terminal potholes. We curved down the winding road to the village of Withington, then left through the hills toward Cheltenham. Since the day we had arrived from Canada, I had never ceased to marvel at the way the small fields of England looked tended to the last blade of grass. The landscape is like a continuous private garden. I sat this day gazing with rapt pleasure at the graceful scene as we purred along through the hills.

Then suddenly, but not suddenly, a feeling, though not a feeling, more a gathering light, or a swelling warmth, started over me. It was like a silent singing throughout my being, a sort of joy lifting me up and flooding me through with rays of an unknown brilliance. Whatever it was it wanted my full attention.

I said to John: "Stop the car."

He pulled off to the side. He thought perhaps I wanted to go into the bushes.

I said, "Something's happened to me. I don't know what, I want to be quiet...." We sat still and quiet. By now he was prepared for anything.

The feeling expanded in my mind. It was very simple, really. It was bliss. A word which had been only a word to me, five letters on a page, a giggle in a guru's throat, became in this instant a reality that bore no relation whatever to its label. It might as well have been called acorn, or rinso, for all the word described the thing.

It was a taste of cosmic consciousness. Not the whole cup; the whole would have burned me up like being dropped into the sun. It was one sip, and it lifted me from those gentle hills to the highest peak my soul could bear.

Yet I felt there was something more to know. I reached for the small Radionic hand instrument I carried with me at all times and asked: "What happened?" and started spelling the answer.

I didn't have to spell it out. It flashed on like a million watts of neon in my brain: PRESENCE OF CHRIST.

I turned to John. "Jesus Christ," I said with a great calm, "has come to me."

Whatever magnetism this was had so permeated the atmosphere that John felt something of it too. Together in our bubble, he accepted what I said.

"What'll we do now?" he asked respectfully.

"We'll go shopping just the same." I waved him forward. Life must go on.

In town, John dropped me at Cavendish House, the elegant small department store where I had already prepared for my Coming by opening a charge account. I walked through the aisles that day on a cushion of exaltation. I smiled upon the salespersons with a radiance that left them visibly stunned. Through my mind roared notes of music and the words, as though sung by a great chorus: Hallelujah, Christ is risen! Signing my name to the sales slips, it's only a wonder I didn't pen "Jesus Christ."

As he picked me up at the front door with my purchases, John asked anxiously: "Is He still there?"

"He is here forever," I said as I loaded up. The Plan was already unfolding in my mind

Of course if I'd waited a few years I could have popped a pill into my mouth and had exactly the same sensation at a lot less trouble and expense. But drugs weren't in yet. I never did take them. From what I've heard, it would have been rather tame for me. As to the ultimate effect of the drug trip versus the psychic trip, I'm inclined to think they are journeys through the same badland — gorgeous though it can look — and where you come out, if at all, depends on your individual makeup.

The drug experience seems designed for individual sensation, whereas the psychic trip is a natural for those with the missionary bug. They both come down to ego trips in the end. The drug kick is honestly selfish, the psychic takes the long, more self-deceptive route.

As I stood alone with my Saviour that evening, beneath the great pine trees in the lower garden, looking out over the expanse of hills, He seemed to talk to me directly. I didn't need the spelling system any more. It was as though a hole had been blasted in my head, and through it He spoke. He spoke in thoughts which unfolded like a flowing stream past my inner eye.

He had returned to earth to complete his mission which anyone could see had failed. (I had only to think back to St. Augustine's school to know what a mess it all was.) He had chosen to work through a human channel because it was the only way He could speak directly to the people. I had been chosen (I! I!) to be His medium. He was going to take me into trance and speak through my vocal chords. That's what our chapel was for, for sacred seances where great new teachings would be transmitted.

Christianity was not only off the rails, it was incomplete. All Jesus's references to reincarnation had been edited out — or nearly all; occultists could still find the traces. His message of eternal life had never been taken seriously. So His great new teaching for the twentieth century necessarily had to come under the spiritualist banner. The new religion would be called Complete Christianity.

Mediums and Psychics

She Is Certainly a Witch

Susanna Moodie

The pioneer author Susanna Moodie (1803-1885) scoffed at the suggestion that the backwoods of Canada might be inhabited by spirits. If there are spirits at all, they haunt the castles of Old England, certainly not the pioneer homesteads of the old Ontario strand. Yet in her own home — which is still standing in Belleville, Ont. — Mrs. Moodie experienced the effects of "spirit communication." What weakened and finally dissolved her innate skepticism was her meeting in Belleville in 1855 with Katie Fox, the famous (or infamous) "spirit-rapper."

Both Katie and her sister Maggie Fox were born in the nearby farming community of Consecon. In 1847 the Fox family moved across Lake Ontario to Hydesville, north of Newark, N.Y. It was here the following year, on 31 March 1848, that Katie and Maggie's "rappings" were heard for the first time. The teenage spiritualists quickly attracted rural, state, national, and finally international attention. They became the best-known spiritualists in the world. Their Hydesville rappings mark the birth of modern Spiritualism which includes mediumship, spirit communication, and what is today called "trance-channelling."

Susanna Moodie's encounter with Katie Fox is described in much detail in the letter she addressed to her British publisher Richard Bentley in the autumn of 1855. The letter was first published in Susanna Moodie: Letters of a Lifetime (1985), edited by Carl Ballstadt, Elizabeth Hopkins, and Michael Peterman.

SINCE I LAST WROTE YOU, I have had several visits from Miss Kate Fox the celebrated Spirit Rapper, who is a very lovely intellectual looking girl, with the most beautiful eyes I ever saw in a human head. Not black, but a sort of dark purple. She is certainly a witch, for you cannot help looking into the dreamy depths of those sweet violet eyes till you feel magnetized by them. The expression on her face is sad even to melancholy, but sweetly feminine. I do not believe that the raps are produced by spirits that have been of this world, but I cannot believe that she, with her pure spiritual face is capable of deceiving. She certainly does not procure these mysterious sounds by foot or hand, and though I cannot help thinking that they emanate from her mind and that she is herself the spirit, I believe she is perfectly unconscious of it herself. But to make you understand more about it, I had better describe the scene first, prefacing it with my being a great sceptic on the subject, and therefore as a consequence of my doubts anxious to investigate it to the bottom.

Miss Fox has near relatives in this place to whom Mr. Moodie had expressed a wish to see the fair Kate should she again visit our town.

One morning about three weeks since, I was alone in the drawing room, when my servant girl announced Miss F. and her cousin. I had seen her the summer before for a few minutes in the street, and was so much charmed with her face and her manners that it was with pleasure I met her again. After some conversation on the subject of the raps, she said, "Would you like to hear them."

I said, "Yes, very much indeed, as it would confirm to do away with my doubts."

She then asked the spirits if they would communicate with Mrs. M--- which being replied to, by three loud raps upon the table, which in *spirit language* means yes, I was fairly introduced to these mysterious visitors.

Miss F. told me to write a list of names of dead and living friends, but neither to read them to her, nor to allow her to see them. I did this upon one side of a quire of paper, the whole thickness being between her and me; writing with her back to me.

She told me to run my pen along the list, and as a test the spirits would rap five times for every dead, and three times for every living, friend.

I inwardly smiled at this. Yet strange to say, they never once missed. I then wrote under the name of poor Anna Laura Harral, a daughter of Mr. Thos. Harral who was for several years Editor of *La Belle Assemblée*, who had been one of the friends of my girlhood, "Why did you not keep your promise."

This promise having been a solemn compact made between us in the days of youth and romance, that the one who died first would appear if possible to the other. The answer to my unseen written question was immediately rapped out, "I have often tried to make my presence known to you." I was startled, but wrote again, "If so rap out your name." It was instantly done. Perhaps no one but myself on the whole American continent knew that such a person had ever existed.

I did not then ask more questions, nor did Miss Fox know what I had asked. She told me to lay my hand upon the table and ask the spirit to rap under it. This I did. The table vibrated under my hand as if it was endowed with life. We then went to the door. Miss Fox told me to open the door and stand so that I could see both sides at once. The raps were on the opposite side to my hand. The door shook and vibrated. Miss F. had one hand laid by mine on the door. I am certain that the sounds were not made by hands or feet. We then went into the garden. She made me stand on the earth. The raps were under my feet, distinct and loud. I then stood on a shallow rock under the window. The raps sounded hollow on the stone pavement under me. Her hand slightly pressed my arm. The strange vibration of the knocks was to me the most unaccountable. It seemed as if a mysterious life was infused into the object from which the knocks proceeded. "Are you still unbelieving." "I think these knocks are made by your spirit, and not by the dead."

"You attribute more power to me than I possess. Would you believe if you heard that piano, closed as it is, play a tune."

"I should like to hear it — " I did not, however, hear it that morning, but two nights after, in the same room. I heard the strings of that piano accompany Mr. Moodie upon the flute, Miss Fox and I, standing by the piano, with a hand of each resting upon it. Now it is certain, that she could not have got within the case of the piano.

Mr. Moodie had on a mourning ring with his grandmother's hair. On the inside of the ring was engraved her birth death, etc. He asked the spirits to tell him what was inside that ring, and the date of birth and death were rapped out, he had to take off the ring, having forgotten the date himself, to see if it was correct and found it so....

I thought I would puzzle them, and asked for them to rap out my father's name, the date of his birth and death, which was rather a singular one from the constant recurrence of one figure. He was born Dec. 8th. I did not know myself in what year, was 58 when he died, which happened the 18th of May of 1818. To my astonishment all this was rapped out. His name. The disease of which he died (gout in the stomach) and the city (Norwich), where he died. The question being mental could not have been guessed by any person of common powers. But she may be Clairvoyant, and able to read unwritten thoughts. I have not time just now to give you more on this subject, and though still a great septic as to the spiritual nature of the thing, the intelligence conveyed is unaccountable.

Can such a thing as witchcraft really exist? Or possession by evil spirits? I am bewildered and know not what to answer.

A Very Ingenious Sort of Spiritoscope

Susanna Moodie

Susanna Moodie (1803-1885) was urged to pursue her new interest in Spiritualism by two people — her husband Dunbar Moodie, a half-pay officer who was a believer, and Katie Fox, the original "spirit-rapper," who was a practitioner. Katie Fox visited Mrs. Moodie in her Belleville home in 1855, produced a handful of special effects, and Mrs. Moodie was never quite the same thereafter.

She described her frame of mind and left a record of her experiences in a long letter to her British publisher Richard Bentley. The letter is dated 2 May 1858 and was first published in Susanna Moodie: Letters of a Lifetime *(1985) edited by Carl Ballstadt, Elizabeth Hopkins, and Michael Peterman. The letter includes a description of her experiments with Dunbar Moodie's "a very ingenious sort of Spiritoscope" — a primitive form of the Ouija board.*

TALKING OF MAGIC, brings before me a subject, which in spite of the battling and opposition of a strong will, has forced itself upon my notice, until I stand astonished, and mentally exclaim — "Can such things be?" — You know how often I have laughed in my letters to you about *Spiritualism*. I was not only a septic, but a scorner. Yet, so many strange things have come under my own immediate knowledge, that though still doubtful on some points, I dare not now, exclaim, as I once confidently did, "It is false. A mental puzzle. A delusion!" It is a mystery, strange, solemn and beautiful, and which I now believe, contains nothing more nor less than a new revelation from God to man. Not doing away with the old dispensation, but confirming it in every particular. As I know that every thinking mind, whether a believer or skeptic on this great question, must feel an interest in it, I shall not hesitate to give you some of my experience in these matters, and leave you to draw your own conclusions. I will not go back to my interviews with Miss K. Fox, the celebrated rapping medium, for she left me as great a disbeliever as she found me, but confine myself to matters of a more recent date. A neighbour of ours, Mr. J.W. Tate, one of the principal engineers upon the G.T. Railway, had in his service a Scotch woman of the name of Mary Williamson, who was a very powerful Medium for physical manifestations, and as a great friendship existed between Mr. M. and this gentleman, I had daily opportunities of testing the powers of this girl. I have seen a large heavy English dining table, rise in air repeatedly, without contact, have seen the leaf of the said table, fly up, and strike the snuffers out of my husband's hand, and put out the candles, have heard drums play, martial tunes where no instrument of the kind was to be found for miles, have been touched by unseen hands, and witnessed many curious phenomenon, which it is needless to my purpose, here to enumerate. Yet after the most diligent investigation, and an utter failure *in my part*, to discover the cheat, I still persisted in my vain un-belief. My husband had become an enthusiastic spiritualist and was much hurt by my obstinacy in refusing all the evidence offered to me, and we had several sharp mental conflicts on the subject, which grieved me much, and one evening last spring, after he had left me to go to the house of another spiritual friend, I went upstairs and wept very bitterly, over what I considered the unpardonable credulity of a man of his strong good sense. As I was sitting alone by a little table, that had been given to my daughter Vickers, by a very talented young friend, long since dead, I suddenly laid my right hand upon the table, and feeling very angry in my own mind at all *spiritualists*, I said tauntingly, enough, "If there be any truth in this doctrine, let the so-called spirits move my hand against my will off from this table, and lay it down in my lap!" You would have laughed to have seen the determined energy, with which I held my hand down to the table, expecting the moon, that was then shining into the room, to leave her bright path in the heavens as soon, as that my hand should be lifted from that table. You may therefore guess my surprise, not to say, terror, when my hand became paralyzed, and the fingers were slowly wrenched up from the table, and the whole hand lifted and laid down in my lap. Not dropped nor jerked suddenly, brought forward, as if held in a strong grasp and placed there.

I left the room and went downstairs into the dining room. My servant had gone out for a walk and I was quite alone. My husband had contrived a very ingenious sort of Spiritoscope. A board running upon two smooth brass rods with an index that pointed to the alphabet in order to save the trouble of culling over the alphabet. I had always refused to put my hands upon this board, which would move for people under the influence and spell out letter by letter messages and names. But being alone, I placed my hands upon the board, and asked, "Was it a spirit that lifted my hand?" and the board rolled forward and spelt out "Yes." "What spirit?" "A friend." "What is your name?" "Thomas Harral!" I must say that this startled me. Mr. H., who for many years, was Editor of *La Belle Assemblée*, was the first literary man for whom I wrote, and I certainly had not thought of him for many years. I did not even know, whether he were dead or living, and I again asked, "Why do you wish to communicate with me?" "Because I felt an interest in you when upon earth."

Knowing that he had been a great sceptic on religious matters, I said, "Was yours a happy death?" The answer was so characteristic of the man, that it made me almost realize his presence — "Susanna — Was mine a happy life?" "Where did you die?" "What matters it to you, where I died. If I were to tell you, what means have you of testing the truth?" "Will you lift my hand again?" "Tomorrow night at this hour." This was done, and for many nights after. I then reversed the thing, and begged the spirit to fix my hands down upon the table, so that I could not raise them. This too was done and so effectively, that my husband had to employ the reverse passes in mesmerism in order to break the spell.

Though, still unwilling to believe, imputing the whole matter to some new and undiscovered power of mind, I did at times consent to put my hands upon the spiritoscope and though at times I got no communication, the board never moving at all, and at other times, had my hands paralyzed and lifted upon from the board, yet at other times it would move rapidly even with my eyes shut, Mr. M. taking the words down letter by letter, as pointed out by the index. The first I got in this matter, was from my dear friend Thomas Pringle the abolitionist, from whose house I was married, it runs as follows —

22 June 1857, Thomas Pringle

"You will not live to see the abolition of slavery in the United States. It will end in blood and great political changes must take place. The corruption of the Government will bring about a great moral reform, and the people will see the necessity of getting rid of the cause of so much crime. But it will not be in your day. A long struggle between the North and South, with the defection of California, Texas and Kansas, will set the poor Negro free, but this will take years to accomplish. God will prepare the mind of the slave, for the great moral change that awaits his condition. When God brings about a great National reform, He works slowly, and uses many instruments because many changes are affected by one. No more. Good night." —

Since obtaining this communication I have watched with great interest the Kansas question. It would be running this communication to too great a length to give you some most curious and interesting communications which I have from time to time, received from a spirit, who calls himself my guardian angel but who will not give his name. I send you, however, the two first communications that we received from him.

June 30, 1857

"A young man, old in the spirit world will communicate with you tonight. Do not too readily give credence to all that mediums tell you. They are often deceived by their own thoughts mingling with the thoughts of the spirit that communicates. Only receive what looks like truth. All great truths are simple. The Circle, the most sublime symbol of Eternity, which is one name for God, is the most simple of forms, yet it is a problem which philosophers cannot solve. Such is God. All can behold his perfect beauty and the harmony which exists in his works, which love unites in the unbroken Circle of divine wisdom. Trust implicitly to Him. It is as easy to gain communications from his spirit, as from souls that have been stained with sins of earth. Pray for this divine influence and it will not be withheld. It can neither lead astray nor deceive, for God is truth. Good night, my friends." My husband asked, "Will the spirit give his name?"

"I have a name in Heaven but not for your ears."

On the 6th July, he gave us the following — "God is a perfect Unity. The great circle and centre of existence. *Death*, is but the returning *wave of life* flowing back to Him. All created existence lives through and to Him, and no man lives for himself alone. He is a link in the chain of life, which would be broken without his ministration.

Hence, bad and good work together for the universal benefit of all. There is no partiality or injustice in this dispensation. God makes no man bad, but their evil passions by forming the trials and temptations of others, bring out their virtues and fit souls for a higher state of existence, and educate them for Heaven. Thus they become ministering spirits to those who are tempted and tried on earth."

Here follows a passage of a personal nature. My husband asked, "Will you give us your name?"

"My name is unknown to you — "

"Can I distinguish you by any name?"

"You will know me by the nature of my communications. Rest satisfied. I wish you well — good night."

I have received some noble communications from this spirit, and if you wish to know more of him, I will give more, in my next letter. He is so unlike all the other communicants, that I know him from the first sentence he spells upon the board.

You will perhaps think, as I too, have often thought, that the whole is an operation of my *own* mind, but my mind must be far cleverer than I, its owner, have any idea of if it can spell letter by letter, whole pages of connected and often abstruse matter, without my knowing one word about it, for, it is not, until, Mr. Moodie reads it over to me, after the communication is suspended that I know what it is about. My sister, Mrs. Traill, is a very powerful Medium for these communications, and gets them in foreign languages. Her spirits often abuse, and call her very ugly names. Had I time, I could surprise you with some that she has received, but could not surprise you so much as she has been surprised herself. She, who was quite as skeptical as me, has been rendered very happy by the intercourse of her dear children, which has quite overcome the fears of death that she till lately entertained. Now, do you think me mad or possessed by evil spirits, like that great Medium of old St. Paul's. I could wish you altogether possessed by such a glorious madness.

But Mother Davis Could Read Minds Fluently

James L. Hughes

James L. Hughes (1846-1935) was a prominent educator, the Inspector of Public Schools in Toronto from 1902 to 1913, and the author of numerous educational manuals and volumes of verse. He was born near Bowmanville, Ont., like his famous brother General Sir Sam Hughes. In later years Hughes puzzled over his chance meeting with Mother Davis in a Toronto general store in 1865. The words exchanged on that occasion suggested to Hughes that mind reading was a reality and that the future could be foretold. Hughes contributed this brief memoir to Benjamin Fish Austin's Glimpses of the Unseen *(1898).*

IN THE YEAR 1865 I attended the Normal School in Toronto. I was then in my twentieth year. I had rooms with three other young men over a small store in a quiet part of the city. On our return from school one evening we found an old negress in the store, through which we had to pass on our way to our rooms. A glance revealed the fact that she was a remarkable woman. Her figure was tall and slight. Her action was quick, definite and graceful, and her animated face reflected very clearly the flashes of thought and feeling that chased each other through her mind and heart. Her manner was weird and her look indicated a half demented condition. When we entered the store she turned promptly from the proprietor, with whom she had been talking, and came close to us — glanced rapidly from one to another, and then seizing my right hand in hers and placing her left on my forehead, she gazed searchingly into my eyes for some moments. Suddenly she said, "Young man, I can tell you anything you ever did or anything you want to know."

"May we ask questions?" said one of my companions laughing.

"Certainly," I said, treating the whole matter as a joke.

"Why, you can't even tell his name," said one of them who had lived for years on the farm adjoining my father's.

"His name is Hughes," she promptly answered.

This was a surprise, and my friend proceeded to make a more thorough test of her power.

"What is his father's name?" said he.

"John."

"His mother's?"

"Caroline."

"How many sisters has he?"

"Seven."

"How many brothers?"

"Three."

"What was he before coming to Toronto?"

"A farmer."

"What direction is the well from the house on his father's farm?"

"They aint got no well. Their water is carried in pipes from a spring."

"In what year did he break his arm?"

This was another catch question, but she was equal to the occasion.

"His arm was never broken; don't try to be too smart, young man," said she with an indignant look of reproof.

His question brought accidents to my recollection, and I asked, "What was the worst accident that ever happened to me?"

"The fall from the gig when the horse ran away with you," was her answer.

Associated in my mind with the runaway was the fact that my favourite dog had been shot the day before the horse ran away. He was bitten by a mad dog and had to be put aside. Some time before his death he was run over by a loaded wagon, and when I ran to pick him up he bit me in his agony. The scars were clearly visible on my hand. My friend's clever question recalled the runaway, the death of my dog, and the fact that he bit me. Almost before I was conscious of the fact that I was looking at the marks on my hand she said: "He did not know what he was doing when he bit you." I was startled to hear her express orally the thought that was passing through my mind. There was now no possibility of doubting her power of mind reading. We proceeded to test her along many lines, and always with the same result. Each question brought the answer to my mind, and she spoke what I thought as quickly and as definitely as I could have done. She had never seen me before. No one in the whole city had known me until a short time previously, when I came from a farm sixty miles away.

Mind reading seemed to me quite a modest accomplishment, however, when she revealed her greater powers. When we tired of questioning she proceeded on her own account: "You are attending the Normal School now," she said, "and you will be a teacher in that school some day."

"Stick to history, Auntie," I replied, "your prophecy is absurd."

"What do you know about it, young man?" she queried. "I tell you, you will be appointed a teacher in that school before you are two years older," she continued, speaking with much emphasis.

Nothing at that time seemed more absurd to me. I was only a few weeks from the farm. My highest ambition was to teach a village school, and I did not allow her prophecy to raise a single hope in my mind; but she was right. I was appointed without an application. If an application had been necessary I should not have obtained the situation. She proceeded to give me information relative to my future, the wisdom of which was accurately shown by after years, but her most remarkable statement was a prophecy which left but an hour for its fulfilment:

"Before you take your tea tonight a gentleman will come to see you who will be a relation of yours by your marriage."

It was nearly six o'clock when she spoke her prophecy. Only one gentleman came to our rooms before we took tea. He came to borrow a book, and years afterwards I married his cousin.

I knew Irving Bishop, I have witnessed Stewart Cumberland's remarkable mind reading; but Mother Davis could read minds fluently, while they spelled their syllables with difficulty. Her prophecies are to me inexplicable. No foundation of even the most shadowy kind existed on which she could logically base either of them, when she made them. None of my professors had ever dreamed for an instant of my appointment as a teacher in the Normal School, when she foretold it. No such hope had ever come to me, nor did I admit it when she presented it to me. No one in authority ever knew till after I was appointed that she had made her prophecy; so her opening up of the future could have no possible influence in securing the fulfilment of her prophecy. This is equally true in regard to my marriage. The lady who afterwards became my first wife, and made me a "relation by marriage" to the gentleman who visited us on the evening Mrs. Davis called, was a fellow-student of mine at the Normal School, but my interest in her was not aroused by anything Mrs. Davis said. We continued at school for nearly a year after her prophecy, and even attended the same Sunday-school, yet we did not become acquainted. I left the city to teach in the country, and became engaged to another lady. I was appointed to a position in the practice department of the Normal School unexpectedly. I resided in the city for nearly a year before I visited the lady whom I married. During this time the possibility of our union had not presented itself to me. We were brought together at last by a chain of circumstances that resulted from no effort of ours, but were wrought out by the absolute overthrow of our plans by causes over which we had no control.

The Appearance of Sir John A. Macdonald

Sir John S. Thompson

Sir John A. Macdonald is alive and well in the pages of history books. But is he alive and well in the afterworld? Did his personality survive bodily death?

Sir John A. Macdonald (1815-1891) was the first Prime Minister of the Dominion of Canada. He was affectionately known as Old Tomorrow for his penchant for procrastination. His residence was Earnscliffe where he resided with his handicapped daughter Mary; the stately home is today the residence of the British High Commissioner. Macdonald died in office on 6 June 1891.

Sir John S. Thompson, Macdonald's successor as Prime Minister, served for only two years (from 1892 to 1894). He also died in office, and did so dramatically, on an official visit to Windsor Castle, 12 Dec. 1894. Thompson is (in part) the author of the political anecdote that follows. Although undated in the original source, it is set in the Muskoka district of Ontario, which is summer cottage country, and it relates to the summer of either 1893 or 1894.

It is not a matter of historical record that Old Tomorrow attempted to communicate his views about private matters and affairs of state to his successor as Prime Minister through "a young man." But the only person in a position to know for sure is the late Prime Minister W. L. Mackenzie King, who as a practising Spiritualist might have entertained an opinion on the matter.

"Anecdote of Sir John Thompson — A Curious Experience Related by Faith Fenton" is the title Benjamin Fish Austin gave this *curious anecdote in* Glimpses of the Unseen *(1898). Nothing is immediately known of Faith Fenton. It seems that she contributed the second half of the anecdote about the newly deceased Sir John S. Thompson; the first half likely flowed from Austin's pen.*

SIR JOHN THOMPSON was never given to much speaking. He lacked the small coin of gossip and light badinage in a marked degree. His words were few and thoughtful. His attitude was that of the onlooker rather than the participant. Yet when time for speech arrived he was always ready.

This was noticeable in the House. When one of those breezes of disagreement so common in parliamentary debate sprang up between member and member, or party and party, Sir John — who usually sat in that atmosphere of absolute quietism which seemed in itself a strength to his followers — waited until the matter had gone far enough or threatened the dignity of the House, then he arose and spoke the few wise, judicial words that made instantly for peace.

In debate it was the same. His was always the final utterance upon any subject; not because of his official position, but because his few words summed up the entire matter. He was judicial always, and his impartial attitude won recognition and favour upon both sides of the House.

In private life he was much the same, speaking little but always a kindly observer; and nothing was more attractive to those privileged to meet him socially than his attitude of readiness to be interested and pleased.

"I know I am not a talker; but I am pleased to hear you talk, and ready to listen," his quiet look and bearing said to all who approached him. And because of these abiding qualities of strong sympathy, and a thoughtfulness that was not secretive, wrapped in an atmosphere of quietism, Sir John was a prince of listeners.

Yet he enjoyed fun, as most quiet people do, and when in the privacy of a friendly circle the merry talk went round, he — the usually silent listener — would frequently arouse himself to contribute something — an opinion, mayhap, or an incident out of high official experience — that was well worth the hearing.

It was on such an occasion, and only a few months before his death, that he related in the presence of the writer one of those curious experiences that, doubtless, occur to all men of high official position, who become naturally a mark for cranks and faddists.

That it relates very closely to the Old Chieftain, and has hitherto been known only to some three or four of Sir John's associates, will render it of interest to Canadians everywhere:

It was an August afternoon that last summer of Sir John Thompson's life, and in the company of his family and two or three friends he sat on the deck of a certain pretty yacht as it rippled its way across the waters of Lake Rosseau. The Premier had been silent, as was his wont, lying back in his chair with closed eyes, with only an occasional smile, showing that he heard the conversation carried on about him.

Presently the talk turned on hypnotism. Sir Mackenzie Bowell, who was an adept at the art in his young days, related certain stirring experiences of his personal explorations into the misty land of psychology; and urged on by the joking skepticism of Senator Sanford, offered to give practical illustration of his power on the spot.

Sir John roused suddenly into a decisive veto against the half-jesting proposal.

"The thing is all nonsense, of course, but we mustn't have anyone tampered with," he said; and as the conversation drifted on naturally to the subject of clairvoyance and dreams, he related the following incident:

I had been premier something less than a year, and Sir John Macdonald had been dead, as you will remember, a year or so, when one morning my private secretary came into my office and said that a young man wanted to see me, but would give neither his name nor his business.

As on enquiry he appeared to be respectable and well-mannered, I gave orders that he should be admitted.

On finding himself alone with me, he told me frankly that he was afraid I would be surprised at his errand.

"What do you want?" I said.

"I have a message for you from Sir John Macdonald," he answered.

I looked him over keenly; but he was evidently in earnest, and moreover seemed conscious of his position.

I enquired quietly what the message was, and in what manner he received it.

Sir John Macdonald had appeared to him distinctly on several recent occasions, he said, urging him to bring a certain message directly to me; and so strong was the influence exerted, that he felt impelled to relieve himself of responsibility in the matter of complying with what he believed to be a request from a departed spirit.

The message related to certain private funds that belonged to Miss Mary Macdonald, and which her father — so the young man asserted — desired to be transferred and otherwise invested.

After the young man departed I made a few enquiries concerning him. He came from Nova Scotia, and was engaged in temporary work at Ottawa in the Buildings. He belonged to a thoroughly respectable family, and up to the present bore no reputation for erraticism of any kind.

I mentioned the matter to the lawyer entrusted with the Earnscliffe interests, and he confessed himself at a loss to understand how the private affairs involved in the "message" could have come to the young man's knowledge since they were known only to himself. But he admitted that the course indicated concerning the funds in question might be sound business advice.

The matter had almost passed from my memory, when one day, several months later, the young man presented himself again with a second "message" from the same source, this time for myself. Sir John Macdonald was earnestly desirous that certain changes should be made in the Cabinet.

I took the young fellow in hand and questioned him closely. As far as I could discover he was honest, and apparently an unwilling bearer of these pre-emptory messages.

Why they were given to him, he said, he did not know; but after they were given he had no peace with the nightly appearance of Sir John Macdonald reiterating his commands until they were filled.

Sir John Thompson's quiet face broke into a smile of amused remembrance at this point in his story.

"You would need to understand Sir John's well-known penchant for planning Cabinet changes," he said, "in order to appreciate the effect of this last 'message' upon my colleagues, whom I took into confidence in the manner."

They listened in silence; but it was Sir Adolphe Caron who voiced their thought in one expressive sentence:

"Good Lord!" he exclaimed, "Is the old man at it again?"

"What were the proposed changes, Sir John?" queried one of his listeners when the laugh subsided.

"Ah, that is another story," he said, smiling. "But again the curious fact is that they were excellent suggestions, and just such changes as I should like to have made myself had it been practicable. Yet this young man knew nothing of politics — much less of the inner workings of the Cabinet."

Experience with a Mind-Reader

Benjamin Fish Austin

The Reverend Benjamin Fish Austin (1850-1932) remains one of the most intriguing figures and controversial characters in the realm of religious and spiritual thought in Canada at the turn-of-the-century. He tested theological tolerance, found it wanting, and made a notable contribution to the cause of Spiritualism.

Benjamin Fish Austin was born near Brighton, Ont., and educated at Albert College, Belleville. He was ordained a minister of the Methodist Episcopal Church and from 1881 to 1897 served as Principal of Alma College, a girls' school in St. Thomas. Along the way he became a confirmed spiritualist and began to proselytize his views within the ministry. In 1899, he was tried for heresy by church officials, pronounced guilty, and expelled from the Methodist Church and its ministry. Thereafter Austin lived in the United States and served as pastor of spiritualist churches in Rochester and Los Angeles. He died in the latter city.

Austin wrote and self-published a dozen or so books on a number of surprising subjects, including studies of the sins of the Jesuits, the needs of womanhood, the lives of leading prohibitionists, memory training, money-making, as well as two turgidly written occult novels. His most notable publication was Glimpses of the Unseen, a large-format, 500-page compilation of the psychical experiences taken from the past and the present and amassed through research and correspondence. The anthology includes "Rev. Principal Austin's Experience with a Mind-Reader," which is

*reprinted below, along with other narratives included elsewhere in
the present book.*

*The full title of Austin's remarkable volume gives some idea of its
contents. The title and subtitles go like this:* Glimpses of the
Unseen: A Study of Dreams, Premonitions, Prayer and Remarkable
Answers, Hypnotism, Spiritualism, Telepathy, Apparitions, Peculiar Mental and Spiritual Experiences, Unexplained Psychical Phenomena: A Book of Personal Experiences, Original and Selected,
Related in their Own Language by Reputable Persons, Together
with Running Comments and a Thoughtful Summary. *It was
illustrated with portraits and published in Toronto and Brantford
by The Bradley-Garretson Company, Limited, in 1898.*

IN THE SPRING OF '94, I was returning from the Ohio State Sunday
School Convention, where I had delivered a lecture on "Palestine,
the Fifth Gospel," and having a short time to wait in Detroit for
Michigan Central connection, I noticed the reports of a celebrated
mind-reader who was then giving experiments in that city.

Having had, for many years, an earnest desire to witness a
genuine case of mind-reading, I resolved to call upon this man and
witness, if possible, an exhibition of his powers. I may say that I had
witnessed, some years before, the experiments of Cumberland in
his so-called feats of mind-reading, but having been able, with very
little practice, to duplicate nearly all his performances, I had long
ceased to regard the most successful experiments in which there
was bodily contact with the experimenter as tests of mind-reading,
and had, indeed, formed my own theory in explanation of such
experiments, which I was pleased to see verified by the experiments
made by the Society for Psychical Research.

I had previously called on a number of professional mind-
readers, but had never been able to secure any satisfactory evidence
that the ideas and emotions of one mind could be conveyed to
another mind except through the recognized channels. Accordingly I called up this Mr. W. --- , but found, after a few minutes'
sitting, he could not give me a successful experiment.

On expressing my disappointment and mentioning my previous
attempts to secure some satisfactory evidence of this power — if it

really existed — and expressing a doubt as to such a power, he confidently affirmed that, under certain conditions, mind could communicate with mind directly and without the ordinary channels of communication, and told me if I would call on a certain Mrs. C---r, a resident of Detroit, I would probably get a successful experiment in mind-reading. He assured me of her ability, of her sincere and religious character, and on the strength of his strong endorsation I called upon her. I found her in a beautiful home on ---- street. She was a lady of medium height, rather slender in body, with a thoughtful, pale face, which carried an air of devotion constantly. I introduced myself as a student of mental science, anxious to test the power of mind-reading, and asked her for an experiment. She received me cordially in her parlour and asked me to be seated, taking a seat directly opposite and a few feet from me. Taking my hand for a moment she dropped it and, closing her eyes, appeared to pass almost instantly into a kind of sleep. Almost immediately she began talking rapidly and loudly in quite another tone from her ordinary speech. I remember quite well her opening statement, and after that will give in summarized form the chief things said to me:

"Sir, I perceive you surrounded by a great crowd of young people. (I had been for nearly fourteen years Principal of Alma College, St. Thomas, Ont., which position I now hold.) Your work is laborious and you and your comrades are carrying heavy burdens. You seem to me like a company of men in a field, with ropes over your shoulders, all striving to draw a stone-boat well filled with stones. The burden is heavy and will so continue, but gradually lightening with coming years. (We had been, and were then, labouring under heavy debt, and her prediction as to gradual lightening of the load upon us seemed justified by subsequent events.)... You have been a term of years in your present position, coming from the east, where you were located near a great river. (We spent our three years preceding my college appointment at Prescott on the St. Lawrence.)"

In a number of her statements she gave remarkable correct accounts of a general character concerning myself and my work, and I could not say that any one statement — though she gave a number of particulars — was incorrect. For example, she particulary referred to one of my fellow-laborers with whom I had been associated a long time, describing very well his general appearance, etc. (Prof. Warner, the Vice-Principal of Alma College, associated with me for fifteen years at Alma, had been a college mate for some years at Albert University, Belleville, Ont.)

Still I professed to be unsatisfied and demanded a more particular test. I said: "Madam, you are able to read the mind, and if so, you can mention the name of my associates in labour."

"Ah, sir," said she, "you have asked me a hard thing."

"I came for that very purpose," I said, "and nothing but a most particular fact will satisfy me you can read the mind."

"Sir," said she, "you must know there are two classes of mind-readers — those who see as in a vision what they relate — clairvoyant — and those who hear what they relate — clairaudient. Very few have the spiritual sight and hearing both well developed; what I have told you I have seen as in a series of pictures. My spiritual hearing is not well developed — though I hear a great deal — but all I hear is confused; I cannot well distinguish the sounds from each other. I am hearing names all the time I am in your presence; I will try and get you one or more."

And then for some little time she was silent; a look of most intent earnestness came over her face. Her whole being seemed to resolve itself into hearing, so intently did she seem to listen. The stillness was death-like and oppressive, when all at once, with a sudden spring as if she would leap from her seat, she cried out loudly: "Professor — Professor — Professor W — I can't get the rest of the name. He is a professor and his name begins with W."

I was astounded, and yet fully convinced of the fact of mind-reading from that hour, for Prof. Warner had been my intimate co-laborer for fifteen years. I never saw Mrs. C---r before or since.

Winnipeg's Psychic Possibilities

Sir Arthur Conan Doyle

Sir Arthur Conan Doyle (1859-1930) devoted the last decade of his life to the Spiritualist cause. He was its able defender for the reading public associated the famous author with his cele-brated fictional creation, Sherlock Holmes, the embodiment of the scientific method of inquiry. Accompanied by his wife, Doyle trav-elled widely, lectured lengthily, wrote copiously, and argued convinc-ingly on behalf of "spirit return." Believers found him compelling; doubters found him credulous. Among his major works in the field is the semi-scholarly History of Spiritualism *(1926).*

Doyle was no stranger to the Dominion, travelling right across Canada on at least two occasions. He took time out from his lecture tour of 1922 to attend two séances in Winnipeg and to examine the report of a poltergeist in Montreal. The author's impressions, psy-chical and other, appear in his travel book Our Second American Adventure *(1923).*

Two Winnipeg séances are described in the passage that follows. The first séance, with its well-defined manifestations, was held at the home of Dr. T. Glendenning Hamilton, the respected physi-cian. The location of the second séance, the one with a more religious air, is no longer recalled.

ON OUR FIRST NIGHT in Winnipeg we attended a circle for psychical research which has been conducted for two years by a group of scientific men who have obtained remarkable results. The medium is a small, pleasant-faced woman from the Western Highlands of Scotland. Her psychic gifts are both mental and physical. The circle, which contained ten persons, included my wife and myself, placed their hands, or one hand each, upon a small table, part of which was illuminated by phosphorus so as to give some light. It was violently agitated, and this process was described as "charging it." It was then pushed back into a small cabinet made of four hung curtains with an opening in front. Out of this the table came clattering again and again entirely of its own, with no sitter touching it. I stood by the slit in the curtain in subdued red light and I watched the table within. One moment it was quiescent. A moment later it was like a restless dog in a kennel, springing, tossing, beating up against the supports, and finally bounding out with a velocity which caused me to get quickly out of the way. It ended by rising up in the air while our finger-tips were on it and remaining up for an appreciable period.

Many of Crawford's Belfast experiments have been duplicated by this group of scientists, which is the more important in view of Dr. Fourrier d'Albe's failure to get the same results. The doctor who presided had a butcher's scale in the room. The table weighed 12$^{1}/_{2}$ pounds. He suspended it to the scale and was able, simply by psychic power, to increase the registered weight to 46 pounds and to decrease it to 7 pounds. He made one novel observation, which was that the raps which accompany the experiments persist and even increase when the weight increases, but disappear when the weight is below the normal.

On the mental side the peculiarity of the sittings is that little quotations which can be traced to R.L. Stevenson's works are rapped out by the medium. So far as is known, the little Scotch woman knows nothing normally of R.L.S., because she is not of a literary turn. Quotation after quotation has been actually verified. One curious line came through which has not yet been located. It is: "It will come at last like grey hair or coffin nails." It sounds like Stevenson, but I cannot place it.

The man who goes upon occult paths does certainly have an extraordinary variety of experience. Let me briefly narrate that which happened on the morning of July 4th, the day after my lecture at Winnipeg, which had been a remarkably successful one to a very crowded house. I had heard of a strange circle and of a very remarkable medium, whom I will call Mrs. Bolton. At 9:00 a.m. one of her devotees, who are absolutely wholehearted in their belief and devotion, was at the hotel door with a car. After a four-mile drive we alighted at a lonely villa on the extreme outskirts of the town, where there were six other men and three women to meet us. The men were all alert, middle-aged or young, evidently keen men of business who might have been accountants or merchants. Yet here they were from ten o'clock onwards on a working day giving themselves up to what was in their eyes infinitely more important than business.

We sat around the room, and presently Mrs. Bolton entered, a woman of the Blavatsky type of rounded face, but less heavy. She seemed gentle and amiable. She sat down while "Lead, Kindly Light" was sung. Then she sank into a trance, from which she quietly emerged with an aspect of very great dignity and benevolence. I have never seen more commanding eyes than those which fixed us each in turn. "It is the Master. It is the High Spirit," whispered my neighbours. Standing up, and greeting each of us in turn with very great dignity, the medium, or the entity controlling her, proceeded to baptize a child nine weeks old belonging to one of the circle. The mother might have stood for a model of reverence and awe. She then handed round bread and wine, as in the Sacrament. The wine, as I was assured by all, was simply water drawn from the domestic supply. It had now become faintly red with an aromatic odour and taste. At every meeting this miracle of changing the water into wine was performed, according to the unanimous testimony of these very same workaday men of the world, who declare that they themselves have drawn the water. I could not give a name to the taste and smell, which were very pleasant. It was certainly non-alcoholic.

We then had a long address, which was in the medium's own voice and dialect, but purported to come from the high control. My growing deafness made me miss some of it, but what I heard was dignified and impressive. After speaking for nearly an hour, a second control took possession. He was more smiling and homely but less majestic and dignified than the higher one. The latter, by the way, unbent in a very charming way when he blessed a little boy who was present, saying, "I remember when I was a little boy myself once." The second control gave messages relating to worldly things to several of the circle, who received them with deep reverence. They assured me that they never failed to be true. He spoke of conditions at death. "The dark valley on the other side waits for all. I am in the glorious city at the end. Those who are prepared by knowledge, as you are, soon pass the Valley. But some linger very long."

Then after some ceremonies which I may not describe the séance ended, and Mrs. Bolton, the plain, homely, uneducated Lancashire woman, came back into her own body. What is one to say of such a performance? It is against all my prepossessions, for I have a deep distrust of ritual and form and sacraments, and here were all these things; yet they were solemn and moving, and nothing can exceed the absolute faith of these men and women. Their faith is founded, as they assure me, upon long experience in which they have seen miracle after miracle, including materializations of these high personages. I cannot claim that I saw anything evidential with my own eyes, and yet I am convinced that my informant was speaking truth so far as he saw it, when he claimed that he poured water into the chalice and that it had been transformed. It all left me with mixed feelings, but the conviction that I had been on the fringe of something very sacred and solemn was predominant. It is true that these High Spirits occasionally used Lancashire speech, but as one of them said, "We cannot open brain-cells which have never been opened. We have to use what is there."

When I considered the wonderful psychical phenomena of the one circle seen with my own eyes and the religious atmosphere of the other, I came away with the conclusion that Winnipeg stands very high among the places we have visited for its psychic possibilities. There are several Spiritualist Churches and a number of local mediums of good repute.

On the Threshold of
the Unknown

John Booth

In the early 1930s an informal psychical research group was formed and met in private homes in Hamilton and nearby Burlington, Ont. One evening the members of the group invited to their séance a medium from Kitchener, and that special meeting was recalled and described in vivid detail many years later by one youthful member.

That young member was John Booth. A native of Minneapolis, Minn., he grew up in Hamilton and later graduated from McMaster University. For many years he worked as a strange magician. His interest in magical effects and parapsychology ultimately led him to California where he now makes his home. He is the author of Psychic Paradoxes *(1984), a lively memoir about a life devoted to magic and psychical research.*

Thomas Lacey is the name of the medium who performed at the séance that Booth described so brightly in his memoirs. Little is now recalled of this "trumpet medium" except that in the 1930s he was in demand throughout Ontario. Booth could not help but view Lacey's performance during the séance through the eyes of a conjurer-in-training. Here is Lacey in action as recalled by Booth in the chapter "Shooting Down the Floating Trumpets."

INFECTED WITH SCIENTIFIC CURIOSITY about paranormal phenomena, fifteen highly salaried professional and executive types in

Hamilton, Ontario, established an informal psychical research group of their own. They met almost monthly for investigative evenings in different homes. Into a kitty each member deposited ten or fifteen dollars periodically to defray the costs of engaging for seances skilled Spiritualists who specialized in physical phenomena.

Several unimpressive meetings occurred with imported mediums before the Canadians excitedly felt that at last they had a winner. Three seances with a Kitchener, Ontario, psychic named Thomas Lacey proved him to be a master at spirit writing and trumpet levitations, i.e., messages and signs from the dead. Professors studying his phenomena at Queen's and McGill universities allegedly had commended him unreservedly.

At this point I was brought in. A darkroom seance was called in the plush Burlington home of a Mr. Christiansen, manager of a prosperous retail store in downtown Hamilton. When I was introduced to Mr. Lacey he remarked cordially: "They say you are an extraordinarily skilful magician. Well, tonight you see things magic can't do."

In spite of this slightly braggadocio statement, the medium was an unassuming, labourer type. This fact he exploited in our educated assemblage of physicians, professors, merchants and retired, well-to-do persons. The more humble and untutored any psychic can make himself appear, the more dramatic and attributable only to spirit world manifestations would seem any high level articulation and phenomena. Such occurrences would theoretically be beyond a man of his personal limitations.

Curtains were already drawn in the living room as we seated ourselves in a circle, joined hands and extinguished the lights. The medium slowly slipped into a trance. Before him, on a table, rested pads of paper and several pencils. On the floor in the middle of the human circle, stood the traditional collapsible tin trumpet. Radium bands painted around it, in four places, glowed softly in the pitch blackness, a constant reminder of its location.

I liked an attitude that prevailed, something that the years since have taught me to be of utmost importance. Although no religious significance was attached to the group's meetings, it conscientiously followed whatever specifications the guest psychic laid down. No hostility, coolness or open skepticism were displayed.

The sitters had promised no scenes and had exacted from me a similar vow. Commendably, they wished each medium to receive a full, co-operative opportunity to produce the best of which he/she was capable.

Thus, at Lacey's request, we sang *a cappella* two hymns: *Rock of Ages* and *Nearer My God to Thee*. By now I had sat through so many seances, without feeling strange in the disorienting total lack of light, that I could croak forth lustily with the tenors and baritones around me. It happened to be an all-male session.

Silence. We waited. A tiny light appeared near the ceiling. It drifted downward and disappeared in Lacey's vicinity. Apparently it was the medium's Indian control entering his body. In broken, gutteral English, this guide from the spirit world brought in the voices of loved ones with messages for persons sitting in the room. The departed spoke of their happiness; one reminded her grown son to wear his nightcap in cold weather. We were permitted to ask a few questions seeking advice. Most of the committeemen, I learned later, took this phase of the seance with maximum skepticism. They were awaiting the phenomena of which the Spiritualist was an unquestioned master.

Automatic writing commenced. A sudden scratching cut through the bony stillness like an etching. Pencil scraping paper. A ripping sound. Sheet torn from pad, crumpled hurriedly and hurled with remarkable aim through the darkness toward whatever it was intended to reach. Four written messages arrived that night.

Still holding hands in a circle, we were asked to join in a mournful religious hymn, one of those traditional pieces with lyrics that, properly analyzed, would discredit a five-year-old's intelligence. As our dirge ended we noticed the delicate radium bands before us begin to sway back and forth. The trumpet was in motion. Easily and hauntingly it floated upward and then swept in graceful arcs across the chamber. In silence we watched and listened as the metal scraped across the plaster ceiling above us, the glowing bands posting us on the location every moment.

No voices came through the trumpet. In theory a spirit can materialize a larynx out of ectoplasm. The discarnate places this at the small end of the sound amplifying trumpet and through it addresses the sitters. Except for the omission of this feature, ours was a typical trumpet seance but exceedingly well done.

After one closing hymn, the lights were gradually snapped on, one by one, so that our eyes would not be hurt by a sudden brilliance. Refreshments were served to a solemn crowd. The medium stood by quietly, obviously tired, answering whatever technical questions occurred to the onlookers. Then we disbanded.

The chairman, Mr. Christiansen, was certain that genuine psychic phenomena had been experienced that evening. Transparent exultation suffused his manner as he sought my reactions. I committed myself to nothing but waited until I had sat through a second seance. Then I was ready.

"I would like you to build a small chimney of sticks, like a box kite," I asked my host. "We will rest it upright in the middle of the living room floor with the trumpet based vertically inside it."

"The radium bands will be clearly visible to us. Under these conditions," I continued, "it will be virtually impossible for any human agency, without much awkwardness and delay, to get at the trumpet in order to levitate it. The contraption would be just high enough so that the trumpet can emerge from the top, underneath the ceiling."

Years afterward, I learned that Sir William Crookes, noted British research scientist, had devised a similar cage for an investigative test. It was introduced to encase an accordion which played melodiously when held under the table in one hand of the remarkable psychic, Daniel Dunglass Home. I was disappointed in Mr. Christiansen's reaction to my recommendation.

"That would be an insult to the integrity of Mr. Lacey," he protested, echoing famous last words of many a balky medium. "He'll never agree, either."

"These are simply tests," I pleaded. "You can't move forward now unless you introduce a new element into the situation. This is it. It is a static control. Lacey can be prepared for it. You aren't springing an unexpected, unfair surprise on him."

Human minds build their own blockages. The group was afraid to push its search for truth to the limits. I could tolerate just so much knowledge and tension but no more. When called upon to energize an innovative research device beyond sitting on their rumps, the folk pulled back. Did they fear what might be learned and cringe from the risk of disillusionment? Were they inhibited by timidity over perhaps offending a medium who realized he was there ostensibly to be judged? What other factors in human nature might help to account for this behaviour on the threshold of the unknown?

A Gypsy Fortune-Teller Beckoned Me

G. Allan Burton

A generation of Canadians grew up knowing and respecting G. Allan Burton, the personable Chairman of Simpsons Ltd. He maintained the tradition that the Simpsons department stores possessed a particular cachet. Was his life foretold by a gypsy fortune-teller in London, England, in 1937? At the time Burton was a twenty-two-year-old apprentice in interior designer. It would be many years before he would assume command at Simpsons. Yet the fortune-teller was right about so many details. Burton recalled the encounter in his highly readable autobiography A Store of Memories *(1986).*

AS THE YEAR WORE ON I became more and more lonely for home and pined for Audrey. One day, I wandered down the Haymarket and from one tiny shop a gypsy fortune-teller beckoned me to have my fortune told, which she would do for half a crown, about fifty cents. On an impulse I undertook this unnecessary extravagance. The woman started on her humdrum routine of palm reading when, suddenly, a great change came over her and she gripped my hand more firmly and peered at it with new intensity and excitement. For the next fifteen minutes she told me a lot about the past, something of the present, and even things concerning the future. In conclusion, breathing heavily from mental exertion and emotion, she assured me that, in the many years she had been reading palms and telling fortunes, she was never so sure she had seen a person's life so clearly. Afterwards, out of amusement I noted down the salient points the soothsayer had predicted for me and sent them off to Audrey in New York.

To begin, she said, I was an artist, draughtsman, or designer, a fact that she could have told from my perpetually grubby hands. I had travelled far, my home being across the sea, which she could have told from my accent. I had a particular loved one who was not at my home but was also in a foreign place. It was at this point that she had changed her pace, her excitement had risen. Her first prediction was that I would leave London within the week to return home permanently. It would be sudden and unexpected and not in my current plans.

She continued that on my return home a new and more important job awaited me, that my love would return, that we would be once more separated from each other for a very long period of time, separated by another assignment, and that I would be surrounded by great danger, possibly a war. I was not to worry because my life-line was long and strong, so once more I would be reunited with my wife and family and accomplish much, until I was head of a large corporation. Her actual words were even more specific, but as I could not see as far ahead as the gypsy, I was amused but unconvinced.

When I returned to my apartment, there was a cablegram waiting for me from my father, ordering me to return home at once. A director's passage had been booked for me on the S.S. *Normandie*, sailing from Southampton in exactly one week. I was astounded at this coincidence, and decided to write down the remaining predictions before I forgot them. In the sober light of next day, I realized that while a new job had been offered, no indication was included as to how much I was to be paid, so I wired Dad: "How much?"

He replied, "$45 a week."

"Not enough!" I wired back, with my last few shillings. "Want $75 a week."

The last cablegram in the series said tersely, "$60 final. Get on the boat!"

I hurried back to the Haymarket to tell the gypsy my good fortune, but she had gone and the shop was closed.

Watching Uri Geller

Abraham Setton

Is Uri Geller a psychic or a conjurer? Or is he a little
of both?

Geller maintains that he has psychic powers. The well-known
Israeli performer and personality is the author or co-author of a
number of popular books which tell about his experiences and
adventures travelling the world, performing in theatres and on
television, bending spoons and keys, restarting watches, reading
thoughts, predicting the future, locating precious minerals, etc.

One of these books, The Geller Effect (1986), written with the
British journalist Guy Lyon Playfair, records Geller's chance encounter with a summer-camp friend from his youth. Avi spotted
Uri in the lounge at the Tel Aviv airport and approached him on the
plane flying to London. At first Geller failed to recognize Avi.

"Uri, look at my face," he said. "Do you remember?"

"Well," I replied, "yes, I saw you in the airport."

"Look again," he went on. "Don't you remember me?"

His face looked vaguely familiar, but I could not put a name to it.

"If it wasn't for me," he said, "you wouldn't be on this aeroplane."

"What do you mean?"

"Don't you remember the day you nearly drowned when you
were ten years old?"

"Avi!" I exclaimed. Of course I remembered now. During my
brief stay at the kibbutz at Hatzor, near Ashdod, in 1955 or 1956,

I had gone swimming in the sea one day with some of the other boys. I was a terrible swimmer then, and had no idea how strong the undercurrent was or what to do if I got myself caught in it, which is just what had happened. What I had done was clutch in terror at the only person within reach, which was Avi. I had nearly drowned the pair of us in my panic, but mercifully he was stronger than I and a good swimmer, and he managed to drag me to the beach. He was right — but for him I would not have been on that aeroplane, or anywhere else.

We had a good chat about old times and promised to keep in touch when we said goodbye to each other at Heathrow Airport. Avi was flying on to Canada, where he now lives, and since I had already begun to plan this book I asked him to write to me with his account of an unusual episode from the same period as my near-drowning, which he also remembered clearly. For the benefit of those who still believe the witch-hunters' claim that I learned all my tricks from Shipi Shtrang (who was only a few months old when the incident in question took place), here is part of the long letter Avi sent me, dated 10 June 1985 . . . .

One of the "witch-hunters" that Geller had in mind is undoubtedly James Randi, the Toronto-born conjurer and psychic debunker. Randi has devoted an entire book to exposing Geller and revealing his methods — how, whether on stage or off, the Israeli is able to perform the psychic feats that Randi calls magical tricks.

The letter that Avi — Abraham Setton — wrote to Geller follows. It is interesting to note that even when Uri Geller was ten years old he was playing with watches and that this youthful audience of one was "watching" him.

THE FIRST AND ONLY time I remember you demonstrating your powers was on a warm summer afternoon. We were walking on a footpath across from the main dining-hall, just past the steps leading to the new swimming-pool. To our left was a good-sized grassed area and to our right a hill with young pine trees.

You took your watch off your wrist and gave it to me so that I could admire it. I think it was a gift from your Dad. I thought it was a great watch, and you said, "See what I can do with it."

I watched you take it in your hand and hold it tightly. Then the hands started to move forward on their own, and later backwards. I thought you were playing tricks, so I said, "I think you're playing with the knob on the watch."

Then I took a closer look. At this point we stopped among some larger trees covering the footpath, and I said, "Do it again, without touching the knob."

You laughed, and did it again. I was sure that you did not touch the knob, but I thought just the same that you were playing some trick on me. I must admit that I did dismiss it as just some crazy thing you were doing, but as a kid twelve years old I put the thought away as "So what?" We kept on walking to our class-house, and that was it.

I really do not think you even knew what it all meant. It was very natural to you, and you liked the idea of "Look what I can do"....

Abraham Setton
Victoria, B.C., Canada

It Was Something I Was Picking Up

Teresa Stratas

The operatic soprano Teresa Stratas was born Ana-
stasia Stratakis in Toronto. She studied at the Royal Conservatory
of Music and made her début as Mimi in the Canadian Opera
Company's production of La Bohème in 1953. The following year
she joined the Metropolitan Opera, New York, where she became a
popular leading singer and recording artist. She is renowned for her
acting ability and her temperament as well as for her marvellous
voice.

"It Was Something I Was Picking Up" is an excerpt from an
interview with Teresa Stratas. It was conducted by an unnamed
interviewer who probed not only the diva's sense of herself as a
performing artist but also her sense of herself as a receptive and
intuitive personality.

The interview appeared as the liner notes on the Nonesuch LP
Album Stratas Sings Weil *released in 1986, with the Y Chamber*
Symphony conducted by Gerard Schwarz.

... YOU TOOK OFF *with your backpack and went to India. Why?*
What did it do for you?

I'll tell you some of the things that I thought were important
about India. Some are simple and I'm not quite sure what they're
about. The very first day I was there, I walked for about fifteen

hours till I was exhausted. I was crazy, manic. Then I wanted to sit down. And as I was stepping around people whose lives took place on the street, eating, pissing, shitting, sleeping, I realized that I could also just sit down there, right on that spot, anywhere. And when I sat down — and this is the truth, I can't really describe it — I had the most incredible feeling, being able to simply sit down. Am I crazy? Say I'm walking on the street, here on Broadway, or on Fifth Avenue, or Park Avenue, and I feel just like sitting down for a few seconds. But I never do. I'd have to look for a bench or a coffee shop. But in India I could sit down anywhere in the street and no one stared at me. It seems a simple thing, but it was immensely important; I thought it might have had something to do with my father having been a shepherd in Crete, sitting down anywhere he liked on his mountain. That happened on the very first day in India. I found a part of myself I'd put aside — no, not put aside, a part of myself I felt I had to hide. We are always afraid of doing anything conspicuous or out of step. There were other things about India. I went to Mother Teresa's Home for the Dying and held a woman in my arms who was dying; someone who was my age, who must have weighed fifty pounds, truly just skin and bones. She was dying and staring into my eyes and I was looking into hers, and for a second something happened. I can't quite say what it was. I was holding her very close and she had these enormous eyes staring up at me. She was already seeing something else and maybe her spirit had left her body, but there was definitely an exchange. She was here and I was over there. There was a definite fusion somehow.

Perhaps it is this quality in you, this ability to enter another person, that makes it possible for you to do the diverse roles that you have played.

I suppose it is. Once you have truly entered, say, a Lulu or a Jenny, it's no longer possible to play them as stereotypes.

You mean you become that person in an uncategorizable way?

Absolutely, but this ability also brings problems, negative aspects, what someone described as "the defects of one's qualities." It really does reduce the scale of what others enjoy as a social life. I'm not sure I can talk about these subjects without using the word "psychic." One of the reasons I don't, or rather can't, go to parties or socialize in a way some people enjoy is that I can really get into other people's skins; I really know what's going on in their heads, their minds, even physically what's going on in their bodies. It can knock me out physically because I seem to take on, for the moment, the disease of that mind, or the sickness of that body. I really do have to protect myself from becoming too susceptible to that kind of experience, and yet you can't cut yourself off from the world, and I certainly don't. I'll give you a small example. The other day I happened to be alone with a woman, and within ten minutes I had a very severe pain in my chest. Things like this often happen to me. And I think: "What's going on?" In this case, I bet that woman had heart trouble. She was a very anxious woman with two deep-furrowed creases on her forehead. The more we talked, maybe for forty minutes, the more this pain in my chest got worse and worse and worse. Either the woman had such anxieties that her heart was beating like crazy, or she did have heart trouble. I realized after she left that I had to shake it off, and after maybe half an hour I got rid of it. It had nothing to do with me. It was something I was picking up from her. And, you know, the next day I found out she really did have heart trouble. Sometimes I feel interchangeable with everybody else. I've often thought I am most "myself" when I am least myself.

And that is the key to your style of performance on stage?
    I think it could well be.

Visions and Premonitions

As One In a Dream I Followed Her

Lydia Leavitt

The Mysterious East is alive and well in the wondrous and romantic account that follows. It tells of a remarkable dance, performed by a strange woman, in an unnamed building in Port Said, in Egypt, before the turn of the century. Characteristic of this eye-witness account is the intangible air or aura of wonder. Is the account a memoir? Is it a piece of imaginative fiction? Do — or did — such things happen?

The account, whatever its provenance, appeared as a letter-to-the-editor in 1894 in the predecessor of The Globe and Mail. *It was signed and contributed by one Lydia Leavitt of Toronto. Nothing is known of Miss or Mrs. or Ms Leavitt. Her letter was reprinted under the title "The Egyptian Dancer" in* Shocked & Appalled: A Century of Letters to The Globe and Mail *(1985) edited by Jack Kapica.*

JANUARY 6, 1894

I was on my way from Australia to England by the handsome steamship *Orizaba*. Everyone knows the weariness of a long sea voyage, when the eye becomes tired of the sight of "water, water everywhere," and the increasing thumping of the huge engines makes one's head ache.

It was with a feeling of relief that I stepped ashore at Port Said, that interesting — if wicked — port, the only place in the world where such a heterogeneous mixture of all nations of the earth can be found. After visiting the Mohammedan mosque and the money changers — of whom we read in the time of Solomon, for nothing changes in the unchanging East — it was growing dusk, and, noticing a crowd gathering about a building, I joined it and waited for the doors to open. After the doors had opened there was a mad rush for seats, and soon the place was crowded almost to suffocation. It was a low, dingy building, and the first part of the entertainment was of the music hall type, poor singing and still poorer playing, but it was evident the people had not gathered there to to hear this. From different parts of the house came impatient cries of "dancer," "ballerine," "tanzer," from dozens of foreign tongues. The noise was confusing, and I was just about to leave the place, thinking the dancer was probably on a par with the performances just witnessed, when the sudden silence of the audience surprised me. There was not a sound in that crowded building, but a silence like the stillness of death. I turned quickly to the stage. A young girl was standing there motionless as a statue, looking not at the people, but beyond them. The eyes were unnaturally brilliant and her long, black hair reached nearly to the floor. My sensations were those of a paralytic, a feeling of numbness came over me, and I was conscious of a great desire to sleep, like one partly under the influence of a mesmeric trance. It may have been five minutes that she stood in that position, absolutely motionless; then slowly she began to dance, but no dance which I had ever before seen was like this, and never before had I seen such a figure, except in my dreams. She was clad in soft shimmery stuff that clung to her shapely limbs as though it liked the contact. Her arms were bare and perfect as the arms of Venus, and as she moved to and fro the white skin on her beautiful limbs glistened like snow on the window pane. I use the simile advisedly, for there was nothing glowing or warm in the flesh tints, but cold and beautiful as a statue. The face, had it been carved in marble, could not have been more colourless and could not have been more beautiful had it been one of Canova's matchless marbles. There was nothing sensuous in her movements, it did not set the pulses tingling, neither did it appeal to the intellect, but seemed to deaden both senses and intellect. As I looked I forgot her beauty, her youth, her grace and saw only motion, and was again conscious of the feeling as of mesmeric influence, and, looking around, I saw many people following the movements of her lithe body by similar movements of head or arm, and evidently unconscious of the fact. Again this strange influence almost overpowered me, and, half sleeping, half waking, I watched and was again conscious only of motion. What was the motion? Not the waves of the ocean, nor the swaying of trees, nor the motion of birds in their flight. Her beautiful arms, as she raised them and stood swaying to and fro, seemed something apart from a human body, and as I looked at her beautiful hair the heavy braids seemed to writhe and twist themselves about her body.

I sprang to my feet with an effort and forced my way through the crowd into the street. When I reached the open air I began to ask myself if it were not all a dream. Soon the people began to leave the building and the graceful figure of the danseuse appeared. There could be no mistaking that figure, with its graceful, undulating movement. As one in a dream I followed her, unconsciously keeping step and watching the swaying of her body. She might have been in a somnambulistic sleep, so little attention did she pay to anything around her. The eyes seemed to be fixed and staring, but no change took place in the peculiar motion of her body. I took no note of time or place until she turned and entered a house with no sign of life about it. As in a dream I noticed the house had an air of decay, tangled vines half hid the entrance. The moon at that moment emerged from a cloud and one room of the house was sufficiently lighted to enable one to see any object within. I walked mechanically to the window, and shall I ever be able to banish from my sight, either sleeping or waking, what I saw there. Like a body without a soul that beautiful creature entered the room and began crooning a low, mournful chant. From out of the darkened corner came gliding toward her a huge snake, and now for the first time the lovely creature seemed to have life. She stood with arms upraised and body bent slightly forward, while the snake came towards her swaying, swaying its horrible body to and fro. She bent forward until her eyes were fastened upon those of the monster, then she stooped until her beautiful mouth touched the slimy folds, and then it drew its body up and around her, coiled its shiny folds through her hair, and, with its horrible head close to her face, she began again the rhythmic motion, gliding into a darkened corner, out into the moonlight, and again into obscurity.

How I reached the ship I cannot tell, but during the remainder of the voyage I was under the doctor's care with brain fever.

Lydia Leavitt
Toronto

The Singular Case of
Mr. M-----

J. W. Garland

The Rev. J. W. Garland of South Stukely, Que., sent the following account of a friend and congregant's clairvoyant deathbed experience to the Rev. Benjamin Fish Austin who published it as "Clairvoyance before Death — The Singular Case of Mr. M-----" in Glimpses of the Unseen *(1898).*

MR. M-----, with whom I have been acquainted for about twenty-two years, died on the 24th March, 1897. He was a thoughtful student of his Bible, and a good, moral man. During my acquaintance with him, he observed at times, and spoke of to me, the inner or spiritual life of certain men with whom both of us were acquainted. I did not remark this very much, as I thought it showed in him only a keen perception.

I attended him during his last sickness, and, during that time, the perception into spiritual things seemed to develop stronger and brighter. He spoke several times of bright visions which he saw, but they were not well defined.

On the afternoon of March 23rd last, the day before he died, about two o'clock p.m., I called on him. He was very glad to see me. During my stay in the house, his wife, who is an intelligent and pretty well educated woman, told me as follows: Some time before I came, she was in the room with her husband. He seemed to be in a dreamy mood; then he woke up quite bright, and said to his wife I was coming. He could not think of my name, but he described me so that she knew whom he meant. He told her several times, but she did not pay much attention. He told her to go and let me in. She did not go at the moment, but in a few seconds after she heard my knock, and, on going to the door, was indeed surprised at what he had told her of my coming.

About an hour before he died, he called his wife to him and pointed upward and described a beautiful, bright sight that he saw, and seemed to be in great ecstasy of delight. Then he said to his wife: "See that place? I see a place for me up there." He knew his children and those about him even up to the last, and died quietly and in peace.

South Stukely, Que., April 15, 1897.

My Days Are Nearly Numbered

Emily McTavish

"*Daniel M'Tavish, While in Good Health, Foretells His Early Decease*" *is the title of the following premonition recorded by Emily McTavish, of Ridgetown, Ontario. It appeared in the volume* Glimpses of the Unseen *(1898) compiled by the Rev. Benjamin Fish Austin.*

MY HUSBAND, Daniel McTavish, died October 30th, 1873, in his 32nd year. About six weeks before he died he attended the funeral of a friend, and on his return, after telling me of the sad circumstance, he said: "My time, too, is short; my days are nearly numbered." I tried to reason him out of the notion, and attributed it to his having been at the funeral, but he said: "No; my days are nearly numbered." Up to this time he had been in perfect health, but he immediately began to straighten up his business. He seemed anxious to go back to our first home, and in two weeks we were there. For two weeks after we got back he seemed perfectly well, and four weeks from the day we reached our fist home he was buried.

Emily McTavish.
Ridgetown, Ont.,

April 6, 1897.

The Tragic Death of Edward Thomson Foreshadowed

James Finch

*E*dward Thomson, *a young brakeman employed on the Grand Trunk Railway running east of St. Thomas, Ont., was killed twelve miles west of the city on a branch of the line on which he had never before worked. He slipped and fell between the cars, striking his head on the iron connecting rods. The fall broke his neck and crushed his skull. The incident occurred about 10:00 a.m. on Friday, 3 March 1893.*

What is peculiar about young Thomson's death is the fact that foreshadowings or premonitions of the fatal accident were experienced and reported by six people, among them James Finch, the night operator on the Grand Trunk at St. Thomas. Some time before the incident he foretold the fact that the young man would be killed and even identified the spot where it would occur, although at the time no one imagined that Thomson would be working on that branch of the line.

Two points of fact are unusual about this case. First is the fact that Finch was not the sole recipient of foreknowledge. Five other people, mainly members of the Thomson family — one of them living more than a hundred miles away — are on record as having received premonitions of the incident. Second is the fact that the circumstances surrounding this case were the object of extensive research conducted by the lawyer and historian James H. Coyne who was the Registrar of Deeds in the County of Elgin in St. Thomas.

Coyne was urged to collect and examine the evidence in this case by Dr. Richard Maurice Bucke, the alienist and a resident of nearby London. Not only was Bucke interested in such matters but he was personally acquainted with the Thomson family, maintaining that the faculty of "second sight" was hereditary in the Thomson family. Coyne took statements from all concerned, noting the discrepancies that crop up. He came to the conclusion that there was, indeed, foreknowledge of the tragedy.

A full account of the case, titled "A Telegraph Message in a Dream Announces in Advance a Young Man's Death — Several Members of the Family Have Premonitions of the Coming Fatality," was included by Benjamin Fish Austin in Glimpses of the Unseen *(1898). Austin reproduces Coyne's observations about Finch (whose statement is reproduced below): "James Finch is not by any means the ordinary telegraph operator. He is a man of perhaps thirty-two years of age, with large, mild eyes, a smooth, clear skin and a heavy curly beard. He looks like a skilled mechanic, a man with a conscientious, careful, mathematical mind. He says himself that he has a great turn for machinery and is always devising things. He is a man of remarkably well balanced though sensitive, nervous organization. It has happened that he has had occasion several times to receive telegrams very similar to the news of Teddy Thomson's death and he had to break the news."*

"Mr. Finch's dream," Coyne concluded, "is an instance of 'second sight,' projecting itself into the future; and is, in my mind, the most extraordinary part of the whole affair."

Dr. Bucke came to the following conclusion: "Suppose you admit the fact that an event may project itself into the minds of these people. Then it is easy enough to understand how the event came to strike Finch with such force. Finch was in the direct road of the event. He knew Teddy Thomson very well. He was interested in him. He saw him every day go and come from the road. He was directly in the way of the event. This is how he came to experience it. Finch's physical peculiarities may have had something to do with it. You would naturally expect these things to occur in certain kinds of nervous organism."

I AM NIGHT AGENT and telegraph operator on the Grand Trunk Railway at St. Thomas.

Between one and two weeks before Edward Thomson's death I had gone home from my work at 7:00 a.m., had breakfasted and gone to bed about nine o'clock. A little after one o'clock I woke up with the impression that a message had come over the wires: "Teddy Thomson is killed. Tell his father."

There was no signature to the message. It came from the west, but I did not recollect the station. I feel pretty certain that it did not state the station. The impression it made on me woke me up. I had felt that I had risen from my desk and gone to the ticket office door and taken the keys out of my pocket to open it, thinking: "How shall I break the news to his father." Just then I woke up.

I lay about an hour trying to sleep again, but could not. I usually sleep soundly, without dreaming, until 6:00 p.m. I only remember once dreaming since then.

I stayed about the house until 7:00 p.m., when I went on duty again. I saw Ted that night and told him I had a dream about him and dreamed that he was hurt, and wanted him to be very careful. He said he'd be careful, but that he did not believe in dreams. Next morning I went into the ticket office after his father came. I told him I didn't believe much in dreams, but that I had a dream about Teddy and wanted him to be very careful. I said the message came from the west and Teddy always ran east. I said dreams always went by contraries and probably this would.

The impression remained strong on my mind from that time on. The second night before he was killed I received a message from the assistant superintendent of the division to send two spare brakemen to Windsor to make a few trips. I look at the list of spare brakemen, and saw that Clark and Thomson stood for this call. I sent out the call-boy to call them accordingly. I remember feeling glad that I had not had to call him out of his turn. Teddy had been call-boy for two years before becoming a brakeman. He was a quiet, steady boy, and I thought a good deal of him.

The day he was killed my wife woke me up to tell me. When she awoke me it was about the same hour as that in which I had received the message I have referred to. I saw the message afterwards at the telegraph office announcing his death. It was the same in effect as the message I had received in my dream, only worded about like this: "Brakeman Thomson is killed. Let the family know."

James Finch.
St. Thomas, Ont.,

April 21st, 1893.

Saved by the Song

Phyllis Harding

*P*hyllis *Harding is an English singer and dancer who resides in Chichester, England. She recalled a frightening experience that involved herself and Beatrice Lillie which took place on the stage of the Grand Theatre in London, Ont., in 1928-29. Her experience was cited by Arthur Koestler in his article "The Mysterious Power of Chance,"* The Sunday Times, *4 May 1974, which adjudicated the best cases of coincidence — or simultaneity — from over two thousand submitted to* The Sunday Times *of London in a "coincidence competition."*

Beatrice Lillie was born in Toronto in 1898. She enjoyed a "brilliant" career and was the "toast" of two continents, singing saucy songs in musical revues in the West End and on Broadway between the late 1910s and the early 1960s.

"Saved by the Song" appeared in Incredible Coincidence: The Baffling World of Synchronicity *(1979) by Alan Vaughan, who asked the following question: "Did Beatrice Lillie have an unconscious premonition which expressed itself as a lapse of memory?"*

I WAS WITH the American Company of Noel Coward's revue *This Year of Grace*. After our New York season we were on a short tour of Canada, playing in London, Ontario. One matinee we were all on stage for a scene which ended with Miss Beatrice Lillie's song, "Britannia Rules the Waves." At the end of the second verse, we were all ranged in an oblique line well away from the centre of the stage, whilst Bee harangued us in the best Lillie manner. As one of the "Mums" in the front line I suddenly caught in her eye a look of anguish, and to our amazement we suddenly realized that she was repeating the entire second verse all over again — keeping us glued to our places on the stage, unable to move.

Suddenly there was a resounding crash and one of the biggest arc lights fell in the middle of the empty stage — where by rights at that moment of time we should have been standing — breaking in two and scattering fragments of glass in all directions. Without a flicker Miss Lillie calmly went on to the chorus, and obediently we moved into our positions covering the entire stage.

What caused this extraordinary lapse of memory on Miss Lillie's part? This had never happened before, and certainly never happened again.

An Odd Thing Happened

Leslie McFarlane

$The\ word$ ghost *is widely used to modify the word* writer, *as in the phrase* ghost writer. *A ghost writer does not take dictation from the world of spirits; far from it! A ghost writer produces the words that are credited to someone else.*

The country's leading ghost writer was the late Leslie McFarlane. A generation of youthful readers grew up thinking that somewhere in the United States there was a Franklin W. Dixon who was writing the Hardy Boy books. Little did they realize that the early books in this popular adventure series for boys were being produced by a freelance writer named Leslie McFarlane in a succession of Ontario towns and cities! McFarlane wrote the first title, The Tower Treasure (1926), *and a good many more until he ended his toil with* The Phantom Freighter (1946).

In his lively autobiography, The Ghost of the Hardy Boys (1976), *he described an odd coincidence while juggling two writing assignments: the last of the Hardy Boy books and a script for CBC Radio. Occurrences like this one, far from being coincidental, are more commonplace than most people realize.*

THE FLICKERING TORCH MYSTERY, 1943, was written in a stifling room during a heat wave in wartime Ottawa. The very thought of it brings out perspiration.

An odd thing happened while I was sweating this one out. I had broken into radio, doing a long series of plays for the Canadian Broadcasting Corporation, and ventured into history with a little piece about Sir John A. Macdonald. In the course of the play it was necessary for the future Prime Minister of Canada to spend a little time in a country blacksmith shop during repairs to his carriage. I thought it would lend authenticity if I could come up with the name of Sir John's coachman. So I spent about a week on research, reading everything I could find out about Macdonald's life, but the coachman's name always eluded me. A week after the play went on the air, with the name of Macdonald's secretary substituted for that of the coachman, I was toiling at *The Flickering Torch Mystery* when I looked out the window and saw a funeral in progress at a house across the street. While the search for the coachman's identity had been going on, I had noticed an elderly man enjoying the shade of the veranda. Then he had disappeared. The next morning the *Ottawa Journal* ran a brief story about the funeral. It provided the name I had been seeking in vain. The funeral was for a man who had once been coachman for Sir John A. Macdonald.

Many Odd Things that Have Happened through the Years

Helen Creighton

No one knows more about the supernatural in the
Maritimes than Helen Creighton. The eminent folklorist was born
in Dartmouth, N.S., in 1899. She is the author of two well-known
books, Bluenose Ghosts (1957) and Bluenose Magic (1968), which
collect and preserve many of the customs and beliefs characteristic
of the "old ways." So it is not surprising to learn, upon reading her
autobiography A Life in Folklore (1975), from which the excerpts
which follow are taken, that she feels herself to be somewhat
special, gifted in a spiritual way, perhaps even psychic.

WAS IT PROPHETIC that I was born with a caul? This thin mem-
branous tissue that sometimes covers the face of a newborn baby is
universally known in folklore, and folklore was to become my life's
work. The most common belief is that the fortunate infant will
never be drowned (sailors used to buy cauls for protection) and will
inherit second sight, or at least a sixth sense, and this is true in a
slight degree in my case.

I learned the most comforting of many old beliefs about cauls in
the 1950s when I visited Mrs. Charles Ritchie in Annapolis Royal
after hearing that she could foresee the future. We made friends
quickly, and after a while I said, "Mrs. Ritchie, were you born with
a caul?" "Yes I was," she said, "but how did you know?" I told her it
came to me by the way she looked at things. She then told me a

person so born need never worry. Things would always work out for them, and this has been true for me. Today in hospital births I doubt if anybody pays attention to this magic veil, but on September 5, 1899, when I appeared, the doctor carefully preserved my caul (on a piece of foolscap paper), and presented it to my mother in the custom of the day. I must have been ten or twelve when it was shown to me and I thought the whole business ridiculous. Like my contemporaries, I had no idea how babies were born and I suppose if I ever asked I was put off with evasive answers — which seems incredible in these days. Mother wisely put it aside for a few years, and now it is one of my most cherished possessions. I also had the cord three times round my neck; if that has a meaning I have never heard of it.

*

I have mentioned various unexplainable things that have happened in my life. In 1960 my dear friend Mrs. Stanley Walker (Ella) was having her first visit in Halifax since her husband's death five years before, and I suggested she join me on a trip. On our second night in a beautiful new motel in Middleton I awoke to see Dr. Walker standing as though on guard at the foot of her bed, and I was struck by the nobility of his appearance. Usually I thought of him with his scholar's stoop and glasses slightly tilted downward on his nose. He had died in the fullness of health, and I had taken his sons to the funeral home to see him. There, as I saw him laid out, I had also been startled by this appearance of nobility. I have concluded that a person who wants to be seen after death will appear in some way that will startle the observer into instant recognition. In a moment the vision was over, and I went back to sleep. In the morning I told Ella rather hesitantly and wasn't surprised when she looked doubtful. For months I wondered why he would guard his wife when she was in one of the safest places in the world and with one of her closest friends so near her. I decided if he had appeared to her she would have been frightened, but if I saw him she might think, "Oh that's just some of Helen's nonsense," but in time might come to accept it and be pleased, and that is what happened. I told this to Dr. Puxley, Dr. Walker's successor at King's who was not at all surprised because he had often felt him in the office looking over his shoulder. His presence brought no sensation of fear to either of us.

*

On my way to the Miramichi Folk Song Festival in 1963, I had stopped off for a night's rest at Marshlands Inn, the nicest place of its kind in the Maritime Provinces, and more of a club than an inn. I decided to sleep in the early evening and go downstairs later for cocoa which is always served at bedtime, and where there are always interesting people to be met. I had wakened and was getting out of bed when I saw a vision of myself coming towards me, but as a child of ten with a very sweet and welcoming expression on my face. I recognized this immediately as the worst omen I could have and put my hands out as though pushing it away. It faded but returned almost immediately but not quite so vividly. Again I made the gesture of pushing it away. It came a third time, but by then was quite faint. I got up and went downstairs as planned, determined to forget it as I always react when anything supernatural occurs. I met other guests as though nothing had happened and afterwards had a good night's rest.

In the morning it began to bother me and I felt I must drive with extra caution. I had kept especially alert when going through a wooded section and had come to a clearing when suddenly, directly in front of my car, I saw a deer. It seemed to have come from nowhere. Isn't it extraordinary how much the mind can think of in a split second of time? I said to myself, "There's a deer; I can't miss it." Then I prayed fervently, "Oh God, *please* help me," and because I believed this possible, I took my hands off the steering wheel. There was a crush — that was inevitable — but I was not propelled forward as I would expect after colliding with a heavy object at fifty miles an hour, nor did the car swerve off the road, but came to a gentle stop. With shaking knees, I got out to survey the damage for I had heard the sound of glass being shattered. The right headlight and lens were broken in many pieces and the metal below the light was pierced. I looked for the deer but it had disappeared, and even though I backed up there was no sign of it. Were it not for the evidence, I would have thought the whole thing an illusion. I concluded that the vision, coming as a child and not an adult, had not been a death omen but a warning. The conclusion was strengthened the following spring when on the train between Toronto and Winnipeg I heard the porter singing and talked to him about Negro songs. We then got around to folklore, and among other things he mentioned that his mother had said a person born with a caul would always have a warning before danger. He of course had no idea I was born with a caul, so it is odd that he mentioned it.

In June of '63 I told my experience in a speech at the Canadian Authors' convention and afterwards a young woman came to me trembling and said she had experienced a similar vision. In her case her father had died within a week. Another author, Frances Shelley Wees, threw further light on it. She said the vision's proper name is *Doppelgänger*, and she gave me this note: "Every individual has a 'spiritual' or non-physical double. This double never appears, nor can it be seen by anyone else. It is in a sense the 'guard,' the archon, the protector of the physical person. To see the *Doppelgänger* (the double-goer) is supposed to be dangerous because obviously at this point strong protection is going to be needed. It is only when the *Doppelgänger* comes too close that death is imminent — the *two* cannot merge on this earth."

The next odd occurrence came in March 1964 as I was writing a cheque for my Northeast Folklore Society dues. It was a small amount, so I thought I might pay for the next year as well. Then I changed my mind and thought, "No, I'll be seeing Sandy Ives at the Miramichi Folk Song Festival in August, and can pay him in person," but a voice inside me objected and said, "You won't be alive by then." I replied, again inside my head, "What?" and the message was repeated. "Don't be silly," I objected, or words to that effect, and sat down to complete my letter, but found I couldn't do it. I knew then that something bad in a physical sense would happen before the middle of August, and therefore I hastened a trip to England to visit my nephew Peter in his home as he and his family had so happily visited me in mine the year before.

My term as Authors' president drew to a close in 1964 with the annual convention held that year in Halifax, and I was thankful to be able to preside and enjoy my office to the end. I felt as well as I ever do, and if I was more tired than I knew was wise, excitement carried me through. Nature will take so much, and, I suppose, this time nature rebelled. At any rate, a week later there were sudden indications of a growth, and it was thought to be malignant. I fully expected the operation to be successful, but was prepared to be told the cancer had spread. As I lay in my hospital bed awaiting the doctor's verdict, my *Doppelgänger* reappeared. This time I seemed to be about thirty-eight years of age. I had a board which I was holding at waist height and I was paddling my way through heavy water and making slow but steady progress. The important thing was that I paid no attention to myself but passed by without so much as a glance.

"I've had a reprieve," I thought, and so it turned out. In 1966 I saw myself again, this time walking away in the opposite direction with one shoulder dropped as in age or from a heavy burden. My fishermen friends have told me that walking away means a long life, so I expect to be around for a while yet. Nonetheless, I had reached a turning point. Whether or not it is true an ailing daughter improves in health when her mother dies, I was much stronger in my forties, fifties, and early sixties than I'd been in the hard twenties and thirties. I had been aware of the passing years, but didn't need to cater to them. I could do that no longer. However I was far from through yet.

*

Another honour had a strange forerunner. On a December morning in 1967 I looked towards the sunrise which was red and beautiful, but a cross stood above it. I'd never seen this before, it didn't strike me as an ill omen. That morning the postman brought a registered parcel, a Centennial Medal given (as declared to 49,999 other recipients) "in recognition of valuable serve to the nation." A ribbon and bow accompanied the medal, and when put in place, these formed just such a cross as I had seen.

I could mention many odd things that have happened through the years — like the time I leaned down to get a log of wood for the fire in the grate. When I straightened up my eyes were level with a picture of my father in an oval frame. In the same oval shape there was mist or cloud about three inches thick enclosing the picture. I presume it was his aura. I had no particular worry at the time nor did anything occur to account for it.

When my sister Lilian died in 1968, I had the most amazing experience, and one that still gives me comfort and joy. Usually when I was worried about her I could feel my parents around, but when I held my lonely vigil in the Tatamagouche hospital, I had no feeling of their presence and missed them. I had gone to church myself to say special prayers for her, but as the moment of death approached, I realized no clergyman had been asked to visit her in hospital. I must have looked stricken as I rushed to the nurse on duty.

The Reverend James Fraser came quickly, and as he stood on one side of the bed and I on the other, the two attendant nurses left. He read a passage from Scripture, said a prayer for the dying and one for me. I didn't realize until later that she had probably stopped breathing during his prayer for me. She was certainly alive when he started. When he was through we sat for a moment in conversation until I realized that the shoulder which had been pulsating with her rapid breathing had ceased its motion.

What happened during the prayer for me was an inflow of strength so vigorous that I knew it would sustain me through the days ahead. In fact it sustained me for most of the following year. I learned later that this is known as the gift of grace. The theological meaning is "strengthening influence" or "divine regenerating." It uplifted me in a way I had never known, like a benediction, and I was in a state almost of ecstasy. Since then I have never thought of her with relief as at the dropping of a heavy burden, but always with love and affection, and usually I find myself smiling. At first I used to feel her close as though things were reversed now and she was looking after me, and one time in that period between waking and sleeping, I saw her. It was just her head. She looked happy and seemed to be flying slowly through the air at the centre of a little group I can only think of as a heavenly host.

An Older Man with Little Hair

Richard Hancock

Memory and imagination operate organically and not mechanically, particularly in children. The experience of Richard Hancock, in concert with that of his younger brother, suggests that it is indeed memory and not imagination that is responsible for the image of "an older man with little hair" that has continued to puzzle him since 1964. Today Richard Hancock operates a photo studio in Etobicoke, Ontario. The details of his experience come from letters written to the present editor on 31 May 1987 and 10 Aug. 1987.

I HAVE ALWAYS TRIED to be a rational and reasonable person, with an open mind regarding the supernatural, etc. My own experience is supported by a disturbing amount of so-called evidence. Here goes....

For many years, while we lived in Barrie, at 10 Jonathan Court, my younger brother and I shared a bedroom. It now seems that we also shared a similar experience. This happened in the winter of 1964, when my brother and I were about five and seven years of age respectively, so my recollection could be a little fuzzy.

We never discussed it at the time, but independently we both remember hearing footsteps coming down the hallway from the front of the house and approaching our open bedroom door, after everyone in the house was in bed. At this point I imagined I saw a greenish head peer around the corner of the doorway. It paused for a moment to look at us, then proceeded back up the hallway again, leaving me (and my brother) stiff with fright.

The apparition appeared to be that of an older man with little hair, of medium height, and in no way threatening. That is why I never cried out, though I was still scared half silly at the time. As best I can remember the incident occurred several times over several weeks or a month. Then it stopped as suddenly as it started. I have not seen it since — I am now thirty years of age — and both my brother and I have turned out to be fairly stable people mentally, with college and university educations.

This past Easter the whole family gathered for Sunday dinner and the talk somehow turned to the supernatural/occult world. My mother remarked that she had sometimes thought that the house in Barrie was haunted. She said she sometimes had heard footsteps in the hallway at night, after everyone was in bed, and she also heard them upon the kitchen floor above her when doing laundry in the basement, when she knew very well that no one was home at the time.

Further talk brought to light the fact that my brother had been awake as well (though I never knew it!) and had seen the same sight on several occasions. The scary part was that he mentioned the greenish tinge before I did — and was just as scared. Father then mentioned that the time frame roughly fit that of his father's death. His father died at the age of seventy-two, and had a white crew-cut and apparently doted on my brother and myself, though we did not realize it at the time.

See what you can make of all this!

Vision of a Body without Legs

Emil S. Zmenak

One day a strange thing happened to Emil S. *Zmenak, who is a Doctor of Chiropractic. In the morning his wife told him that she had the vision of "a body without legs." In the evening that is precisely the sight that greeted Zmenak's eyes. "An Odd Experience Involving a Prediction" is the title of Zmenak's account of the curious and rather chilling incident. It was published with some explanatory notes by Iris M. Owen in the Summer 1972 issue of* New Horizons: The Journal of the New Horizons Research Foundation.

ABSTRACT: The fulfilment of a prediction is described.

In the fall of 1970 while I was preparing to attend a meeting of the Toronto Society for Psychic Research, my wife urged me to stay at home, having received a strong feeling that something was going to happen. She received an impression of being awakened by a phone call from the police and visualized a body without legs.

At any rate, I attended the meeting, and on leaving, I commented on being uneasy about the drive home to other members of the committee.

[*In fact, his words were as he went out of the door — to me — "Iris, you had better make a note of this, Carol did not want me to go out tonight — she says she sees a death if I do — I don't know*

219

whether she thinks I will be killed, I don't think I shall be." (Note added by Iris M. Owen.)]

As I was driving home and reaching the Stoney Creek traffic circle I ran into trouble with my battery and my car lights quit, and my brakes (which are power assisted) failed. At that moment a large transport truck was barrelling down behind me and just avoided hitting my Viva. I made it as far as the next road and walked from the Queen Elizabeth Way to Highway 8 where I found a telephone. As I was phoning my wife to ask her to pick me up a police cruiser pulled up beside me. I asked my wife to hold the phone and I arranged to have the cruiser drive me part-way to Grimsby where my wife could meet me.

I got in the car and as it started to pull away, another car stopped on the other side of the road and a man got out and signalled us to stop. He came across the road and asked for directions to a motel. The policeman spoke to him for a few minutes and the man started to return to his car. The policeman called him back again as he suspected he had been drinking. The man returned and the policeman spoke again with him and smelled his breath for alcohol. He decided to let him go back to his car, and as he turned to go he walked directly into the path of an oncoming car, and was killed instantly.

The impact of the car broke both the man's legs and his body was crumpled up so that only his torso was visible. Since I had to stay behind as a witness, the police had to contact my wife and let her know what had happened, thus both parts of her premonition were true.

(Signed) Emil S. Zmenak, D.C.

[*The tragic death was, of course, a matter of judicial record; Dr. Zmenak attended the inquest. The date and names have been suppressed to avoid distress to relatives. (Note added by Iris M. Owen.)*]

Toronto Society for Psychical Research   10 April, 1971

An Out-of-Body Experience

Herbert J. Smith

*H*erbert J. Smith had a strange experience while
driving alone in his car, a LeMans, on the Queen Elizabeth Way in
Metropolitan Toronto one Sunday afternoon in 1980. The experience frightened him, then puzzled him, and finally enriched his life
and that of his wife in an unexpected way.

Smith, a native of Saskatchewan, served with the army in the
Second World War. At the time of the odd incident, he was in his
early sixties and working as a machinist and millwright for
STELCO. Smith's account is based on a letter written to the present
editor in July 1987.

THIS HAPPENED ON MARCH 23, 1980.

I had to work this day and was returning home along the Queen
Elizabeth Way, going in a westerly direction. I was in excellent
health, feeling perfectly well, and alone in my car. The road was
dry and clear though there was a fair amount of traffic.

I had left Windemere Avenue and Lakeshore Road in Metro
Toronto at 3:00 p.m., and it was about 3:15 p.m. when I reached
No. 10 Highway. I had just completed changing lanes from the
inner to the outside lane in readiness to exit south at Mississauga
Road about one and a half miles farther on.

Quite suddenly the scenery was rapidly changing and the other
cars on the road were turning around in a very strange way. There

was confusion around me! The road had become very black and the white lines very white. I felt extremely alarmed and my impulse was to pull over to the side of the road. But now the right-hand side of the road appeared to have vanished; there seemed to be nothing there but a deep precipice. Then, on the left-hand side, the road was curling up like a huge ocean wave.

Although I was still moving along, it seemed the car itself had vanished, and I found myself out in some bright countryside. Now I seemed to have stopped moving along, and the feeling of alarm and concern appeared to have subsided. Here I remember feeling amazement and interest; the greenest and healthiest-looking grass I had ever seen stretched out in front of me, and on either side of me, and appeared to go all the way to the horizon. I could see no weeds.

The land was quite flat and some distance ahead of me there was a very unusual-looking tree. There was another one over to my left and another one to my right. The latter two appeared to be a little farther away. I don't think I can adequately describe what they looked like. Very vaguely a cactus comes to mind. I would judge that they might have been about twelve to fifteen feet tall, with a centre trunk, and a branch growing out on either side about three-quarters of the way up. The top of the trunk and the branches were rounded and looked something like a large bud. I saw no smaller branches or leaves. The bark was a brownish colour and seemed to be made up of overlapping scales. They stood in a round bed of earth that appeared to have been well tended, with the grass edges neatly trimmed.

The sky was blue and there were a few small flecks of white clouds. I remember feeling surprised at being able to see so far into the distance, even to the horizon, so clearly. I also thought how perfect and beautiful it all looked.

Then suddenly the whole scene vanished and I became aware of the tops of normal-looking trees on either side of me, and I felt I was descending, as the lower parts of the trees and houses and fences came into view.

Then everything around me was confusion again, and my feelings of alarm and concern had completely returned. But soon the confusion started to clear and I began to see familiar things again, the road, the inside of the car. Then I found myself behind the wheel in the usual position and now apparently in control of my car. I now became aware I was on Mississauga Road, just south of the CNR bridge and about 150 yards from my home.

I cannot find words to describe how completely mystified I was feeling, nor how relieved I felt when I turned into my own driveway.

In summary, I have driven over this road constantly for the past twenty-nine years and nothing unusual has ever happened to me, before or since. While I was having this experience, the car travelled from No. 10 Highway to the CNR bridge on Mississauga Road, with no one else in the car, apparently not under control, in what would be about the usual time, and seemingly without mishap. The estimated mileage travelled was three and two-tenths miles; the estimated time is four minutes and thirty seconds. I find it impossible to draw a picture of the tree that I saw. However, this is vaguely the idea.

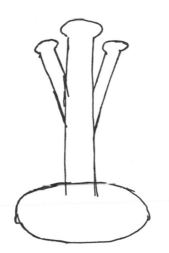

I would like to say that up until that time I knew nothing of, nor would I have been interested in, psychic matters. I am sure I had never heard of an out-of-body experience. However, when I arrived home after this experience, feeling bewildered and really quite afraid, I discussed it with my wife. We decided to call our son, who is a Sociology professor. Almost immediately he got in touch by telephone with Ian Currie, the author of *You Cannot Die,* and Ian contacted Carole Davis who, we afterwards learned, is a well-known medium.

We talked with Carole Davis and she told me I had had an out-of-body experience of some kind, although she said she had never heard of one quite like that one before. As she was talking, she was apparently getting messages for us. We clearly understood them and my wife and I were told we should get involved in spiritual development. The Spiritual Science Institute started a three-year course in Toronto shortly after this, and my wife and I joined. Now we are both graduate members of the Institute and very involved in this field.

A Mystery of
Memphremagog

Jacques Boisvert

Jacques Boisvert lives in the city of Magog on the
shore of Lake Memphremagog in Quebec's Eastern Townships. He
is an insurance broker, a scuba diver, and a president of the Lake
Memphremagog Historical Society.

It was in 1986, while serving in the latter capacity, that he co-
founded the International Dracontology Society of Lake
Memphremagog. Its purpose is to draw public attention to
Memphré, "the friendly creature of Lake Memphremagog," and
one way of doing this is to document the lake creature's many
appearances. Boisvert has accomplished this by collecting and
computerizing references to more than one hundred sightings of
Memphré from the first recorded appearance in 1816 to the present.

Lake Memphremagog is a lake much like Loch Ness, its better-
known counterpart in Scotland. "I am preparing a study of the
similarities of Loch Ness and Lake Memphremagog," wrote
Boisvert in 1987. "Surprisingly, they are many. Both the loch and
the lake are twenty-five miles long and one mile wide and very
deep. There is a Benedictine Abbey at Fort Augustus on Loch Ness;
there is another on the shore of Lake Memphremagog; it is called
l'Abbaye St-Benoît du lac. Both lakes run diagonally from northeast
to southwest; the waters of both run from south to north.

"I fool people by showing them pictures of the scenery around
Loch Ness and asking them to identify it. Most people tell me that
the pictures were taken at Lake Memphremagog. An airplane, a

Wellington bomber, crashed in Loch Ness in 1940; the same thing happened here in 1942, a Harvard II; both accidents claimed one life. There are many, many more similarities — mountains, latitude, etc. This will be the subject of a very lengthy article."

In the meantime, Boisvert has contributed the following account about a strange experience. It has nothing to do with the "friendly creature" but it does have a lot to do with the depths of both Lake Memphremagog and human experience.

I WAS 220 FEET BELOW the surface of Lake Memphremagog, moving through the cold and inky waters, and I knew I was getting close. I could feel him near me. I came to the foot of an underwater cliff, turned my light slowly toward the right, and spotted at once the whiteness of an air cylinder, then the black and red of a diving suit. Yves St-Martin's feet rested against the cliff, his head towards the open lake, face towards the surface, eyes open, and hands raised — exactly as the clairvoyant had pictured him to me two weeks earlier!

It was three in the afternoon of Thursday, October 31st, 1985. Yves St-Martin, a diver with ten years' experience, had drowned on August 22nd while attempting to set a personal record of 200 feet off the village of Georgeville. Since that depth far exceeded safe working norms set down by the Commission de Santé et de Sécurité au Travail (CSST), the Sûrété du Québec decided against sending police divers down to recover the body. Volunteers tried without success. Canadian Armed Forces divers, who had recovered one of Jacques Cousteau's divers who had drowned while filming *Danger in the St. Lawrence*, were summoned but, for some reason, did not come.

A team from Trois-Rivières, which called itself Aqua Marina, explored the site with a miniature submarine on August 31st and September 1st. But the four-foot sub was powered by current from a 200-foot cable which made manoeuvering extremely difficult. The whole experiment cost the taxpayers around $20,000 and accomplished nothing.

A few days later, Jean-Marc Gaudreau came to inform me he had been hired by St-Martin's family to recover the body. He asked me for my advice and assistance. My first reaction was, "Why risk human lives to bring a body from the bottom of the lake only to bury it in the earth?" My second reaction was more sympathetic. I agreed to help him but I declined any money consideration because Yves had been a friend and a colleague and I felt I owed it to the memory of our friendship and to the solidarity of divers.

But Jean-Marc was persuasive and I began to train myself to dive at depths of more than 200 feet, far deeper than I had ever dived before. We dropped an anchor in 200 feet of water, attached a buoy to the line, and began making descents day after day, deeper and deeper. The day I reached the bottom, I had the sensation of spinning like a top, and I had to stare at the lake floor to reassure myself that nothing was moving. I signalled to Jean-Marc to return to the surface because I knew I had begun to experience "the rapture of the depths," a type of nitrogen narcosis.

I had a terrifying experience at 190 feet on my third training dive, and I told Jean-Marc that I would thereafter dive by myself, in my own time, and in my own way. Back home, I took down my books on diving to study the decompression tables and the phenomenon known as nitrogen narcosis or "the bends." The books told me that the human body can habituate itself to great depths and, since I had often dived to 160 feet, I was encouraged to persist.

On October 7th, a team of divers from Montreal and Calgary arrived with yet another miniature sub or Remote Operational Vehicle (ROV). They made an attempt to locate the body, but they finally had to admit that it was impossible to operate their machine at depths between 200 and 250 feet. After several hours of searching, they weighed anchor and returned home.

A few days later, on Sunday, October 13th, I received a visit around four in the afternoon from a person new to me, a clairvoyant from Alexandria, Ont., who was accompanied by his nephew, Jean-Paul Poulin, of Magog. The clairvoyant produced a sketch that he had prepared and explained that the body of Yves St-Martin was to be found at 220 feet of water at the foot of a cliff 540 feet from shore. He said that he had seen the body lying on its back with its feet on the cliff, eyes open, face towards the surface, arms raised. He said that if the body was not recovered soon, it would take a very long time to raise it to the surface of its own accord. He also told me that he saw red spots on the diving suit. I recorded our entire conversation on tape.

After my thirty-second dive in search of the body — my 238th dive of the year — I told Jean-Marc that we were going to follow the clairvoyant's directions. After all, we had nothing to lose.

From the shore, we strung out a line 540 feet long, tied the end to a rock, and sank it to the bottom. I swam out from the shore following the line and to my surprise my depth gauge was reading 220 feet, exactly what the clairvoyant had told me. On my next dive, I followed the line out to a depth of 190 feet, left it to explore to the south, and returned to shore. On my thirty-fifth dive, I did the same towards the north and swam out about 60 feet beyond the end of our cord to a depth of 240 feet. This was a personal record. Then I returned, using a forty-five degree on my compass. When I reached 220 feet, I saw the bottom of a cliff. I was 540 feet from the shore. I swung my light towards the right and found the body of Yves St.-Martin. Its location and position were exactly as the clairvoyant had described them, right down to the red stripes on the diving suit.

As a diving instructor, I insisted on respect for one cardinal principle: In a dangerous situation, before undertaking any operation whatsoever, count to five. I took my own advice. Needless to say, I had often considered what I would do if and when I found the body. But I was down 220 feet, without a cable, and without assistance. I first attempted to lift the body but found that it was very heavy. Yves had four weight-belts on. I unfastened one of these on the left side. Then I pressed the button that released air from his cylinder to inflate his dry suit. I had the satisfaction of hearing air pass through the valve. After a few seconds, slowly, the body began to rise.

It popped to the surface in about thirty seconds. In the boat Jean-Marc was so startled that he almost fell over backwards. Although desperately impatient, I took a good five minutes to surface to avoid all danger of pulmonary or cerebral embolism. The whole dive had taken no more than fourteen minutes.

We notified the police and Jean-Marc submitted the chart on which he had carefully plotted each dive and recorded the exact spot where the body had been found. But even that was not the end of this mysterious story.

A few days later I had the honour of meeting Leon Perron of St-Valérien, another clairvoyant. He had prepared a chart on October 5th that he had sent to Denis Boisvert (no relation) on October 12th, which was the day prior to my interview with the psychic and two weeks before the finding of the body. On that chart he had indicated that it was lying at a depth of 220 feet and close to a "mass of lead." I was astounded because, on September 19th, I had lost my 40-pound, lead weight-belt on that very spot. No one knew about it save Jean-Marc and myself.

Yves St-Martin was a very good diver. The spectacular spot on the bottom of Lake Memphremagog where he had drowned will now be known as Cap-St-Martin in his honour, and in remembrance of the strange circumstances surrounding the recovery of his body — an ordeal that had lasted 67 days.

Jacques Boisvert,
December 5th, 1985

The Vision of a Crime

Allen Goldenthal

Is it possible for someone who is living today to "tune in" to the events of the distant past and witness them now as they must have unfolded decades ago or even centuries ago? Mediums and psychics claim to have this power — this ability to be "sensitive" to the past. They maintain that far from being "dead," the past is very much "alive." From time to time there are disturbing reports from other people — individuals not known for their mediumistic gifts or abilities or talents or predilections — who supply some out-of-the-way evidence that they have accidentally "tuned in" to the past. A good instance of this type of sensitivity is the remarkable experience of Allen Goldenthal, B.Sc., D.V.M.

Dr. Goldenthal is a veterinarian with the City of Scarborough as well as the owner-operator of the Birchmount–Steeles Animal Clinic in that city. His account comes from a letter to the present editor written on 9 June 1987. It gives one pause....

I READ with interest your request in the Sunday *Sun* for people with any insight into psychic phenomena to share this information with you.

If I had seen this request a year ago, I would have ignored it completely, as I was made to feel apprehensive about revealing some of the strange, unnatural events that have occurred to me over the years. In the past I shared these stories only with the closest of my friends, and even some of them were quite skeptical about them. Regardless of that, one event left me more relaxed and free to talk of my psychic experiences.

In January of 1987, I was driving north up Warden Avenue towards Highway Seven. Suddenly, up ahead, on the west side of the road, a south-bound car pulled over. It was an old car, lime to faded green in colour. The driver of the car was a man. A woman got out of the car, pulling a child behind her. The woman was about six feet tall. She had a build that was almost masculine. She wore a long black dress and a high collar. The dress went down to her ankles. She had silver-platinum hair, a high-up hair-do, done in a Fifties style.

At first I thought she was taking the child into the field to pee. But then I noticed the child struggling and trying to pull away. The child's hair was cut short, almost in what they used to call a Prince Valiant hairstyle. I placed the child between four and six years of age. Then the woman started dragging the child across the road to the field on the east side. I could hear the child yelling for help, even though my windows were up. At one point she paused in the centre of the road and looked directly at me. Even though I was in the north-bound lane doing 70 km., I did not seem to be getting any closer to her. It began to bother me that the cars in the south-bound lane were passing by this scene as if nothing was happening.

When I came alongside the parked car, the man in the driver's seat turned to face me. He was Greek or Italian in appearance, with an oblong head, full moustache, and balding pate. His eyes were dark and cold.

Finally I had driven past the scene. I was about fifty yards down the road when the strangeness of everything suddenly dawned on me. I turned the car around and stopped. There was no one there and no longer any car. Then the name of the car — BelAir or Belmont — suddenly hit me. I don't know why, because I am not at all familiar with these automobiles.

The next day I related what had happened to me to some friends and inquired of them what I should do. Their reply was that if I had witnessed a crime I could expect to read about it in the papers in a day or so and then I could give my information to the police. Obviously nothing had happened, or at least nothing had appeared in the newspapers, so I stored the scene in my mind. I could no longer sleep well at night, however, as I was troubled by the events I had witnessed.

It dawned on me that what I had witnessed might have occurred in the past, long ago. Nevertheless I refused to tell anyone else about the vision, even though it weighed heavily on my mind. There is a certain amount of fear connected with talking about such things. As a public servant, I have to consider what my clients' reactions would be if I talked about such things. So I kept quiet about it for four months. By April I knew that I would no longer be at peace with myself unless I investigated the matter more fully. So I resolved to act.

One of my clients was a constable with 41 Division, as I remember. I asked him to do me a favour and investigate the first vision for me. I told him I believed that it took place in the time period between 1956 and 1960, that some crime or other was committed farther into the field on the east side, and that I believed the child was a boy between four and six years old.

Constable Adams did some inquiring for me and got back to me a few days later. He had created quite a stir because the oldest officer in York Region had only had twenty-five years of service on the Force. But the officer did recall coming onto the Force with an unsolved murder in the files. My client protected my interests by not telling him why he was interested in this case and where he had received his information about it until he had talked to me.

The facts of the case are these. On Jan. 9th, 1955, young Judy Carter was abducted from her Toronto home on Sherbourne Street and taken to Warden and Highway Seven where she was murdered. She was six years old. Her body was found on Jan. 11th beside the creek that at one time flowed past Warden which, at that time, was only a concession road. Somehow I had witnessed a crime that had occurred four months before I was even born! The Chief of Police for York who investigated the crime was Harvey Carps and he retired without ever closing the case. Constable Adams informed Metro Homicide that I was willing to talk about the case I had seen. He told me that they would call me in the future for what information I could give. But that was some time ago. I'm still waiting, but at least I can sleep at night.

Unidentified Flying Objects

A Cloud of Very Remarkable Appearance

Charles Cooper

What strange sight attracted the attention of Charles Cooper? The farmer observed something strange crossing the sky in the middle of the afternoon of Tuesday, 3 Oct. 1843. At the time of the sighting he was working his fields outside Warwick, a small farming community located between Strathroy and Sarnia and south of Lake Huron. There was unquestionably "a cloud of very remarkable appearance." But what about "the appearance of three men, perfectly white, sailing through the air"? Cooper testified that he saw them too. The cloud but not the men was observed by two labourers not very far away, but other witnesses in the community claimed they saw "the cloud and persons." These testimonies are included in a millennialist tract called Wonderful Phenomena: Wonders of the Age... Carefully Compiled by Eli Curtis, Proprietor and Publisher, New-York, 1850.

WARWICK, C.W., NOV. 1, 1843.

On the 3rd day of October, as I was labouring in the field, I saw a remarkable rainbow, after a slight shower of rain. Soon after, the bow passed away and the sky became clear, and I heard a distant rumbling sound resembling thunder. I laid by my work, and looked towards the west from whence the sound proceeded, but seeing nothing returned tó my labour. The sound continued to increase

234

until it became very heavy, and seemed to approach nearer. I again laid by my work, and looking towards the west once more, to ascertain its cause, I beheld a cloud of very remarkable appearance approaching, and underneath it, the appearance of three men, perfectly white, sailing through the air, one following the other, the foremost one appearing a little the largest. My surprise was great, and concluding that I was deceived, I watched them carefully. They still approached me underneath the cloud, and came directly over my head, little higher up than the tops of the trees, so that I could view every feature as perfectly as of one standing directly before me. I could see nothing but a milk-white body, with extended arms, destitute of motion, while they continued to utter doleful moans, which, I found as they approached, to be the distant roar that first attracted my attention. These moans sounded much like Wo—Wo—Wo! I watched them until they passed out of sight. The effect can be better imagined than described. Two men were labouring at a distance, to whom I called to see the men in the air; but they say they did not see them. I never believed in such an appearance until that time.

I Knew Then that They Were Space Beings

A.H. Matthews

Arthur Henry Matthews is a native of England who was brought up in the Province of Quebec. In recent years he has lived on the secluded family farm at Lac Beauport outside Quebec City. Matthews explains in the full narrative that follows that his father was an electrical engineer who had worked with Lord Kelvin, and that as a youngster he had first met the eccentric but brilliant Serbo-American inventor Nikola Tesla.

Matthews further explains that before Tesla died in 1943 the inventor entrusted to his safekeeping the unpatented plans for certain radical new inventions, some of which Matthews later perfected and constructed. Among these inventions are two that are mentioned in the narrative that follows: the Tesla Anti-War Machine, of which little is known, and the Tesla-Scope, an "interplanetary communications set."

Mention was made of the narrative. The full title of Matthews's own narrative is The Wall of Light: Nikola Tesla and the Venusian Space Ship the X-12. *It was reproduced in a limited edition in California in 1973. Only part of the opening section of that work is reprinted here, as the full illustrated work is approximately 70,000 words in length. It consists of Matthews's first-person account of his encounters with the Venusians, their numerous landings in their Space Ship the X-12, his visits to their ship, and his own voyage to the planet Mars and back. Of the latter he noted, "It reminded me of our beautiful Eastern Townships." The mission of the Venusians was to ensure that Tesla's inventions were not misused and to deliver a message of peace and hope for all mankind. As Matthews wrote at one point, "I expected wonders. I saw a miracle."*

IN RELATING THIS ACCOUNT of the landings of a large spaceship on my property at Lac Beauport, of my strange experience in meeting with people who claimed they were from Venus and what I learned about life on their planet, I would like to emphasize that I consider myself of little importance in this story. If my name is known at all, it is due to my long friendship with Nikola Tesla and an intimate knowledge of his great work for mankind. Perhaps I may be excused if I say that it affords me a certain amount of amused satisfaction to realize that I am now probably the last living person who knew and loved Tesla, but in all humility, I am aware that it was only because Tesla left me some of his ideas to develop that I was thus able to meet these people from Venus who claimed Tesla as one of their own.

Due to the fact that my story covers several visits of the Venusian spaceship, I am, for space reasons, condensing its details into one account and will therefore leave out dates. It is sufficient to say that the first visit was in Spring, 1941, with continued landings about every two years until 1961, which, to date, included the last landing. These landings took place on my 100-acre property in the hollow of a large meadow formed by the sloping mountainside at the back and the rise of ground at the front.

It was on a spring morning of 1941 that I was standing near my workshop with my son, Humphrey. We were discussing some matter relating to electrical waves when suddenly Humphrey looked up and exclaimed: "There's something wrong with the sun!" I looked to the east and gasped in astonishment. Exactly in the centre of the golden disc there was a round black spot about one-quarter the apparent diameter of the sun. It was too big to be a sunspot and, besides, it was moving. As we watched, it crept slowly to the upper edge of the sun and in about ten minutes had left the solar disc when it simply vanished from sight. We saw nothing more of it that day.

I went to bed early that night but could not sleep. An oppressive sense of something strange impending descended on me like a pall. Finally, I arose and dressed. I went outside and looked up at the sky but all I could see were the stars sparkling in full brilliancy. I returned to the house and settled down to read — but not for long, for suddenly the alarm signal on the Tesla Scope rang shrilly. I ran outside and at first saw nothing except the sparkling stars. Then I noticed something queer toward the mountain. It appeared to be darker than usual. It was, indeed, for some huge object seemed to cover most of the mountain! I began to walk toward it and as I came near to our barn, I was suddenly confronted by two persons.

Both men were nearly six feet tall and in the brilliant starlight I could discern their bright blue eyes and golden hair, but what registered with me most was that these beings radiated an aura of perfect health and happiness. Immediately I sensed a feeling of good will emanating from them which took away any fear I might have had at this sudden meeting. They were wearing grey coveralls and somehow I knew then that they were space beings. I noted with interest that both were bare-headed, with no helmets or other apparatus, and yet they seemed to have no difficulty in breathing Earth air. I have since been asked if there were any physical differences from Earthmen about these space people and I can only say that I saw none — and why should there be? Are we not all built the same, in the likeness of God?

Then one of them spoke to me in very good English, saying, "Good morning, Arthur Matthews. May we go with you into your workshop?" If this was a surprise, there was a greater one to follow, as he continued, "We are from Venus and we have come to see what you are doing with Tesla's inventions."

Completely taken aback, I could only blurt out, "How am I supposed to believe you are from Venus?"

The one who appeared to be the leader answered calmly, "When you see our ship, you will believe. But before we go, I will make a sketch of Tesla's Anti-War Machine. No one on Earth but you knows its secret. Will *that* convince you?"

I nodded and led them to my workshop. With a few deft strokes, he drew a sketch for me which I could only accept as the truth. A brief inspection and explanation of the work I was doing on the

Tesla devices followed. No comments were made and I was left to assume they were satisfied with my efforts.

Then the two Venusians said they would take me to their spaceship. We walked toward the mountain and soon I was staring wide-eyed at the gigantic proportions of the mother-ship X-12, hardly believing my senses, while my two companions chuckled at my bewilderment. The landed ship, which appeared to be made of grey metal (?), looked like two gargantuan saucers put together rim to rim. Circling these rims about twenty feet away from the main body of the craft was an unsupported band of material (later referred to as the "Guide Ring") which was not attached to the ship by any visible means and appeared to be held in place by some magnetic force. Penetrating the centre of the ship was a tubular shaft fifty feet in diameter and three hundred feet in height, the top and bottom ends of which protruded from the ringed saucers which were seven hundred feet in diameter. The bottom end of this large tube rested on the ground and I could see an opened doorway in which stood two of the crew who greeted us with a hand salute.

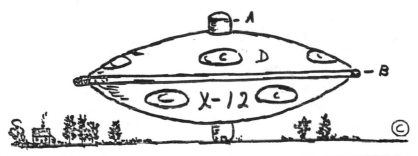

VENUS SPACE SHIP THE X-12. 700 feet in diameter. 300 feet high. the body of ship "D" is 200 feet high. the center elevator and control "A " is 50 feet diameter. 300 feet high.
A CENTRAL CONTROL 50 FT DIA. 300 FT HIGH.
B UNSUPPORTED "GUIDE RING" SURROUNDING SHIP 20ft away FROM MAIN BODY.
C HATCHES? 125 feet diameter,for release and return of the 24 small space-craft carried by this "mother " ship.

My companions invited me in for an inspection tour of the great ship and we stepped into an elevator which I was told had no cables and was operated by will power! We stopped off at the level which was devoted to the storage of some of the twenty-four small spacecraft this mother-ship carried, ground vehicles and other equipment. The second level comprised the living quarters of the crew, gardens, recreation area, study rooms and a meeting hall. Living quarters were compartments for single persons or "married" couples (for the crew was made up of both sexes) and these units comprised a small hallway, a large living room, bedroom, bathroom with toilet and storage locker. All rooms were carpeted with some form of pliant plastic and the walls were hung with beautiful paintings. I discovered the outer wall of the living room was in fact "see through," giving a full view of space outside. The outer door of each compartment led out on to a small flower-bedded garden. At this point, I commented on the lack of a kitchen in these units and was informed that Venusians never spoil their food by cooking it. They grew their own produce aboard and ate it fresh.

We then came to the recreation area which was covered with some form of simulated grass on which a number of the crew were playing a game somewhat like basketball. This gave me an opportunity to study these Venusians more closely and I noted that they ranged from five feet six inches to six feet in height. They were blue-eyed, skin colouring a bronze sun-tan and their hair ranged from golden blonde to a reddish brown. They all appeared in glowing health and their eyes sparkled with a natural *joie de vivre*. Climbing to the third level, I found this was the horticultural section where all their food produce was grown and there were attractive gardens where the crew relaxed and ate their food. The fourth level was divided between storage of more of the small scout ships, heavy material, water supply, etc., and a number of workshops. I had noted that throughout the entire ship all floors were completely covered with some form of plastic material and that all the outer walls were of the same "see through" type. On each wall there was a circular viewing screen, somewhat like television, showing a full view of outer space and the exact position of the X-12 in relation to other planets, and its directional trajectory in space, this changing picture being projected from the control tower to all parts of the ship. I was also informed that built into these walls were "accumulators" for storing solar energy which gave constant light and power to operate heating and air conditioning systems.

We then rose to the exposed top of the tubular shaft which I was told was the control room. My Earthly mind had conjured up visions of all kinds of complex devices to operate this enormous spacecraft, but to my great surprise, there were no visible controls or equipment at all! In the centre of the room was a raised circular platform on which had been built a circular couch and seated with their backs to this and facing outward to the North, South, East and West, were four persons — two women and two men. I was informed that these four operators, chosen specially for their great mental powers, controlled and directed this giant ship! It all seemed completely unbelievable until across my doubting mind there flashed the biblical verse: "Faith can move mountains."

My leader-companion then took me to a lower level and introduced me to a lovely woman whom he described as his "life companion." She was indeed a most beautiful creature, with sapphire-blue eyes, golden-blonde hair and her face glowed with an inner spirituality delightful to behold. He stood beside her and said simply, "You may call us Frank and Frances, for we stand for Truth."

The Biggest and
Weirdest Ship

Al. Mac Nab

*The author of this account of the sighting of "the
biggest and weirdest ship" is now retired and living in Guelph, Ont.
The sighting took place in 1948 in West Hill, Ont., but it remains
imprinted in the observer's memory. As he wrote in letters to the
present editor on 7 June 1987, and again in July, "The experience did
not change my life in any way. However, I have the memory of it
printed in my mind — unlike all the other memories of things I have
witnessed before or after."*

I AM WRITING to tell you about a UFO sighting which took place
thirty-nine years ago. I had the experience on a Saturday in the
middle of summer of the year 1948 at West Hill, Ont., at that time a
little suburb east of Toronto. I was then twenty-five years old. At
the time the incident took place, I was the driver of a truck for
Acme Paper Products on Carlaw Avenue, Toronto.

My wife Mary and I owned small house at the end of Elmwood
Road, off Livingston Stop 29, Scarborough. It was south and a little
west of the Guild of All Arts Inn, about three hundred feet from the
Scarborough Bluffs which overlook Lake Ontario.

It was a nice summer afternoon. We were in our living room, the
picture windows of which face south toward the lake. Our young
son Eddy was in his crib in his bedroom. I suppose we were reading

or listening to the radio, when suddenly bright flashes of light reflected into the room from something outside.

Startled we ran outside and looked up and around to try and see where it had come from. Next we found ourselves running along the path through the trees to the Bluffs where we would be able to get a better look at the sky.

Reaching the Bluffs, we looked and saw what I first thought was the biggest and weirdest ship I ever seen on the lake. Suddenly I realized that this thing was not on the lake. Looking straight ahead, I held my arm straight out, fingers spread, thumb on horizon, little finger on object — it was about that far away, visibly hovering, dead still above the lake.

It was unbelievably huge, like nothing I'd heard described or even seen before — although many years later the movie *Close Encounters of the Third Kind* showed the "mother ship," which had a very close resemblance, though that one was far more flashy than the one we observed.

I know we stood for I don't know how long, probably with our mouths open, staring at this thing. Then we suddenly came to our senses — we had left our son alone in the house! In another panic, we both raced to the house to get him. With our son in our arms, we ran back to the Bluffs.

About four minutes had lapsed since we had left the Bluffs to get our son. The UFO had gone. We had heard no noise. We noticed no more bright flashes of light. It just up and disappeared.

Shortly after, we told relatives about it. They thought we were joking. I think they never did believe us, or anyone else for that matter. The few other people I told always thought I was putting them on. If I had been alone at the time of the sighting, I would not have told anyone. We never reported it to any authority. I hope you believe me.

There were about fifteen people living in that area at the time. None of them had noticed it. We checked the newspapers, listened to the radio, but there were no reported sightings at the time.

I was an average drinker. Mary did not drink at all. We did not take drugs. So we always ruled out the hallucination theory.

For information purposes: From the position the object was in, it would take a lake-going ship, travelling either westerly or easterly in direction, approximately one hour, even more, to disappear from sight.

It Spun Rapidly in the Bright Sunlight

Hazel L. Mack

Hazel L. Mack is an historical researcher who lives in Guelph, Ontario. The experience that she recalls in this memoir-like writing (excerpted from her letter to the present editor written on 19 March 1987) occurred about 1949.

In the literature devoted to flying saucers — nowadays they are more generally called UFOs — it is accepted that there is a relationship of antipathy between the UFOs and members of the animal kingdom. It seems all sorts of animals, including birds, hate or fear UFOs, either cowering before them or (as in this account) attempting to assault them. In turn, UFOs seem indifferent to wildlife, as indeed they usually are to human life.

PERHAPS THE MOST AMAZING THING that happened to me occurred on a Sunday, around noon, in the spring of, I think, 1949. I had moved to Eramosa Township in Wellington County, Ontario, and was living then in the most beautiful surroundings, forty acres of rich cedar growth, a bird sanctuary. There were, here and there, a few openings where the sky could be seen. The day before there had been a heavy snowfall but it wasn't to last, as the ground was already warming up. The day was so beautiful that I stood with my collie dog, just enjoying a few minutes of the lovely sunshine.

Suddenly I heard the crows. They began screaming, about a dozen of them. I looked up expecting to see a hawk. I was standing close to a large pheasant pen. (They were ornamental pheasants.) The crows flew together, still crying out just above the bird pen, perhaps twenty feet above it.

Then I saw what had frightened them. The crows closed in on the object. It seemed to be silvery, very shiny. It was, I suppose, what could be called a "flying saucer." But it appeared to be more like a large child's top. Not big enough for a human being but good-sized. It spun rapidly in the bright sunlight. It might have been the size of a medium-sized wash tub. It was beautiful in the sunlight. The crows were frantic, for they won't stand for something strange in their areas. Then as suddenly as it had come, it vanished. It had made no sound.

I had a good look at it, all silvery and revolving rapidly, but not *too* fast either. I have thought it might have been a photo-taking machine of some sort. It almost touched the bird pen. Later I searched through the deep snow that was to be gone in two days, tramping into the swamp, though walking was rough. No sign of the flying saucer, of course. It was my opinion that — if my guess is correct — the gadget had the ability to make itself invisible when it wished. It certainly was gone like a flash.

I would have doubted my own eyes but for the crows. They did not want the object in their territory. (On one occasion I'd seen them rout an unlucky owl, even though it took them until dusk to move the bird.) I told the Ontario Provincial Police about the experience. They believed me but we could not understand what it was.

This Machine Was Going Away from Us

Mike Johnson

The following report of the sighting of a UFO was written by Mike Johnson who was born in 1911 and now lives in Lethbridge, Alberta. At the time of the sighting, in the spring of 1950, he was living with his wife on their farm near Barons, a village north of Lethbridge.

In letters written to the present editor on 1 June, 3 Aug., and 24 Dec., 1987, Johnson explained that during the war he was with the RCAF as pilot and observer and electrician. About his UFO sighting he expressed the following opinion: "I have seen a real live one. Nobody can tell me it was marsh gas. In the driest part of Southern Alberta you can't even find a marsh! And also, I don't think it was Venus looking my farm over.

"My wife Mildred still talks about the UFO, as she saw as much as I of it," he added. "Seeing it did not make much difference to me, as I was quite busy at that time, but I would like to see another one! My friends said they would like to have seen it too."

IT WAS ON OUR FARM, four miles southeast of Barons, Alta., on a spring 1950 *clear* morning, about eight o'clock, that we saw our UFO.

My wife and I were in the farmhouse. We went outside to see where the cows were. I had cattle on the lakeshore. When we looked to the east, I said, "What the hell is that?"

This machine was going away from us, not very high. I'd say about 150 feet. It was oscillating at right angles to the direction of travel, i.e., the right side would go down, while the left would go up, etc. While the right side was down I could see the reflection of the sun on its top. Then it would go blank till the right side was up and the sun was reflected from the bottom of the craft. It operated like clockwork, about four seconds from top to bottom.

The material it was made of had all the appearance of aluminum. I'd say it could be about 35 feet across and maybe 12 feet deep. It was travelling in a straight line, not fast, about a hundred miles an hour. If it made any sound, it wasn't very loud. It no doubt went fairly close to our house, but we heard nothing.

We watched it till there was just a speck left, there were still reflections. Then there was no speck, but a few reflections were still there.

I had seen a lot of aircraft by that time, having spent three years in the RCAF, in Africa in 1943 and in England. But nothing like this one!

That's all I can think of now. I am sending you a map, etc., of the UFO. I'm not much of an artist, but I'll do the best I can.

A Motionless, Noiseless, Stationary UFO

Frederick C. Dally

The following description of "a motionless, noiseless, stationary UFO" comes from a letter sent to the present editor and dated 21 July 1987. The description refers to a sighting that occurred almost three decades earlier. Frederick C. Dally, the correspondent, was born in 1912 in Preston, Ontario, and was employed until his retirement in 1974 as an accountant at the B.F. Goodrich Rubber Company in Kitchener. About the sighting the correspondent added, "It is the closest of anything from outer space that I have encountered."

I SIGHTED a motionless, noiseless, stationary UFO over Boehmer Street in Kitchener, Ontario.

It was a beautiful day, Monday, May 12th, 1958. While I was at work I had a phone call from my mother who stated that there were some flames coming from the hot-air register in the room in which she was sitting and knitting in our house at 22 Boehmer Street. I stated that I would be right home. By car I was there in about ten minutes or so. I went into the house and saw nothing and spoke to her. She pointed to the hot-air register at the other side of the room and stated that it had some flames coming from it at very short intervals.

I went down to the basement but everything seemed to be normal. The furnace was not then in operation. Then I went upstairs and we talked for some time. She stated that she actually saw some flames. I stated that this could not possibly be so and that everything appeared to be all right. Well, she insisted that she saw them. Then I said that I would return to work.

The time was around 10:15 a.m. when I went out the side door. I looked up and across the street and I saw this object in the sky. I stated to myself, "Good grief, there is a UFO." It was stationary over my neighbour's house, above his TV antenna, some thirty feet above the house. It was motionless because I could see the bottom and I was close enough to see that it was not rotating or spinning. It just hung there in the air and I wondered just what was holding it up. It looked like two saucers were welded together. It was circular in shape. It had the dull appearance of aluminum, not polished steel. It made no sound while it remained there. There were no windows, portholes, doors on the bottom. It was all one sheet of metal. The top I cannot describe as I could not see it.

The houses here are 24 feet by 36 feet in size and I was looking at it lengthwise. I would say that it was some 20 feet in diameter. Then it seemed to sense that I was observing it and it took off at a fast rate of speed without sound or exhaust. It flew about 50 feet above the houses on the street and I wondered how this object could fly from a stationary position to a great speed and also in a straight line. The depth of this object was such that a normal person could not stand upright in it.

Another person who was driving along Margaret Avenue some three or four blocks away saw this UFO and reported it to the *Kitchener-Waterloo Record*. This is the only one that I have seen. I thought that you would be interested.

Two UAO Sightings

E. Walker

These two accounts of the sightings of strange lights in the skies over the British Columbia interior are taken from a long letter dated 9 June 1987. The letter was written to the present editor by Mrs. E. Walker who is of Welsh, Scottish, and English stock and presently lives on Vancouver Island, B.C. She explained in her letter that she has reason to believe herself to be "slightly" psychic, but she added a cautionary note:

"I am not a 'kook' or similar entity. I raised and supported my daughter alone after my first husband and I separated and then divorced. I held jobs with a great deal of responsibility and interaction with many people. I am one of those people who wants to know why, what, when, where, why — and to do anything and everything within reason to learn the answers. I also like to observe things, not just look at them. I am an active Anglican, but see no reason why earth should be the only object in the universe to have the ability to support life, though other planets' life-forms may be very different than those here on Earth, and their levels of intelligence and development far ahead, behind, or equal to our own. For that matter, I don't think we have yet discovered all the life-forms here on Earth!"

I HAVE HAD a number of strange experiences as well as two definite UAO experiences. (I prefer "Unidentified Aerial Objects" to the commoner "UFO," partly because of the connotations of the latter in the minds of many people — e.g., little green men from Mars.)

This is the first time I've written these experiences down for anyone else to see, and I do not know if I can put down on paper the UAO sightings, as something seems to inhibit me when I try to do so. First of all, I may as well say that I have had periods of very heightened perception, a.k.a. ESP, and have had such a faculty for almost as long as I can remember. (I am now nearly fifty-five.) Whether those with this faculty attract, or are attracted to, paranormal events is, I suppose, a moot point. However . . . .

My first UAO experience occurred in either 1959 or 1960. I was living in Abbotsford, B.C., with my daughter by a previous marriage. It was spring, at night, about ten-thirty or eleven. A southwest gale was blowing. There were clouds scudding across the sky, obliterating the stars as they went by. The leaves of the weeping willow clearly showed the wind direction and strength and the branches of the tree whipped about rather strongly. I was taking a last look outside before going to bed, watching the clouds whip along, commenting to myself how bright the stars were and wondering if I could see the moon out the bedroom window. I noticed that the houses on the low hill just across the yard were in darkness, and wondered if they knew how beautiful a night it was. Then I noticed a strange star, strange because it was brighter and bigger than the rest. It took a time for it to sink in that it wasn't — couldn't — be a star, because the clouds were going behind it! Then, I began to get goose pimples. The object began to change colour — blue, green, red, white — very, very bright, clear true colours. It then bounced up and down a few times, and then did something that was not possible as far as I knew — it went against the wind in a pattern that formed the sides of perfectly equilateral triangles before zipping back along the base of the sides of the triangle to its original point. It bounced up and down several times, then followed the same path as before, against the wind. All the time it was moving, it kept changing colours, but not in any definite pattern that I can remember. I watched the object for almost thirty minutes before creeping into bed and covering my head with a pillow. I had had no lights on during the last twenty minutes or so in order that I could see the object better, but could make no sense of something that was doing what it was doing against a southwest gale. It was so obvious that it was between the clouds and the earth!

My second UAO experience was along Highway No. 16 between Vanderhoof and Prince George, B.C. My husband and I were eastbound to Prince George. It was about eight at night, in the winter, with about two or three feet of snow on the ground. We were coming up Mud Hill when I first saw something odd in the trees on the side of the hill. I knew there were houses at the top of the hill, but I didn't know there were any on the side of it facing the road down in the valley of Mud Creek. But there were what at first glance appeared to be flashing Christmas lights. (It was just about a week before Xmas in 1970 or 1971 or perhaps 1972.) But these lights were blue and green, and flashed in perfect sequence, one after the other — in other words, they blinked on and off in order of rotation, so to speak, and were down among the trees about fifty or sixty feet below the top of the hill and about one hundred to one hundred and fifty feet away from the highway. I didn't think any more about it until we had gotten over the top of the hill and were going along a straight stretch. On the right the trees thinned out rather rapidly across a field. Beyond the trees was a long, low mountain. There was a moon, and the snow reflected both moonlight and starlight. The temperature was probably about -30 F. Through the trees, I saw a light that was moving in the direction we were going, the trees blocking it from view for very short periods of time. I tried to open the window to see more clearly, but it was frozen shut. I knew that on the other side there were no trees like that — they were scarcer and not the tapering off of a forest as on the side of the object I was viewing. Whatever it was it was keeping pace with our vehicle but we could not stop because of the snow piled up on the edge of the road and the traffic going in both directions. So I continued to watch out the window (actually, I wanted the window open so I could listen for the sound of a motor!) which was clear. I also leaned far forward and looked through the windshield. Both the side window and the windshield were clear of frost and ice because he had the heater on full blast. The object was the size of a round fifty-cent piece held at arm's length (with the elbow bent at a ninety-degree angle), and seemed to glow from within. It was orangey-yellow in colour. Once it got into full view as the trees gave way to a cleared field, the object was clearly visible: it was low — lower than the tops of the trees, it was quite bright, still keeping pace with the truck — but there was no sign of a glow or light reflected on the snow below it! It began to change colour, the deeper orange colour coming over the surface of the object in the shape of the Technocracy sign's division of colours. As we turned a slight corner to our left, the object suddenly sped up and in a few seconds disappeared up a draw slightly to the right of its previous path. I checked with the airport when I got to Prince George, thinking it was a helicopter, and was told that helicopters were not allowed to fly at night. I thought about it some more, and after a few days realized that its path, upon leaving our sight, would have taken it very close to the Baldy Hughes RCAF radar base. My sister, who lived south of the area of my sighting (she lived in the Backwater Ranches country), told me that she had seen several UAOs in the years they lived on the ranch.

Sorry to have carried on like this, but it is a nice feeling to be able to put it down on paper, and whether people believe me or not, I've told it as it happened, and there is nothing more I can do than that.

This Long, Dirigible-shaped Object

John E. Grosskurth

*John E. Grosskurth describes in two letters, the first
dated 1 June 1987, the second dated 22 July 1987, here combined,
how he sighted "this long, dirigible-shaped object" in 1971 in
Medicine Hat, Alta. The correspondent was born in Toronto in
1911. He operated an insurance agency in Toronto and in Medicine
Hat; for twenty-five years he worked as an insurance company
inspector. He is now living in a senior citizen's apartment in Medicine Hat.*

*The account of the sighting is detailed and dramatic in its own
way. When the present editor queried the correspondent as to
whether or not the UFO experience had changed his life in any way,
the correspondent replied: "I'd say I find it both amazing and
frustrating that close friends exhibit doubts when I relate to them
the events of the evening I saw the UFO."*

YES, I HAVE WITNESSED, close up, a UFO. However, it happened in
1971, sixteen years ago. Being elderly, my memory has dimmed
considerably. However, I will try to give you as much information
as I can now recall.

It was late August, close to seven o'clock in the evening. The
weather was perfection itself. I was in the front bedroom of my
home at 466-12th Street, N.E., Medicine Hat, Alta., packing for a
trip to New Glasgow, N.S. From the open window came the voices

of children yelling and hollering. I heard them shout "Saucer"! The word "saucer" was an attention-getter, so I moved outside to see what was happening.

I was amazed to see this long, dirigible-shaped object, about 100 to 150 feet long, cigar-shaped, moving slowly from the east, toward us. It kept to the centre of the paved street, less than 40 feet above the pavement. It continued to inch along, without any sound whatever coming from it.

From the underside at the forward end of it beamed this brilliant, white, searchlight-type beam of light. When it finally reached opposite the house next door — to the east, on the north side of 12th street — it stopped stock-still. The kids were continuing to holler and shout.

Darkness hadn't yet overtaken the daylight. To get a better view of its underside, I lay down on the lawn and looked up. I wanted to see, first, where the beam of light had originated. I saw that the underside of the object was flat. On the underside at the front was housed a terrific-sized "ring of dozens of lights." I had the impression the front end was substantially wider and it narrowed as it grew closer to the aft. Here is a small diagram showing the mass of what looked to be lightbulbs and ringed by what could be described as huge white teeth (reminding me of cemetery stones!).

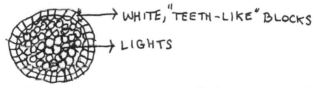

The huge object remained immobile till the skies grew dark. This took between 20 and 45 minutes. Then it "slid" in a southerly direction, changing to a straight bee-line as it sped southwest. Green and red lights were prominent as it moved.

Only too well do I *know* how bizarre this account sounds. But I'm telling it the way it is. There have been dozens of people I've told of it but, quite frankly, no one has yet said: "Sure, I believe your story." But it is, nonetheless, the *truth!*

Let me add, I was living alone with my dog Topper at the time. My wife and I had lived in the house for less than one year, but she had left me (for good) to go to Chicago and it was my decision to leave Medicine Hat. I was packing my clothes, etc., the evening the UFO was sighted.

Topper disappeared under the bed when I went out to the front lawn. Later I quizzed the kids about the huge object. One lad from across the street *did* see it, but immediately his parents talked him into a mental "blank," and he refused to discuss the matter of having sighted it with me. I made three or four attempts to track down other children involved in the sighting, but it turned out to be a really discouraging and futile exercise. Feel free to ask me any question; if I know the answer, I'll tell you; if not, I'll say so too. Thank you for giving me the opportunity to remember that weird night.

The Appearance of Lights and Ships

Nancy DuPlessis-Merrill

Nancy DuPlessis-Merrill and her family moved from the city of Fredericton to an isolated farm not far from Scotch Lake, York County, N.B. The move took place in the year 1973 and thereafter they began to see the lights and the ships...as she reported in this letter sent to the present editor on 10 June 1987. The reader of this strange account might well wonder whether the strange, luminous phenomena continue to this day....

FIRST I'll HAVE TO ADMIT that I was never a believer in anything supernatural. But after moving out of Fredericton to the area I'm living in now, York County, I do have doubts about certain things.

I have been living in an area known as Scotch Lake. It is twenty miles from the city of Fredericton. I moved here fourteen years ago, buying a house that is now 195 years old. When I first moved here I was the only full-time resident. Now there were a lot of camps around the lake which is a quarter of a mile from our house. I live right in a wooded area and it is still the same except that two new families have moved in full-time a mile from me. The area is very isolated and swampy in places.

In 1974, I saw my first strange sighting, a huge light moving on top of the pine trees without making any noise. The lights are clear and move in all directions. My husband and I started watching the skies and saw more and more of them. They would follow the car and at times I would feel nervous. A few times the lights have shone into our bathroom window. One time, about midnight, I went out to the barn to check on the calves when the whole yard lit up. The light was blinding. Then it went straight up without a sound, leaving a darkness so black I had a hard time getting my bearings to head for the house.

On another occasion we saw three small lights across from the house. They were moving around. We looked over by the huge pine tree and saw a huge, huge light. We watched for some time and saw there were three smaller lights that went inside (or whatever) this big one and up it went.

We never really saw a form until 1982. About eleven one evening I was lying on the couch. My one dog ran upstairs and hid under a bed. My other one started barking. I went to look outside and there it was, this huge, oval-shaped machine, silver, all three levels of it, with lights or windows on the first two levels, but around the bottom were a lot of little lights, all clear and revolving. I called my daughter and she came and we just couldn't move. The ship left. It went over towards the pine trees again, but this time there was the largest orange blast you ever saw. I thought it blew up. But again there was not a noise.

Since then all we've had are the usual moving lights. We had a blue light go across in front of the car. Everything inside went dead, but the key was still turned on. Thinking it was a second later we started the car and drove home. It was an hour later. When we first spotted the lights I phoned the radio station. They told us they would like to have what we're drinking and made a joke about it. Afterwards a few more people said that we were over the edge, so we just kept it quiet.

If I had not had these experiences I would have my doubts had I heard someone else telling them.

The Platform of Light

Robert J. Hazzard

*F*or *many hours during a summer night in 1976,*
Robert J. Hazzard and his wife were able to observe a platform of
light seemingly suspended over the St. Lawrence River west of
Brockville, Ontario. At the time of the sighting Hazzard was the
co-ordinator in charge of scheduling and sales of Orlon and Lycra
at the Maitland Works of DuPont of Canada Ltd. He retired from
that position in May of the following year.

Hazzard reported seeing the luminous object in the sky to the
National Investigative Committee on Aerial Phenomena (NICAP)
which published its account in the March 1977 issue of UFO
Investigator. *The account here is based on the text of letters written*
by the witness to the present editor and dated 2 June 1987 and 16
July 1987. Hazzard added the following explanation in the latter
letter: "The model I made is rather fragile or I would send it to you."

ON AUGUST 14TH, 1976, my wife and I were in our cottage on the St.
Lawrence River, nine miles west of Brockville. At this point the river is
approximately three miles wide, with a couple of islands about four
hundred yards from shore in front of us. The air and sky were clear,
although I noticed some lightning to the southwest, indication of an
approaching storm. There was also a light wind from the southwest.

I was reading a newspaper when, at 10:15 p.m., my wife called my attention to a brilliant white light in front of the cottage and over the river. It was about the size of the full moon, but many times brighter. I turned off our lights, but there was plenty of light to still read the paper.

By 10:20 p.m., I had set up a pair of 20 x 65 binoculars on a tripod outside and was watching it. By adjusting the glasses so that the light was just out of centre, I could see everything in complete detail.

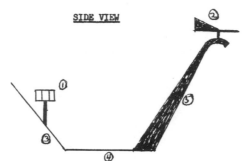

SIDE VIEW

1. Light - 2 light bars inside, 4 bars on outside rim separating top and bottom
2. Weather vane
3. Light platform (estimated about 25 feet in length)
4. Bottom platform
5. Weather vane supports (estimated about 40 feet in length)

OTHER VIEWS OF INDIVIDUAL PARTS

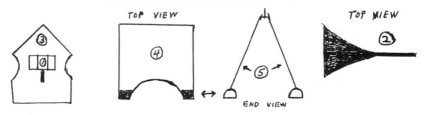

TOP VIEW

TOP VIEW

END VIEW

It appeared to be a platform made of a very thin, satin-finish, silvery-grey material. When it was sideways to me it didn't obscure any of the sky. It was very steady, and when it did move very slightly, it moved so that the bottom stayed flat as though it were suspended from both ends. I raised my glasses but could see no means of suspension at all. It appeared to me to be about 1500 feet in the air and possibly a mile out over the river. A ship going down the channel on the opposite side of the river shone a spotlight at it but it was not strong enough to reach. Other people on the shore also noticed it, but I was the only one with glasses on it.

As the storm approached from the west, the wind suddenly shifted to the northeast, exactly the opposite direction, and became very strong. It didn't affect the cottage as there is an eighty-foot-high cliff behind us. The light platform turned very slowly to the northeast. As it turned, I noted a large weathervane, which I had been unable to see before, shipping quite violently in the wind, but the platform itself appeared to be very stable.

About 1:30 a.m., it started to rain lightly, but lightning was quite frequent, so I went inside and watched through a window. The storm passed very quickly, and after it passed I noticed a very large "halo," well out from the platform but completely around it.

At 2:00 a.m., we retired. At 4:00 a.m., I woke up and it was still there, but it was gone by daylight.

I sent a report to NICAP and discussed it on Brian Smith's CBC-TV talk show (by phone) with a panel of scientists. I am enclosing a couple of sketches. I also made a model of it, which I still have.

You Should Find It Interesting Reading

Stan Mickus

A *number of the contributions which appear in this book were sent to the present editor by correspondents otherwise unknown to him who were replying to requests for information on such matters carried by daily newspapers in their classified columns. The letter which follows is one of these contributions.*

Stan Mickus of Calgary, Alta., responded with the letter which is included here. It is reproduced pretty well the way he wrote it. The only changes that were made were routine editorial alterations — the original letter was typed in capital letters; spelling and grammatical errors have been eliminated. Unfortunately, the correspondent neglected to include his return address.

Letters like this one raise a number of questions and suggest a number of answers about reports of sightings and accounts of abductions. Yet it compellingly combines the possibility of nuclear annihilation with the notion of extraterrestrial visitors and the promise of a religious revival — Atomic Armageddon, ET, and the Second Coming.

MARCH 11, 1988

Dear John,

I had planned to write to you earlier but I wasn't able to. This information might be too late for your book, but you should find it interesting reading at any rate. I've been writing letters to the editor to be printed in the papers but they don't seem to be interested any longer in what I have to say.

I find myself sitting on probably one of the biggest stories since the birth of Jesus Christ and no one to tell it to. So I thought you might be interested in what I have to say since you requested information concerning UFOs.

There isn't much time left. I believe beings from another planet have played a part in man's development over a period of thousands of years. They may have even started it all, whenever it was that life started on this planet. I won't go into that much detail about my own UFO encounters, mostly because I can't. But I will tell you what I know and give you my opinions as to what is going on.

Let's deal with the reality first. As far as I know my first encounter with a UFO was when I was about nine years old. It was summer time. I believe it was in the month of May 1951 on a Saturday. I was playing outside at my friend's place and we saw this object. I believe the surface of it was like stainless steel, maybe a little bit shinier. It was about fifteen feet above us and about fifty feet away. It was moving in a straight line and I don't remember any sound coming from the object. When I realized it would be passing my friend's bedroom window on the second floor, we raced up to his room. We couldn't open the window because it was freshly painted and difficult for us to get the window opened. But we saw this object pass right by. We could have touched it if we had gotten the window open. Then we raced back downstairs and saw the object continue on its way. It was moving about the same speed as a brisk walk. I believe this object was used in gathering information.

My next encounter with a UFO was some twenty-two years later. I was living in Toronto at the time and had an apartment in High Park overlooking Glenlake Avenue. My apartment was on about the second floor from the top. It was a damp evening in November 1974. I believe it was a Monday about 8:00 p.m. I had the curtains closed and it was quite foggy outside. I remember I was sweeping the floor at the time. I heard nothing and saw nothing, but I had a very strange urge to get over to the patio door. I almost tripped over the footstool, I was in such a hurry to get over there.

When I pulled the door open and stuck my head out, I saw a white light, just a bit to the west of me at about the same height up as I was on. It moved over Glenlake Avenue to the east and then turned straight for me.

When I say *turned*, that's an understatement. I never saw anything that manoeuvered the way that object did. It just changed direction on a dime and headed straight for me. By this time I was out on the balcony and can still remember thinking to myself, if I hang onto the balcony tightly, they won't get me. (That was later on to be proved wrong.) The light seemed to go over my head and that was it. I stuck around for a while but they didn't return and as it was spitting rain I went inside. I was amazed at what I saw and probably somewhat dazed because I didn't fully realize what I had undergone. I don't know if I had noted the time or not, but if I had I would have known that something was terribly wrong.

I moved to Calgary in 1975 and quite a few years later I was watching a CBC program called *Man Alive*. It was about people who had been kidnapped by these beings and taken aboard their aircraft. It also mentioned on the show that a lot of these people had scarring on their legs and surgical cuts that couldn't be explained. I was amazed at hearing this because I too had scars and a crater-like hole on my right leg which I could not explain. I always felt that there might have been a good chance that I was abducted on that November evening in Toronto.

It was in April of last year that I got in touch with a hypnotist to find out what happened in Toronto. Under hypnosis I saw two beings coming straight down by the balcony. I was taken aboard their craft and placed on a table while they did a number of tests on me. I believe they took skin samples and maybe bone marrow. I heard that they use our cells and combine them with theirs to create another kind of being which they are populating on another planet.

Something else was also revealed to me. While I was living in London, Ontario, I took a trip to Salt Lake City in June of 1976. When I was returning to London, I had decided to take a nap in the car because I was getting low on loot and wanted to be sure that I wouldn't run out. Under hypnosis I recalled driving east out of

Denver, Colorado, on an expressway. It was about 1:00 a.m. on a Saturday morning. I had to pee, so I turned off the expressway onto a lonely road. When I got out of the car to pee, I saw this UFO hovering over me. I remember telling the hypnotist that the lights were honeycombed under this particular UFO. After the session he commented that it was the first time he had ever heard of the lights under a UFO being honeycombed. I believe that on the following evening when I was in Kansas near the Indiana border I was kidnapped again by these beings.

I can recall under hypnosis seeing two aircraft. One had a pennant on top of it and I can recall the other looking exactly like the UFO in the movie *The Day the Earth Stood Still*. A fitting title. I believe that movie came out in the Fifties.

There's something else I would like to share with you. In 1979, right after I had my heart attack, I was at a meeting. There was a priest, a social worker, and three young fellows like myself. The meeting was recommended to me by a social worker in the hospital. I think this meeting was to help us out of our problems. At any rate I was doing all the talking, I forget about what. I volunteered to shut up and let the other fellows talk, but they wanted me to continue so I did.

The subject came up about life in the Eighties. I think the priest asked us where we thought we would be in the Eighties. Now, I don't have any special powers to see into the future, but here I was bold as brass, telling them what they could expect to see in the Eighties. I told them I could tell them about half a dozen major events that would happen in the Eighties.

The first thing I said would happen would be that Ronald Reagan would be elected President and would be the first two-term president since President Eisenhower, and President Reagan would launch an attack against Libya in the Spring of '85 or '86. I also mentioned that between 1981 and 1987 there would be an expansion in the economy, that boom times were coming. I predicted the signing of the INF Treaty in the fall of 1987 and told them that there would be talk of peace and better co-operation between the U.S. and Russia. But while the Russians were talking peace they were really planning for war. (I still believe this. As I have said earlier there is not much time left. The whole purpose of the INF Treaty is to make it possible for Russia to attack Europe and the Middle East. I believe we will see this happen in thirty to forty days.)

I also told them that the Dow Jones would hit around 3000 and a crash would take place in the fall of '87, that the Dow would drop to 1800 and then come up to about 2100 where it would remain. I also predicted the cunning of the Soviet leader and how he would fool and is fooling the Western leaders, especially President Reagan.

When I left that meeting I was amazed at myself for predicting the Stock Market crash. I had a gut feeling for the other predictions. They were the sort of predictions anyone could make, but the Dow Jones hitting 3000! I doubt that I even knew that night where the Dow Jones average was, much less predicting where it would be in 1987. At any rate, as you know, these predictions have come and gone and while I would like to pat myself on the back I now realize that I had a lot of help with these predictions. I believe I had a look into the future, thanks to our friends in the sky. There's no way that I would have known about the Dow Jones average or even the crash that came in '87.

My final prediction was, and still is, that in May of 1988 the Soviet Union will launch an attack against Europe and the Middle East. It will be a massive blitzkreig-type of attack with millions of soldiers involved. I remember saying that in a few days they would overrun Europe and the Middle East. Their success will be their undoing and ours as well. The United States will have no other choice but to launch an ICBM attack against the Soviet Union. When they see the attack coming they will have nothing to lose but to launch an all-out attack against us which is what they will do. Five billion people will perish in thirty to forty days. The only ones that will be saved (about one hundred million) will be taken off the planet. They will travel at a high rate of speed in space and will be returned to Earth. What will seem like a day or two to them will actually be seven years here on Earth.

I believe these beings have a complete catalogue of all living things here on Earth and they will replenish the Earth with all living things, for everything on the planet will perish, that includes vegetation and the fish in the sea. There is still time to save yourself and your family. I don't know if you are a religious man or not but I urge you to read the Holy Bible and come to Jesus Christ. I forgot to mention Him, but Jesus Christ is alive and will return to Earth to rule over His Kingdom.

They gave us Jesus Christ.

Stan Mickus
Calgary, Alberta.

The Falcon Lake Encounter

Stephen Michalak

The Falcon Lake Encounter is the name given to the sighting of not one but two unidentified flying objects in Manitoba's Falcon Lake Provincial Park on 20 May 1967. There is more information available on this sighting than there is on any other UFO sighting reported in Canada.

The sole observer of the two UFOs was Stephen Michalak, a fifty-one-year-old Polish Canadian. Later that year Michalak offered the following account of himself: "In 1949 I came to Canada, and some years later, settled in Winnipeg, Manitoba. I live with my wife, two sons and a daughter in a modest home. I have a steady income from my job as a mechanic at the Inland Cement Company. Two of my children attend the University of Manitoba. We live a happy, satisfied life of average Canadians, fully enjoying all the blessings this country is offering us."

It was Michalak's passion for amateur prospecting that took him that weekend to Falcon Lake. What he saw that Saturday is open to interpretation. What is laudable and sincere is his desire to tell others what he saw and how he felt. His account comes from a privately printed, forty-page booklet called My Encounter with the UFO (1967). Michalak wrote about his experiences in Polish; the manuscript was translated and printed by Paul Pihichyn.

There were unexpected consequences of the sighting. The encounter left Michalak, as he wrote, "desperately in need of medical attention." He suffered nausea and first-degree burns on his *chest. He was admitted to the Misericordia Hospital in Winnipeg, his first hospital treatment for recurring, sighting-related health problems. This did not deter him from leading investigators to the exact place where the sighting had taken place. "Landing traces" were found there. Earth analysis showed "some radiation but not enough to be dangerous."*

The case was widely reported by the media. There were investigations by the RCMP and the RCAF, by representatives of the National Research Council and the Atomic Energy Commission, as well as by the Aerial Phenomena Research Organization. A question about the government's silence connected with the case was asked in the House of Commons by Ed Schreyer, then a Member of Parliament, not yet Governor General. The Minister of National Defence replied, "It is not the intention of the Department of National Defence to make public the report of the alleged sighting."

IT WAS 5:30 A.M. when I left the motel and started out on my geological trek. I took with me a hammer, a map, a compass, paper and pencil and a little food to see me through the day, — wearing a light jacket against the morning chill.

The day was bright, sunny — not a cloud in the sky. It seemed like just another ordinary day, but events which were to take place within the next six hours were to change my entire life more than anyone could ever imagine. I will never forget May 20, 1967.

Crossing the Trans-Canada Highway from the motel on the south side, I made my way into the bush and the pine forest on the north side. After travelling some distance I got out my map and compass and orientated myself.

By 9 o'clock I had found an area that particularly fascinated me because of the rock formation near a bog along a stream flowing in the southward direction. I was searching for some special specimens that I had found on my earlier expedition.

My approach had startled a flock of geese, but before long they became accustomed to my presence, quieted down and went about their business.

At 11 o'clock I began to feel the effects of the breakfast I did not eat that morning. I sat down and took out the lunch I had brought with me. Following a simple meal of smoked sausage, cheese and bread, an apple and two oranges washed down with a couple of cups of coffee, and after a short rest, I returned to the quartz vein I was examining. It was 12:15, the sun was high in the sky and a few clouds were gathering in the west.

While chopping at the quartz I was startled by the most uncanny cackle of the geese that were still in the area. Something had obviously frightened them far more than my presence earlier in the morning when they gave out with a mild protest.

Then I saw it. Two cigar-shaped objects with humps on them about half-way down from the sky. They appeared to be descending and glowing with an intense scarlet glare. As these "objects" came closer to the earth they became more oval-shaped.

They came down at the same speed keeping a constant distance between them, appearing to be as one inseparable unit, yet each one completely separate from the other.

Suddenly the farthest of the two objects — farthest from my point of vision — stopped dead in the air while its companion slipped down closer and closer to the ground and landed squarely on the flat top of a rock about 159 feet away from me.

The "object" that had remained in the air hovered approximately fifteen feet above me for about three minutes, then lifted up skyward again.

As it ascended its colour began to change from bright red to an orange shade, then to a grey tone. Finally, when it was just about to disappear behind the gathering clouds, it again turned bright orange.

The "craft," if I may be allowed to call it a craft, had appeared and disappeared in such a short time that it was impossible to estimate the length of the time it remained visible. My astonishment at and fear of [the] unusual sight that I had just witnessed dulled my senses and made me lose all realization of time.

I cannot describe or estimate the speed of the ascent because I have seen nothing in the world that moved so swiftly, noiselessly, without a sound.

Then my attention was drawn back to the craft that had landed on the rock. It too was changing in colour, turning from red to grey-red to light grey and then to the colour of hot stainless steel, with a golden glow around it.

I realized that I was still kneeling on the rock with my small pick hammer in my hand. I was still wearing goggles which I used to protect my eyes from the rock chips.

After recovering my composure and regaining my senses to some degree I began watching the craft intently, ready to record in my mind everything that happened.

I noticed an opening near the top of the craft and a brilliant purple light pouring out of [the] aperture. The light was so intense that it hurt my eyes when I looked at it directly. Gripped with fear and excitement, I was unable to move from the rock. I decided to wait and watch.

Soon I became aware of wafts of warm air that seemed to come out in waves from the craft, accompanied by [the] pungent smell of sulphur. I heard a soft murmur, like the whirl of a tiny electric motor running very fast. I also heard a hissing sound as if the air had been sucked into the interior of the craft.

It was now that I wanted a camera more than anything else, but, of course, there is no need for one on a geological expedition. Then I remembered the paper and pencil that I had brought with me. I made a sketch of what I saw.

By now some of the initial fear had left me and I managed to gather enough courage to get closer to the craft and to investigate. I fully expected someone to get out at any moment and survey the landing site.

Because I had never seen anything like this before, I thought it may have been an American space project of some sort. I checked for the markings of the United States Air Force on the hull of the craft, but found nothing.

I was most interested in the flood of lights that poured out of the upper reaches of the craft. The light, distinctly purple, also cast out various other shades. In spite of the bright midday sun in the sky, the light cast a purple hue on the ground and eclipsed the sunlight in the immediate area.

I was forced to continually turn my eyes away from the light which made red dots to appear before my eyes every time I looked away.

I approached the object closer, coming to within 60 feet of the glowing mass of metal. Then I heard voices. They sounded like humans, although somewhat muffled by the sounds of the motor and the rush of air that was continuously coming out from somewhere inside. I was able to make out two distinct voices, one with a higher pitch than the other.

This latest discovery added to my excitement and I was sure that the craft was of an earthly origin. I came even closer and beckoned to those inside:

"Okey, Yankee boys, having trouble? Come on out and we'll see what we can do about it."

There was no answer and no sign from within. I had prepared myself for some response and was taken aback when none came. I was at a loss, perplexed. I didn't know what to do next.

But then, more to encourage myself than anything else, I addressed the voices in Russian, asking them if they spoke Russian. No answer. I tried again in German, Italian, French and Ukrainian. Still no answer.

Then I spoke again in English and walked closer to the craft.

By now I found myself directly in front of it and decided to take a look inside. However, standing within the beam of light was too much for my eyes to bear. I was forced to turn away. Then, placing green lenses over my goggles, I stuck my head inside the opening.

The inside was a maze of lights. Direct beams running in horizontal and diagonal paths and a series of flashing lights, it seemed to me, were working in a random fashion, with no particular order or sequence.

Again I stepped back and awaited some reaction from the craft. As I did this I took note of the thickness of the walls of the craft. They were about 20 inches thick at the cross-section.

Then came the first sign of motion since the craft touched down.

Two panels slid over the opening and a third piece dropped over them from above. This completely closed off the opening in the side of the craft.

Then I noticed a small screen pattern on the side of the craft. It seemed to be some sort of ventilation system. The screen openings appeared to be about $3/16$ of an inch in diameter.

I approached the craft once again and touched its side. It was hot to the touch. It appeared to be made of a stainless steel-like substance. There were no signs of welding or joints to be seen anywhere. The outer surface was highly polished and looked like coloured glass with light reflecting off it. It formed a spectrum with a silver background as the sunlight hit the sides.

I noticed that I had burned my glove I was wearing at the time, when I touched the side of the craft.

These most recent events occurred in less time than it takes to describe them.

All of a sudden the craft tilted slightly leftward. I turned and felt a scorching pain around my chest; my shirt and my undershirt were afire. A sharp beam of heat had shot from the craft.

I tore off my shirt and undershirt and threw them to the ground. My chest was severely burned.

When I looked back at the ship I felt a sudden rush of air around me. The craft was rising above the treetops. It began to change colour and shape, following much the same pattern as its sister ship when it had returned to the sky. Soon the craft had disappeared, gone without a trace.

Sources

Bibliography

Austin, Benjamin Fish
Glimpses of the Unseen: A Study of Dreams, Premonitions, Prayer and Remarkable Answers, Hypnotism, Spiritualism, Telepathy, Apparitions, Peculiar Mental and Spiritual Experiences, Unexplained Psychical Phenomena. Toronto and Brantford: The Bradley-Garretson Company, Limited, 1898.

Barton, Winifred G.
Psychic Phenomena in Canada. Ottawa: PSI-Science Productions Ltd., 1967.

Booth, John
Psychic Paradoxes. Buffalo: Prometheus Books, 1984.

Bucke, Richard Maurice
Cosmic Consciousness: A Study in the Evolution of the Human Mind. Philadelphia: Innes & Sons, 1901. New York: E. P. Dutton. 1969.

Bucke, Richard Maurice
Proceedings and Transactions of the Royal Society of Canada, Series II, Volume 12, date ?????, pp. 159-196.

Burton, G. Allan
A Store of Memories. Toronto: McClelland and Stewart, 1986.

Creighton, Helen
A Life in Folklore. Toronto: McGraw-Hill Ryerson Ltd., 1975.

Curtis, Eli
Wonderful Phenomena / Wonders of the Age! / A Thrilling Narrative of the Facts Relating to The Dixboro Ghost!... / The Wonderful Appearance of Three Angels! / Apparitions of the Human Form, in White Robes, Passing through the Midst of Heaven, Uttering Voices in Thunder Tones — As Witnessed by Several Persons of Undoubted Veracity, in Warwick, (C. W.), ... [etc.] ... / Carefully Compiled / By Eli Curtis, / Proprietor and Publisher / New-York: 1850 / Price, One Shilling.

Doyle, Sir Arthur Conan
Our Second American Adventure. London: Hodder and Stoughton, 1923.

Geller, Uri, and Guy Lyon Playfair
The Geller Effect. London: Jonathan Cape, 1986.

Green, John
On the Track of the Sasquatch. Agassiz, B.C.: Cheam Publishing Ltd., 5th edition, 1968.

Ham, George H.
Reminiscences of a Raconteur. Toronto: Musson Book Co. Ltd., 1921.

Hearne, Samuel
A Journey from Prince of Wales's Fort in Hudson's Bay to the Northern Ocean 1769, 1770, 1771, 1772 (1795). Edition of 1958 published by Macmillan of Canada, Toronto, 1958, edited by Richard Glover.

Joudry, Patricia
Spirit River to Angels' Roost: Religions I Have Loved and Left. Montreal: Tundra Books, 1977.

Kane, Paul
Wanderings of an Artist among the Indians of North America from Canada to Vancouver's Island and Oregon through the Hudson's Bay Company's Territory and Back Again (1859). Edition of 1925 reprinted by Hurtig Publishers, Edmonton, 1974 introduced by J. G. MacGregor.

Kapica, Jack, editor
Shocked & Appalled: A Century of Letters to The Globe and Mail. Toronto: Lester & Orpen Denys, 1985.

McFarlane, Leslie
The Ghost of the Hardy Boys: An Autobiography. Toronto: Methuen, 1976.

Matthews, A. H.
The Wall of Light: Nikola Tesla & the Venusian Space Ship The X-12.
Mokeluhmne Hill, Calif.: Health Research, 1973.

Michalak, Stephen
My Encounter with The UFO. Winnipeg: Osnova Publications, 1967. Translated
from the Polish by Paul Pihichyn.

Moodie, Susanna
Susanna Moodie: Letters of a Lifetime. Toronto: University of Toronto Press,
1985. Edited by Carl Ballstadt, Elizabeth Hopkins, and Michael Peterman.

Morrisseau, Norval
The Art of Norval Morrisseau. Toronto: Methuen, 1979. With an interview and
essays contributed by Lister Sinclair and Jack Pollock.

Prince, Walter Franklin, Editor
Noted Witnesses for Psychic Occurrences. Boston: Boston Society for Psychical
Research, 1928.

Sanderson, Ivan T.
Abominable Snowmen: Legend Come to Life. New York: Jove/HBJ Book, 1977.

Slocum, Joshua
Sailing Alone around the World. New York: Century Company, 1900. Reprinted
by Dover Publications, Inc., 1956.

Stratas, Teresa
Stratas Sings Weill. Record album liner notes. New York: Nonesuch Album,
1986.

White, Howard, editor
"The Cadborosaurus Meets Hubert Evans." *Raincoast Chronicles: Sixteen:
Collector's Edition.* Madeira Park, B.C.: Harbour Publishing, 1983.

Acknowledgements

Every reasonable attempt has been made to contact the individual copyright owners of the selections included in this anthology. In not every instance has this proved to be possible. The editor and publisher hereby acknowledge their use of previously copyright passages written by the following authors: JOHN BOOTH: *Psychic Paradoxes*. Used by permission of Ridgeway Press, Los Alamitos, California. Copyright © 1984 by John Booth. G. ALLAN BURTON: *A Store of Memories*. Used by permission of the Canadian Publishers, McClelland and Stewart, Toronto. HELEN CREIGHTON: *A Life in Folklore*. Reprinted by permission of McGraw-Hill Ryerson Ltd. PATRICIA JOURDRY: *Spirit River to Angels' Roost*. Copyright © 1977 by Patricia Joudry. Reprinted by permission of the publisher, Tundra Books, Montreal. FRANK McINNIS & IRIS M. OWEN: "The Spoon that Moved." Reprinted from *New Horizons* with permission of the editor. A. H. MATTHEWS: *Wall of Light*. Reproduced by permission of the publisher, Health Research, Box 70, Mokelumne Hill, California. NORVAL MORRISSEAU: Interview in *Morrisseau*. Copyright by Methuen Publications. ABRAHAM SETTON: Letter in *The Geller Effect*. Copyright by Uri Geller and Guy Lyon Playfair. Reproduced with permission of Jonathan Cape Ltd., London, England. ROBIN SKELTON: *The Memoirs of Literary Blockhead*. Copyright © 1988 by Robin Skelton. Reprinted by permission of Macmillan of Canada, A Division of Canada Publishing Corporation. TERESA STRATAS: Interview on linernotes accompanying the album *Stratas Sing Kurt Weill*: Copyright by Nonsuch Records, New York. EMIL S. ZMENAK: "Vision of a Body with Legs." Reprinted from *New Horizons* with permission of the editor.

Printed in Canada